Living with Chronic Illness

First published in 1988, *Living with Chronic Illness* presents a vivid account of the reality of life with chronic illness – from the perspective of patients and their families. The authors look at the expectations, priorities, and problems of those most affected by chronic illness, and examine the strategies they have developed to cope with their considerable disadvantages. The experience of carers, the ways in which their problems change over time, are also major themes in the book.

The book looks at the everyday life of people with the following conditions: stroke, renal failure, multiple sclerosis, Parkinson's disease, arthritis, heart attack, epilepsy, rectal cancer, psoriasis, and diabetes. In each case, an overview of the consequences of a particular illness is presented, before discussion of specific problems in daily life – maintaining family relationships, managing treatment regimes, coping with work and home commitments, and living with bodily change and social stigma.

This volume will be of importance to all those concerned with providing support and planning care for the chronically ill – in the health and social services and in voluntary organizations. Students of medical sociology, policy makers and planners will also find the insights and research presented here valuable in the understanding of the daily life of people with chronic illness. It will also be of use for those in professional training, in nursing, social work, general practice and related areas.

Living with Chronic Illness
The Experience of Patients and Their Families

Edited by Robert Anderson and Michael Bury

Routledge
Taylor & Francis Group

First published in 1988
by Unwin Hyman Ltd

This edition first published in 2024 by Routledge
4 Park Square, Milton Park, Abingdon, Oxon, OX14 4RN

and by Routledge
605 Third Avenue, New York, NY 10017

Routledge is an imprint of the Taylor & Francis Group, an informa business

Publisher's Note
The publisher has gone to great lengths to ensure the quality of this reprint but points
out that some imperfections in the original copies may be apparent.

Disclaimer
The publisher has made every effort to trace copyright holders and welcomes
correspondence from those they have been unable to contact.

A Library of Congress record exists under LCCN:

ISBN: 978-1-032-83182-4 (hbk)
ISBN: 978-1-003-50817-5 (ebk)
ISBN: 978-1-032-83185-5 (pbk)

Book DOI 10.4324/9781003508175

Living with Chronic Illness

The Experience of Patients
and their Families

Edited by

Robert Anderson

Institute for Social Studies in Medical Care, London

and

Michael Bury

Royal Holloway and Bedford New College, University of London

London
UNWIN HYMAN
Boston   Sydney   Wellington

© This volume, R. Anderson and M. Bury, 1988
This book is copyright under the Berne Convention.
No reproduction without permission. All rights reserved.

Published by the Academic Division of
Unwin Hyman Ltd
15/17 Broadwick Street, London W1V 1FP, UK

Allen & Unwin Inc.,
8 Winchester Place, Winchester, Mass. 01890, USA

Allen & Unwin (Australia) Ltd,
8 Napier Street, North Sydney, NSW 2060, Australia

Allen & Unwin (New Zealand) Ltd in association with the
Port Nicholson Press Ltd,
60 Cambridge Terrace, Wellington, New Zealand

First published in 1988

British Library Cataloguing in Publication Data

Living with chronic illness: the experience
of patients and their families.
1. Families with chronically sick persons and families with
handicapped persons. Personal adjustment
I. Anderson, Robert, 1953–   II. Bury, Michael, 1945–
306.8'8
ISBN 0–04–362066–3
ISBN 0–04–362067–1 Pbk

Library of Congress Cataloging-in-Publication Data

Living with chronic illness.
  Bibliography: p.
Includes index.
1. Chronic diseases—Social aspects.
2. Chronically ill—Family relationships.
I. Anderson, Robert, 1953–   .   II. Bury, Michael, 1945–
RC108.L57   1988   362.1   88-71
ISBN 0-04-362066-3 (alk. paper)
ISBN 0-04-362067-1 (pbk.: alk. paper)

Typeset in 10 on 11 point Imprint by Computape (Pickering) Ltd,
North Yorkshire and printed in Great Britain by Billing and Sons, London
and Worcester

Contents

List of Contributors

Robert Anderson *Institute for Social Studies in Medical Care, London.*

Michael Bury *Department of Social Policy and Social Science, Royal Holloway and Bedford New College, University of London.*

Ray Jobling *St. John's College, University of Cambridge.*

David Kelleher *Department of Sociology, The City Polytechnic, London.*

Lea MacDonald *Department of Clinical Epidemiology and Social Medicine, St. George's Hospital Medical School, University of London.*

John Morgan *Social Administration Department, University of Birmingham.*

Ruth Pinder *Parkinson's Disease Society, London.*

Ian Robinson *Association for Research in Multiple Sclerosis Research Unit, Brunel, The University of West London.*

Graham Scambler and Anthony Hopkins *Department of Psychiatry, University College and Middlesex School of Medicine, University of London.*

Thomas Schott and Bernhard Badura *University of Oldenberg, Federal Republic of Germany.*

Introduction

This book brings current research and thinking in the social sciences to bear upon the experience of chronic illness. The chapters have been written specifically for the book by social scientists who are active in research and who have drawn upon their own work to prepare contributions about the experience of adults and their families living with chronic physical illness. Much of their investigation is new and exploratory, and the conclusions are tentative, but the contributions reflect current developments with a diversity of approaches and themes in research.

The realities of living with chronic illness have generally failed to receive focused attention from social scientists, despite their importance. The many detailed studies of doctor–patient relationships, use of services, and even the patients' perspective on, or satisfaction with, health care have seldom been presented in the context of specific illnesses; on the other hand, broad surveys of disablement or health services have often been silent on the more subjective aspects of patients' experiences. It is increasingly recognized that family and social factors influence response to illness and subsequent outcome (Kasl, 1983); that the family is a key resource in care and rehabilitation (Smith, 1979; Anderson, 1987) and furthermore, that chronic illness may lead to disadvantages not only for patients but for those close to them. Planners and service providers have identified a lack of information about the expectations, priorities and assessments held by patients and their families; and about the problems associated with everyday life with long-term illness (Royal College of Physicians, 1986).

A sound, effective and ethical approach to chronic illness must lie in awareness of and attention to the experiences, values, priorities and expectations of patients and their families. The individual chapters are designed to enhance understanding of what it means to live with chronic illness and to draw out some of the implications for response by service providers. This is associated with a reorientation of the focus for care from repairing damage caused by disease to education and understanding for living with chronic illness. In an age of changing consumer demands and expectations the contributions reflect the need for providers increasingly to offer choices, not to make them. In addition, the contributions attempt to link the experience of chronic illness with environmental conditions, with material resources and with the demands of contemporary culture and social structure. They point to implications for both professional practice and public policy, while indicating an agenda for research in the social sciences. It will be clear that most of the contributions reflect some level of collaboration between social scientists and service providers – a collaboration which this book is designed to underscore and encourage.

Taken altogether, the chapters do not provide an integrated text in which the experience of different conditions is compared systematically. Rather, the aim has been to highlight the main difficulties and dilemmas over the course of living with different conditions and changing needs. In a world of complex theories about factors influencing recovery and the course of disease (Kasl, 1983), we remain relatively ignorant of the everyday social, emotional, work, and family consequences of chronic illness. Little is known about the complex and sophisticated decisions made by patients and families to manage or control their illness through entering care, communication with professionals, or the management of treatment regimens. Many people living with chronic illness have been excluded from full participation in community life; there is increasing, but limited, public and professional awareness of their existence, but probably less of their needs. Gouldner (1973) makes an argument for sociology to which this book is in part a response: 'suffering of some is simply and literally unknown to many in society. This is a special part of reality which, I think, is one of our important responsibilities to understand and communicate.'

The category of chronic conditions is a far from homogeneous one, but the various conditions exert, by definition, some long-term influence upon the lives of sufferers. They are generally conditions for which treatment of the underlying disease process is not available; the emphasis of care and rehabilitation is therefore more on enhancing and sustaining the quality and fullness of life than on reordering the disease process. Martin (1984), for example, argues that

> most of the common conditions that strike the nervous sytem are of great chronicity and debilitating not only to the patient but to the family . . . To emphasize that these disorders, like many others in neurology, are 'untreatable' is to overlook the great requirement for sensitivity and endurance in their clinical management . . . patients with 'untreatable' neurologic conditions

are those who require and benefit most from the care of a skilled clinician. (p. 149)

Patients with chronic conditions share this general need for continuing support not only from service providers but largely from those giving informal care, especially the family. This continuing support may be in the context of relative stability in expression of illness symptoms or in a process of decline or relative improvement. While the external manifestations of illness may appear relatively constant, chronic illness presents a series of challenges at several levels.

Despite the range of conditions and disabilities encompassed by the category, a number of common features are concomitants of each illness. All chronic illnesses represent assaults on multiple areas of functioning, not just the body. Patients with various chronic illnesses may face separation from family, friends, and other sources of gratification; loss of key roles; disruption of plans for the future; assault on self-images and self-esteem; uncertain and unpredictable futures; distressing emotions such as anxiety, depression, resentment and helplessness; as well as such illness related factors as permanent changes in physical appearance or in bodily functioning. (Turk, 1979, p. 291)

The goal of occupying as normal a place as possible in the life of the community has implications for many aspects of the patient's life – from the management of treatment regimen and the control of symptoms to the management of social isolation, changed vocational status and family relationships.

Three particular foci are employed by contributors in this book to organize and present the difficulties and needs of people living with chronic illness. First, patients are considered as interdependent members of a social network, principally that of the family. Many of the chapters move towards the family rather than the individual patient as a unit of experience and analysis. Lay involvement in long-term care is significant; contributors seek to demonstrate just how extensively patients and families are actively engaged in processes for rehabilitation, recovery and management. The authors underline that patients and families are knowledgeable agents, not merely the passive recipients of influences that irresistibly condition their conduct. It is argued that given the responsibility and extent of caring by the family there is much that formal rehabilitation services can learn from their experiences and concerns. The contributors look at the strategies developed by both patients and families to cope with their daily problems. However, as sociologists, they attempt to show how the organization of society and cultural demands are related intimately to features of coping with illness and management of daily life. These social factors influencing the experience of chronic illness may be patterned by stage in the life-cycle, gender, ethnicity, or social class (Macintyre, 1986).

A second focus of the book is upon problems from the perspective of the sufferers and their families, considering how they feel about the different constraints at work, at home, or in leisure. The contributors pay as much attention to the personal and social as to the strictly physical disadvantages associated with the illness. The patterns of problems and responses are likely to change over time; this process of change is the third focus of the chapters. The authors are here attempting something relatively new – to document change in the nature and priority of problems over time. Furthermore, many of the chapters consider the longer-term outcomes of chronic illness, given that the shorter-term psychological and social consequences are better known. They consider how, at stages in the course of illness, patients may make different sorts of compromises or 'trade-offs' between different priorities. The aim is to move our knowledge beyond the banal listing of potential problem areas in everyday life, to recognize the complexity of coping and disadvantage, and through this, to provide a basis for making programmes of treatment, rehabilitation and support more relevant to the lives and concerns of patients and their families.

The Nature of the Problem

Care for people with chronic illness has, in the last decade, risen high on the political, social and medical agenda. This reflects the force of a variety of trends – in demographic patterns, public services, cultural assumptions about care, and the prevalence of chronic illness. An interesting illustration of the various factors involved is found in the work of the Dutch Steering Committee on Future Health Scenarios (1987). Although the Dutch group recognize the need for caution in looking at the future, they present a clear picture of increasing strain – for families, the medical care system, social services and the economy – associated with levels of chronic illness in the population. Even if the proportion of people with chronic illness is assumed to remain constant, absolute numbers in the population will increase as a consequence of the ageing population. The scenario group predict this will result in increasing numbers of consultations for chronic illness in general practice, and increasing emphasis within medical care upon palliative measures designed to improve the quality of life. As Hasler (1985) notes for the United Kingdom, disability caused by chronic disease has become 'the very stuff of general practice'.

The scenario committee is especially disturbed by the prospect of decreasing care of parents by children. The authors point to widely acknowledged trends such as decreasing level of fertility (fewer children), increasing geographical mobility of the population, growing emancipation of women (lessening their willingness and ability to provide informal aid), and moves towards an increasingly individualistic life-style, decreasing the potential for family care. This picture of decline in 'family care' will depend greatly on changes in attitudes to care and to future values: for example, the priority accorded to the quality of material possessions compared with quality of family relationships. At the least, the social trends indicate 'considerable uncertainty' about the likelihood of increasing levels of informal care.

The contribution of family and other informal carers has become the main ingredient in recipes for 'community care' – a strategy that itself has become the central guiding principle in the development of health and social services for people with chronic illness (Walker, 1982). The future for community care is dependent on the assumption that women will continue, as the most common carers (Anderson, 1987), to make the sacrifices demanded. When this assumption is called into question, the implications for policy are clearly dramatic. Little is known about attitudes to or changing expectations for caring, but the authors in this volume have begun to tease out some of the problems for families that are associated with different chronic conditions in order to provide some realist material for the rather pious calls for 'supporting the carers'.

The numbers of people affected by chronic illness are difficult to assess. Prevalence studies produce highly variable results due to problems of both definition and measurement, and to real variations associated with, for example, geography or the age of the population. Altogether, the picture is of widespread chronic illness (Harris, 1971) and of physical disability affecting about one-tenth of the adult population (Hermanova, 1985). The figures in Table I.1, drawn from studies by Harris (1971), Fry (1979) and the Royal College of Physicians (1986), indicate how common these chronic diseases are, although only a proportion of the sufferers are appreciably disabled (Bury, 1979).

A variety of recent studies of incidence and prevalence, particularly of neurological conditions (Wade and Hewer, 1987), indicate that the estimates of prevalence in the last two columns are reasonably good. The differences in estimates are probably accounted for largely by the

Table I.1 *Prevalence of disability and disease estimated for a population of 200,000*

Condition	Disability Harris	Disease RCP	Fry
Parkinson's disease	100	400	240
Multiple sclerosis	125	160	160
Stroke	520	1100	1400
Chronic bronchitis	550	}16000*{	2800
Emphysema	115		NA
Rheumatoid arthritis	540	2000	8000
Osteo arthritis	600	25600	NA
Diabetes	120	NA	1600
Epilepsy	85	1000	1600

* Respiratory conditions (excluding cancer of lung).

numbers of people who suffer from different conditions, but who are not significantly disabled by them. The main causes of severe or significant disability appear to be stroke, Parkinson's disease, rheumatoid arthritis, multiple sclerosis and cardio-respiratory conditions (Harris, 1971; Wood and Badley, 1978). All of these conditions are represented by chapters in this book with the exception of the experience of living with a chronic respiratory illness – an observation which we believe reflects an omission of research rather than of the editors.

The Meaning of Disablement

We have chosen to look at the meaning of chronic illness in relation to ten specific conditions. Notwithstanding the common elements in living with chronic illness, most management by service providers is in relation to specific conditions and information for patients is likely to seem more relevant when organized around their particular problem. The aim of the chapters is to systematically build up data using conditions as the base, with a view to documenting what they share, but also to emphasize the heterogeneity of experiences within conditions. It is intended to provide concrete information on the specific disadvantages associated with conditions and therefore to identify appropriate foci for management. Much is known about the general problems of patients and, to a lesser extent, their families – usually adduced from general studies on disability (Blaxter, 1976) – but the identification of the main problems and concerns associated with different conditions has been rare. The selection of conditions for this book was based upon the identification of the most disabling chronic conditions, reflecting those that affect both younger (for example, diabetes, psoriasis, epilepsy) and older (stroke, Parkinson's disease, rectal cancer) people, and the availability of research on the experience of living with these conditions.

Biomedical classifications of disease by, for example, degree of threat to life, may not distinguish the psychological or social consequences which are also due to disability, pain, interpersonal implications, and requirements for daily management. Harper and colleagues (1986), for example, have found that in the case of multiple sclerosis, psychosocial disability bore little relationship to the underlying disease or, indeed, to socio-demographic variables such as social class. They concluded that 'Psycho-social handicaps accompanying chronic disease and the associated reduction in quality of life need to be studied as health problems in their own right' (p. 309). As a basis for distinguishing the elements of disablement, the conceptual framework developed by Wood (1980) has been employed for contributions in this volume. He and his colleagues distinguished between impairment (loss or abnormality of physiological or anatomical structure or function), disability (restrictions in the ability to perform an activity or task in a manner considered normal), and handicap (the disadvantage associated with the inability to fulfil a role that is normal). Handicap represents the consequences – social, environmental, economic – that stem from the presence of impairment and disability. It is probably the most appropriate level for consideration in primary health care (Warlow *et al.*, 1987) since it ultimately defines the needs of a person with physical disability (Anderson, 1985). The framework provides a systematic way of classifying illness consequences, although it is more of a taxonomy than a rating scale. Whatever its limitations as a research instrument or in daily medical practice (*Lancet*, 1986), it has proved extremely useful in directing attention to the systematic disadvantage associated with chronic illness and the different levels or dimensions of experience that are associated with this (Bury, 1987). There is, in the framework, no necessary link between the severity of problems at the different levels. Handicap may be both more and less than disability, depending upon social, cultural and economic values attached to the restriction. The authors in this volume are not preoccupied with the definitions but with making use of the general distinctions to document the social reality, and the contribution of the social environment to the experience of illness. It is worth noting that the handicap of chronic illness may fall as heavily on the family as on the patient, in terms of problems created for daily living and family life, and through the search by the family for adequate responses to these problems.

The perspectives of patients and their families, rather than of service providers, are the main foci in this book which basically takes the 'insider's' view of illness. The perspectives of providers and patients may differ on both the definition and treatment of illness (Blaxter, 1976). Unless providers are able to recognize and respond to these differences in views and expectations, they are unlikely to bridge the resulting gaps in communication and co-operation (Bury, 1985). Equally, it is becoming clearer that patients and their families may have different problems, priorities and expectations. The experience of chronic illness is a process of change and adjustment over time; of resolution and renegotiation of roles and relationships. Not only may the patient's physical condition change but so may attitudes and inclinations (to care, independence, future, relationships). Chronic illness may modify family dynamics and power, so that both the objectives and strategies of patients and families are, at certain stages in the illness, in conflict with each other. The contribution that families make to c ,ring with chronic illness may exact a severe toll on them; but fami ies may have a negative effect on the quality of life of patients – through overprotectiveness, intolerance, or neglect. As Walker (1982) has noted, it cannot be assumed that either formal or informal care is better; both may enlarge or restrict freedoms, increase or decrease dependency, deny or facilitate rights. This balance of benefits and hazards in the relationships between patients and families and patients and formal services is a key issue in this volume.

The current picture of professional involvement in chronic illness is not heartening. Reports of unclear responsibilities, inadequate co-ordination and poor communication between general practice, hospital and community services are common (Blaxter, 1976; Royal College of Physicians, 1986). Formal services for care and rehabilitation may be fragmented but nevertheless undermine the efforts of patients and their families or be misdirected (Elian and Dean, 1983). The general dissatisfaction with disability services (Tulloch, 1985; Royal College of Physicians, 1986) may reflect a poor system for the identification and management of problems of chronic illness in general practice. Hasler (1985) comments that the need is for education and advice, not prescription, but that a supportive, enabling strategy demands an understanding of the ideas, concerns and expectations of patients. Some indication of the character and proportion of these values and beliefs can be generated from research, which should inform individual contacts as well as offer a guide for public policy. In this context of improving the fit between needs and services, the unintended consequences of information, treatment, or other interventions demand examination.

The contributions in this volume offer a framework for considering the value of formal treatment and care, both by giving a platform for the views of patients and their families and by seeking to enlarge our vision about the range of needs that are experienced. Each chapter begins with a brief overview of previous research, to assess the level of systematic knowledge of, and attention to, needs, particularly in the social and psychological domains. This is not done simply to identify gaps and argue that professional services should meet all needs – they cannot and, in any case, neither patients nor families expect the professional to have all the answers or solutions (Hasler, 1985). Rather, the point is to identify ways of furthering the self-care expertise of patients and their families, by enhancing their skills, not by replacing them, and thus increasing their control over the illness and its consequences.

Over the last twenty-five years, a variety of studies by social scientists have addressed questions about how people manage illness in their everyday lives: how they live with reduced options for employment, with loss of spontaneous behaviour, with routinization and regulation of everyday life, with uncertainty, ambiguity, loss of independence and control. The research and ideas represented in the collection of Strauss and Glaser (1975) are important reflections of work in North America. More recently, Locker's (1983) study in the UK looks at the ways in which patients with rheumatoid arthritis adapted by reconstructing everyday life in order to avoid, minimize, or otherwise manage its disruptive effects. He considers both coping strategies and the availability of resources as influences on the process of adaptation. These twin themes of coping (for example, Folkman and Lazarus, 1980) and the armoury of resources (Croog and Levine, 1977) have contributed substantially to the development of explanatory frameworks on adaptation to chronic illness (for example, Turk, 1979; Mechanic, 1977). However, while the abstract development of models has proceeded and the investigation of coping behaviours has become even more detailed, there appears to have been relatively little sustained or co-ordinated application of concepts from the social sciences to analyse the daily life of people with specific chronic conditions.

This volume brings together work which has sought to employ concepts such as 'stigma' (Goffman, 1963) or 'biographical disruption' (Bury, 1982) to consider their usefulness in understanding the lives of those affected by chronic illness. A sociological approach to chronic illness attempts to establish the nature of links between individual experience and social position, rather than, say, degree of impairment or psychological predisposition. These latter are factors to be taken into account, but alongside these is recognition of the influence of the mundane features of daily life dictated by contemporary culture and material conditions (Macintyre, 1986), and the significance of the social organization of daily life seen, for example, in the formal remits of the helping services (Blaxter, 1976). The aim of several chapters in the current volume is precisely to identify those key variables in the social environment that affect the experience of illness, strategies for coping, and the resources for doing so.

This process of analysing experiences is complemented by attempts to enlarge our understanding of illness by good description and ordering of qualitative material. In each chapter, the authors have sought to give space to the words and views of patients and their families. Both qualitative and quantitative approaches are represented as tools for describing and increasing understanding of the complexities of disablement. In different ways, the diverse methods employed, in studies here of from ten to one thousand people, are evaluated by the extent to which they reflect the 'real world' of people affected by chronic illness. The questions of validity and reliability are addressed in individual chapters, against a background of relative immaturity in the development of sensitive, meaningful measurement, especially to capture the social aspects of disablement. The problems of research in this field lie not only with a lack of appropriate measuring instruments but also in: the ethical constraints on approaching ill patients; the identification of adequate samples; the effects of the interviewer during in-depth contacts; the hazards of both joint and independent interviews of patients and carers; the availability of adequate frameworks for interpretation and analysis; and the lack of longitudinal data sets for considering change over time. The authors in this volume highlight the methodological problems that beset them in their own research – problems which they acknowledge have often not been resolved. The various chapters indicate that no single methodology is always feasible or desirable, but that a diversity of approaches may contribute to illuminate the experience of chronic illness.

In summary, the book is intended to inform a wide community of people engaged in supporting patients and their families with chronic illness – this embraces service providers, policy makers, researchers, and people in training. The individual chapters show how people affected with various chronic conditions feel about themselves and their lives; how the illness has changed these lives; what they view as major difficulties in different domains, and how they might be helped. Each chapter begins with an overview of the nature of the chronic illness and associated problems; it goes on to describe the author's research and how the concepts of social science are employed.

The main themes of the chapters are different, though with considerable overlap. So, for example, the effects of chronic illness on personal identity are taken up in nearly all chapters, but specifically in those on psoriasis, Parkinson's disease and diabetes; stigma is a central theme of the chapters on epilepsy and rectal cancer; the impact of chronic illness on family life is a focus of the chapters on stroke, multiple sclerosis, heart disease and rheumatoid arthritis; its effects on employment are discussed more extensively in the chapter on renal failure. Nearly all the chapters direct attention to experiences in use of the professional health system, looking at decisions to use formal care, especially in the chapters on rheumatoid arthritis and epilepsy; managing medical regimens, from high technology in the case of patients on renal dialysis, to potions for psoriasis, and the daily drugs to control Parkinson's disease and diabetes; and satisfaction with care, particularly among people affected by rectal cancer, multiple sclerosis and heart disease.

Taken together, the chapters point to the main differences between the daily lives of people with and without chronic illness, and they identify some of the factors which appear to distinguish the coping and adaptation of different people with the same condition. For reasons alluded to earlier, many of the conclusions for policy and practice are modestly formulated. Our approach has been to describe the current situation as a basis for developing ideas, policies and services that are relevant and sensitive to the changing needs of people with chronic illness and their families.

References

Anderson, J. A. D. (1985), 'Physical disabilities resulting in handicap', in W. W. Holland, R. Detels and G. Knox (eds), *Oxford Textbook of Public Health Vol. 4* (Oxford: Oxford University Press), pp. 412–26.

Anderson, R. (1987), 'The unremitting burden on carers', *British Medical Journal*, vol. 294, pp. 73–4.

Blaxter, M. (1976), *The Meaning of Disability* (London: Heinemann).

Bury, M. R. (1979), 'Disablement in society: towards an integrated perspective', *International Journal on Rehabilitation Research*, vol. 2, no 1, pp. 33–40.

Bury, M. R. (1982), 'Chronic illness as biographical disruption', *Sociology of Health and Illness*, vol. 4, no. 2, pp. 167–82.

Bury, M. R. (1985). 'Dilemmas facing patients and providers in disablement', *International Journal on Rehabilitation Research*, vol. 7, pp. 162–6.

Bury, M. R. (1987), 'The international classification of impairments, disabilities and handicaps: a review of research and prospects', *International Disability Studies*, vol. 9, no. 3, pp. 118–22.

Croog, S. H., and Levine, S. (1977), *The Heart Patient Recovers* (New York: Human Sciences Press).

Elian, M., and Dean, G. (1983), 'The use of health services by patients with multiple sclerosis', *Lancet*, 14 May, pp. 1091–3.

Folkman, S., and Lazarus, R. S. (1980), 'An analysis of coping in a middle-aged community sample', *Journal of Health and Social Behaviour*, vol. 21, pp. 219–39.

Fry, J. (1979), *Common Diseases* (Lancaster: MTP Press).

Goffman, E. (1963), *Stigma: Notes on the Management of Spoiled Identity* (London: Penguin).

Gouldner, A. (1973), *For Sociology* (London: Allen Lane).

Harper, A. C., Harper, D. A., Chambers, L. W., Cino, P. M., and Singer, J. (1986), 'An epidemiological description of physical, social and psychological problems in multiple sclerosis', *Journal of Chronic Diseases*, vol. 39, pp. 305–10.

Harris, A. (1971), *Handicapped and Impaired in Great Britain*, Part I (London: HMSO).

Hasler, J. C. (1985), 'The very stuff of general practice', *Journal of the Royal College of General Practitioners*, vol. 35, pp. 121–7.

Hermanova, H. M. (1985), 'Need for a data base on consequences of disease', *International Rehabilitation Medicine*, vol. 7, pp. 61–3.

Kasl, S. (1983), 'Social and psychological factors affecting the course of disease: an epidemiological perspective', in D. Mechanic (ed.) *Handbook of Health, Health Care and the Health Professions* (New York: Free Press), pp. 683–708.

Lancet (1986), Editorial: 'The assessment of disability', *Lancet*, vol. 1, pp. 591–2.

Locker, D. (1983), *Disability and Disadvantage: The Consequences of Chronic Illness* (London: Tavistock).

Macintyre, S. (1986), 'The patterning of health by social position in contemporary Britain: directions for sociological research', *Social Science and Medicine*, vol. 23, pp. 393–415.

Martin, J. B. (1984), 'Whither neurology?' *New England Journal of Medicine*, vol. 311, pp. 1048–50.

Mechanic, D. (1977), 'Illness behaviour, social adaptation and the management of illness', *Journal of Nervous and Mental Disease*, vol. 165, pp. 79–87.

Royal College of Physicians (1986), *Physical Disability in 1986 and Beyond* (London: Royal College of Physicians).

Smith, R. T. (1979), 'The rehabilitation of the disabled: the role of social networks in the recovery process', *International Rehabilitation Medicine*, vol. 1, pp. 63–72.

Steering Committee on Future Health Scenarios (1987), *Growing Old in the Future* (Dordrecht: Martinus Nijhoff).

Strauss, A. L., and Glaser, B. G. (1975), *Chronic Illness and the Quality of Life* (St. Louis: Mosby).

Tulloch, A. (1985). 'Prevalence of disability observed in an Oxfordshire practice', *Journal of the Royal College of General Practitioners*, vol. 35, pp. 368–70.

Turk, D. C. (1979), 'Factors influencing the adaptive process with chronic illness, in A. Sarason and C. D. Spielberger (eds), *Stress and Anxiety Vol. 6* (Washington DC: Halsted Press), pp. 291–311.

Wade, D. T., and Hewer, R. L. (1987), 'Epidemiology of some neurological diseases', *International Rehabilitation Medicine*, vol. 8, pp. 129–37.

Walker, A. (1982), *Community Care: The Family, the State and Social Policy* (Oxford: Basil Blackwell).

Warlow, C., Wade, D., Sandercock, P., Muir, J., House, A., Bamford, J., Anderson, R., and Allen, C. (1987), *Strokes* (Lancaster: MTP Press).

Wood, P. H. N. (1980), *The International Classification of Impairments, Disabilities and Handicaps* (Geneva: World Health Organization).

Wood, P. H. N., and Badley, E. M. (1978). 'An epidemiological appraisal of disablement', in A. E. Bennett (ed.), *Recent Advances in Community Medicine* (London: Churchill Livingstone).

1 The Quality of Life of Stroke Patients and their Carers

ROBERT ANDERSON

> Being promptly blooded, however, by a skilful surgeon, he rallied;
> and although the doctors all agreed, on his being attacked with
> symptoms of apoplexy six months afterwards, that he ought to die,
> and took it very ill that he did not, he remained alive – possibly on
> account of his constitutional slowness – for nearly seven years
> more, when he was one morning found speechless in bed.
>
> (Dickens, 1841)

Stroke (or apoplexy, or cerebrovascular accident) was common in the
nineteenth century; Dickens himself survived less than a day after a
'paralytic stroke' in 1870 (Johnson, 1979). However, scientific
research into the role of personal and social, as well as medical,
influences on survival and recovery after stroke has developed only in
the last quarter of a century. The growth of research has been linked
to the increasing provision of rehabilitation services for stroke
patients, and the allied belief that the recovery of stroke patients
could be assisted or encouraged. Such research has also been stimu-
lated by awareness of the number of deaths and disabilities due to
stroke, and the escalating costs to society of medical care, welfare
provision and lost productivity. More recently, the problems associated with caring and the stress on carers have moved towards the
centre of debates about the prospects and conditions for stroke
patients in the community.

The Stroke Problem

In England and Wales in 1983 cerebrovascular disease (ICD430–438)
was recorded as the main cause of death for about one woman in every

seven and one man in every eleven. Altogether more than 65,000 people died from a stroke, that is 12 per cent of all deaths, and stroke was the third most common cause of death after heart disease and cancer (Office of Population Censuses and Surveys, 1985). In the same year about 100,000 people in England and Wales are likely to have suffered a stroke, and half or more of these will have survived for at least one year (Aho *et al.*, 1980; Warlow *et al.*, 1987). Weddell and Beresford (1979) calculated that the prevalence of stroke survivors in the community was about four times the annual incidence rate.

In the national survey of handicapped and impaired people in Great Britain, Harris and colleagues (1971) found that 71 per cent of people reporting a previous stroke were very severely, severely, or appreciably disabled, and that stroke was the most common cause of very severe disability. They estimated that there were about 130,000 adults in the community who were disabled by stroke.

Altogether, it has been estimated that the care of stroke patients absorbs about 6 per cent of hospital running costs and nearly 5 per cent of all National Health Service costs (Carstairs, 1976). Supporters of stroke patients also incur economic costs. They often have to give up their jobs or reduce their working hours; Mackay and Nias (1979) found that 12 out of 28 relatives looking after young (under age 65) stroke patients at home were employed before the stroke; when the patient returned home, 8 abandoned their jobs and 2 had to work reduced hours.

Relatives, mainly close family, are the main source of help and support for stroke patients. The suffering of carers has been obvious for many years, as an editorial in the *British Medical Journal* more than a decade ago illustrates:

A sense of isolation is felt as much, or more, by the relatives than by the patient in many households; only those who have experienced it fully appreciate the despair which sometimes overcomes a wife or husband who, without warning or training, has to assume for months or years, a responsibility combining the skills of nurse, remedial therapist, psychologist and speech therapist. This role which calls for unfailing optimism, resilience, and the patience of Job, also calls for a measure of sympathetic understanding and support from community services and society which is seldom forthcoming.   (1974, p. 122)

The evidence to support these observations has become increasingly emphatic in the years since that editorial. A high proportion of people who support the survivors of a stroke identify deleterious effects of caring on their health and emotional well-being (Brocklehurst *et al.*, 1981). Depression among carers has been related to the patient's physical disability in some studies, but not others. However, the Frenchay study (Wade *et al.*, 1986) indicates that in the first year after stroke, the carer's depression is related to the patient's emotional condition. Changes in the patient's mood or personality are often referred to, but their frequency among patients and their serious effects on the lives of supporters have been documented only for a sample of younger stroke survivors (Coughlan and Humphrey, 1982).

Isaacs and colleagues (1976) point out that the stroke patient's increased dependency upon contacts with close family and relatives may contribute to increasing conflict and hostility at home. For carers, the loss of the patient as an active social partner and the demands of patients which reduce the time or energy available for social activities, may be an important cause of problems and distress. Among the spouses of younger stroke patients, the loss of companionship and interference with social and leisure activities were described as the major reasons for a loss of enjoyment in life (Coughlan and Humphrey, 1982). However, among the chief carers of patients in south Manchester, it is reported that the disruption of leisure activities, which had been a significant feature for chief carers shortly after the stroke, was minimal by the end of one year (Brocklehurst *et al.*, 1978). The process of adjustment to a stroke makes certain issues more salient at different stages after stroke, but there is little evidence about how this pattern changes over time.

The aim of this chapter is to contribute to an understanding of these issues: it deals with the problems associated with caring for the stroke patient and the main causes of distress for carers; and then considers more specifically problems caused by changes in the patient, in the supporter's relationship to the patient and in the supporter's social life. Secondly, the chapter discusses the link between these problems and the ways in which patients and carers feel that their enjoyment of and satisfaction with life change following a stroke.

The Concept of Quality of Life

Although there are a wide range of problems to be faced by patients and their carers, researchers have concentrated on the patient's physical disability. They have assessed the contribution of rehabilitation services in terms of reduction of physical disability, as indicated by diverse measures of activities of daily living. Evaluation of services has generally ended at the patient's discharge from hospital and return to home (Garraway and colleagues', 1980 trial of a stroke unit in Edinburgh is a notable exception). The longer-term experience of living with a stroke and the quality of life of stroke patients and their carers, have received scant attention.

The concept of quality of life has gained currency in medical practice and related research, in part to reflect an orientation to 'caring' within health services, to enhancing well-being, in addition to 'curing' and survival after illness. It draws attention to the significance in chronic illness, of living every day with an impairment that may have consequences for social, emotional, working and family life. Perhaps the growing professional interest in the quality of life of stroke patients reflects the visibility of suffering which might be alleviated, against a backdrop of physical impairment which it is very difficult to change.

However, this concept of quality of life remains vague and has rarely been explicitly defined in other research among patients with chronic illness (De Haes and van Knippenberg, 1985). It has often been used interchangeably with concepts and measures of well-being and positive affect (Badura and Waltz, 1984). In general population surveys, there appear to be two primary categories in which quality of life has been investigated: as an objective examination of resources, such as health, housing and income (for example, Hunt, 1978); and as subjective evaluations of conditions or experiences such as satisfaction with health or housing. (George and Bearon, 1980, provide a useful review.) A number of studies with stroke patients have begun to ask questions to establish some of the conditions of life (for example, Brocklehurst *et al.*, 1978) and to assess aspects of psychological well-being (for example, Wade *et al.*, 1986); but none have really sought to capitalize on the value of obtaining evaluations from the patient (Najman and Levine, 1981; Mayou, 1986).

Research on quality of life can be further differentiated into assessments of life in specific domains (for example, work, housing, leisure) and assessments of life in general. Global assessments of life satisfaction are rare in terms of chronic illness (Brown *et al.*, 1981), although they are very common in the gerontological literature (George and Bearon, 1980) and a variety of validated measures have been developed (see Andrews and Withey, 1976). One of these measures was employed in this study to assess the global life satisfaction of patients and their carers. Their general views on quality of life are analysed in relation to their more specific comments, particularly those of the carers, about the aspects of living with stroke that cause them most problems.

Methods

The patients investigated in this study were people aged 60 or over, registered with a general practitioner from Greenwich health district in London who, between April and December 1983, had a stroke, irrespective of severity, and survived for 3 weeks or longer. Altogether 176 patients were identified.

Some of the eligible stroke survivors are likely to have been 'missed' simply because only 54 per cent of general practitioners in the health district confirmed their participation in the study. However, in inner London, perhaps more so than in other urban areas (Brocklehurst *et al.*, 1978; Wade *et al.*, 1985), relatively few patients are cared for exclusively by the general practitioner at home. A crude estimate of the completeness of the sample can be made using epidemiological data from other community registers. Since this is not a study of incidence, but essentially of survivors, the results from four studies in southern England (Weddell and Beresford, 1979; Stevens and Ambler, 1982; Oxford Community Stroke Project, 1983; and Wade *et al.*, 1985) have been aggregated to give rough estimates of: incidence (2 per 1000), proportion of patients aged 60 or over (85 per cent); and survival to three weeks (65 per cent). Altogether, in a health district with a population the size of Greenwich (216,000) about 180 survivors could have been expected over the duration of the research – there were 176. However, none of the other studies was based in London and it seems reasonable to conclude that there is some shortfall in registration of strokes, largely due to a failure to identify a small number of milder cases managed at home.

Response to Interviews

Altogether 98 per cent of the patients were interviewed by the author around 4 weeks after their stroke, when two-thirds were still in hospital. Only three patients refused to participate – two patients did not want their diagnosis passed on to the researcher, and one patient decided, after considering for some time, that he did not wish to participate – this patient believed his diagnosis was psychiatric rather than stroke. It was intended that for each patient a supporter should be identified as 'the person who, in general, gives you most help and support'. This was not necessarily, therefore, someone who gave practical help, but someone who could be providing support by visiting, giving information, showing concern, helping to sort out problems, or improving the patient's morale. If the patient was unable to communicate for any reason then the identification of the

Table 1.1   *The Response of Patients and Supporters*

	Patient's interview			Supporter's interview		
	1st	*2nd*	*3rd*	*1st*	*2nd*	*3rd*
Eligible	176	116	96	148	101	80
Interview	173	110	93	147	95	76
Response rate (%)	98	95	97	99	94	95
Number of deaths before next phase (patients + one supporter)	57	14	—	46	15	—

main supporter was sought from the patient's family or a ward nurse. Altogether main supporters were identified for 160 of the patients: in 6 cases no one appeared to act as a supporter for the patient, and in 7 cases the patient refused to pass on the name of their main supporter. Patients were reassured about the confidentiality of the supporters' interviews and that they would be conducted by another interviewer who knew nothing about the patient; but the patients' main objection was to having their supporter 'bothered' when the supporter was already worried or burdened enough.

Many patients were still very unwell when first seen and 11 died in the next few days before their main supporter was visited. One supporter also died in the days between the patient's interview and their own. So, altogether 148 supporters were available for a first interview. The response rates at the first and subsequent interviews are shown in Table 1.1. The interviews with the patients, and shortly afterwards with their supporters, took place at around four weeks, nine months and eighteen months after the stroke (88 per cent were seen between the third and fifth weeks; 96 per cent between the eighth and tenth months after the stroke).

The next section describes some characteristics of the patients and their supporters before going on to present findings from the study about how patients and their supporters viewed problems caused by the stroke, and its effects on their quality of life.

The Patients and their Supporters

The patients in this study are a cohort of *survivors* from stroke – of people aged 60 and over who lived beyond the acute phase of three weeks after a stroke. There was a small majority of women (55 per cent) and a high proportion of people aged 75 or over (58 per cent). As would be expected the age and sex of patients were related: 19 per

Table 1.2   *Physical Disability among Patients at Different Stages after the Stroke*

Barthel disability rating:	1 month (%)	9 months (%)	18 months (%)
Severe	48	16	17
Moderate	16	23	20
Mild	27	37	40
None	9	24	23
Number of patients for whom information was available (=100%)	172	109	93

cent of men were aged 80 or over compared with 38 per cent of women.[1] Associated with this age difference, 65 per cent of women were widowed and 21 per cent married, compared with 29 per cent of men who were widowed, and 59 per cent who were married at the time of the stroke.

Although these patients had survived the first few weeks many were significantly disabled. The rating of disability was based upon the Barthel system (Mahoney and Barthel, 1965), with patients grouped into four main categories of severity of disability – these are shown in Table 1.2 for patients interviewed at each phase of the study. Changes in the pattern of disability with time were partly because those with more severe disability were more likely to die in the months following the stroke (the proportion who survived to twelve months increased from 46 per cent of the patients who were classified as having 'severe' disability one month after the stroke to 100 per cent of those classified as having 'no' disability); and partly because the functional ability of most patients improved (among patients who were severely disabled one month after the stroke, and were alive eight months later, 37 per cent were still severely disabled, but 35 per cent were rated as having moderate disability, 23 per cent as mild, and 5 per cent as none).

Altogether 88 per cent of the main supporters were relatives of the stroke patient, compared with 96 per cent reported in the stroke studies from Manchester and Edinburgh (Brocklehurst *et al.*, 1981; Murray *et al.*, 1982). This small difference possibly reflects efforts in this study to identify 'carers' for all patients, as well as the higher age of the patients in the Greenwich study. The age of the patient, not surprisingly, affects the identity of the supporter, since older patients

Table 1.3   *Sex of the Patient and Relationship of Supporter*

| Relationship | Sex of patient | | All |
| of the supporter: | Male | Female | supporters |
	(%)	(%)	(%)
Wife	52	0	24
Husband	0	19	10
Daughter (-in-law)	15	38	27
Son (-in-law)	12	22	17
Sister	7	5	6
Brother	0	1	1
Other relative	4	3	3
Friend	7	6	7
Other carer	3	6	5
Number of patients (=100%)	68	79	147

are less likely to have a living spouse. In Manchester, three-fifths of the carers were spouses, in Edinburgh the proportion was somewhat less than half; in Greenwich it was just over one-third. Among patients aged 60–79, 46 per cent of carers were spouses and 35 per cent were children (an inappropriate label considering that no supporter was aged under 25); among patients aged 80 or over only 5 per cent of the main supporters were spouses, and 67 per cent were sons or daughters (including in-laws).

Two-thirds of the supporters were caring for a patient of the opposite sex. The relationship of the supporter to male and female patients is shown in Table 1.3. If spouses are excluded from consideration, then 33 per cent of women patients were receiving their main support from a man (usually their son), and 76 per cent of men had a female supporter. At the time of the stroke half of the supporters were living with the patient, including all spouses and 28 per cent of sons and daughters. Male and female supporters were equally likely to be sharing their home with the patient. All the supporters in the categories of 'other relatives' and 'carers' (four home helps, two care assistants and a social worker) were women; altogether 70 per cent of the main supporters were women. So, in this study as in others, most of the burden of caring falls on women (Anderson, 1987). Nevertheless, the presence of men as carers is substantial; carers are a heterogeneous group and there is a need for caution in the use of simple stereotypes.

Coping with caring

Eighteen months after their stroke two-thirds of patients could carry out fewer activities of daily living independently than they had before the stroke. Their carers were asked about the support they were then giving. In comparison with life before the stroke nearly half the carers, 45 per cent, said they were now spending 'much more' time helping with practical jobs – like getting the patient about, bathing, shopping and doing housework; 21 per cent of supporters said they were spending 'slightly more' time on this, 25 per cent said there had been no change, and 9 per cent said that they were giving less practical help than they had before the stroke. Only 24 per cent of the carers of patients rated as having 'no' disability reported giving 'much more' help compared with 52 per cent of the carers of 'disabled' patients; but among those who were disabled, the severity of the patient's disability was not related to the proportion of carers who felt they were giving 'much more' practical help. It was clear that spouses and the few other supporters who lived with the patient were more likely to be spending 'much more' time giving the patient practical help: 64 per cent of supporters who were living with the patient reported this compared with only 35 per cent of the supporters of patients who were living in their own homes.

Characteristics of the supporters, such as age, sex and social class were not related to their assessments of how much more practical help they were giving. However, there was a major difference between male and female supporters in their views about whether any increase in helping caused particular problems or difficulties: only 44 per cent of men said the increased help had caused problems compared with 79 per cent of the women. This was not because women were caring for patients who were more disabled – they were not; nor simply because more of them cared for men. It may be that women carers were doing more and more frequent work than men, or that they were stretched by other commitments to home, work and family. But perhaps also they were more inclined to identify and respond to problems (see Pearlin and Schooler, 1978); or it may be that, contrary to stereotypes, the men who took on the role of carer were less troubled about this than women. This complex issue about attitudes to caring responsibilities has only recently begun to receive systematic investigation (Allen *et al.*, 1987, especially chs 2 and 3).

The difficulties caused by giving more practical help were not usually a simple product of physical overload. Only two of the carers made direct reference to difficulties caused by lifting or the sheer physical capacity required to do things for the patient. However, the single most common problem was tiredness, which was mentioned by about a quarter of the carers who identified a problem, all of them women. Two of the wives associated the problem with being older themselves:

> I get tired which is only natural because I'm coming up to 68. It isn't as though you're young is it? I'm nowhere near methodical like I used to be because you haven't got the time to be like it.

> Just that I'm getting older and I'm getting very weary. It does put a lot of strain on the wife doesn't it.

The monotonous, repetitive nature of the practical tasks and of the 'strain' was referred to by several other supporters. Among those who did not live with the patient, several mentioned the problem of finding time, as well as energy, to visit and meet the patient's needs. The resources of one daughter were stretched by the problems of getting to her mother's flat:

> I'm there practically every afternoon. I'd much rather be at home. You come out of work absolutely exhausted and all you want to do is get home. It's three bus rides from here to Thamesmead.

The problem of being tied, of being constantly available, rather than the tasks involved, was a source of difficulty for other carers. A woman caring for her 'severely' dependent husband identified the main difficulties as:

> I don't get the sleep that you should have. When you're stuck in for so long you get short-tempered. You just can't put your coat on and run up the shops.

Other difficulties that supporters related to giving more practical help included being 'on call' all the time, feeling worried or depressed about how the patient was coping with practical tasks, and having too little time for other people.

In general, practical tasks were not reported by the supporters as serious difficulties. In part, perhaps, other problems were more distressing; or if the tasks were difficult for the carers then nursing and social services or a neighbour might step in to help. At the second interview, nine months after the stroke, supporters were asked if they helped the patient with various activities of daily living, with housework and with communication; if they did they were asked if this caused them no problem, some problem, or a great problem. The responses are in Table 1.4.

Table 1.4   *Supporters' Attitudes to Helping the Patient with Various Tasks*

This help causes the supporter:	Getting about (%)	Self-care (%)	Help with: Using toilet (%)	House-work (%)	Commun-ication (%)
No problem	70	74	61	77	80
Some problem	30	26	39	23	20
A great problem	0	0	0	0	0
Number of supporters giving help (=100%)	46	46	18	70	51

In these interviews, not one carer who was giving help with practical tasks in these five areas reported that this constituted a great problem. Why not? Most supporters simply said they accepted or did not mind doing what they did. In many cases those who said they had 'no problem' made similar comments about helping in all five areas: these comments broadly reflected values that supporters linked to their marital or filial relationship to the patient, and variously expressed sentiments of pleasure, natural response, acceptance and resignation. Supporters therefore appeared to cope with the direct practical and physical problems of caring. They were asked at both the second and third interviews, 'Of all the things we have discussed what difficulty or problem has upset you most?' Their responses were coded into the general categories shown in Table 1.5.

It was distressing for many supporters to see the patient dependent and restricted; and this helplessness among some patients was particularly striking to carers eighteen months after the stroke, possibly because by then few expected the further improvement that they had been hoping for nine months earlier. The wife of a man in his seventies said she was most upset:

Seeing him like this ['moderately' disabled]. Sometimes I think it would be better if he had been taken when he had the stroke. It's no life at all for him, and it could go on for years like this.

It was, not surprisingly, difficult for some carers to accept that the active partnership of many years was over. One couple had continued working in their early seventies, but now the woman was only able to get about in her wheelchair. Her husband was upset most:

Table 1.5 *Reports from Supporters about the Difficulty or Problem that Upset Them Most*

	After 9 months (%)	After 18 months (%)
Nothing/not distressed (now)	16	15
Social restrictions on supporter (including loss of companionship with patient)	15	14
Carer's isolation (especially lack of support from family/services)	8	7
Patient's mood/personality	19	7
Patient's (physical) dependency, helplessness, lack of recovery	15	30
Practical problem for supporter:		
general	6⎤	4⎤
dealing with incontinence	2⎟	2⎟
communicating with patient	2⎬ 17	8⎬ 15
lifting	2⎟	1⎟
doing housework	5⎦	0⎦
Patient's housing/accommodation	5	5
Other problems of patient	3	3
Other problems of supporter	2	4
Number of supporters (=100%)	87	73

To see the helplessness of a woman that's always been so active. She was able and so capable. She was never no trouble to me physically.

Inevitably, many of the supporters who lived with patients who were unable to walk were doing more practical work, but the poignancy or distress for them appeared to be generated less by the demands caused by disability and more by what the disability represented:

To think that he can't walk. He lived in the garden; if he could walk that would be the best thing. Sometimes he looks out the window and you know what he's thinking.

Carers, then, often felt sorry for patients who were often distressed themselves. The daughter of a woman who was rated as 'no' disability was upset by:

How much it depresses her. To see her in these depressive states, that upsets me. And I don't like her feeling incapable.

Altogether, 60 per cent of supporters compared with 45 per cent of patients felt that the patient had changed as a person in the eighteen months following the stroke. These changes, whether viewed by patient or supporter, were generally negative, and were a particular source of distress for supporters around the period nine months after the stroke. For example, the two spouses quoted above who, eighteen months after the stroke, were upset by seeing the patients unable to care for themselves had different concerns at nine months after the stroke:

This change of character; but everybody has said that this is something that is so common with this complaint.

He goes at me. There's not a day goes by he doesn't go at me. Every day I go to the hospital I think what am I going to be greeted with this time.

This woman was one among several carers (though she did not know this) who were feeling tired and upset by the patient's bad humour:

When she can't see right from wrong: she drives me mad at times.

I don't really know. I can't express it – very difficult; cussedness I suppose really. He can be very cussed at times. This is when he does cause me stress – when he's awkward.

The wife of a patient who was both moderately disabled and had a major loss of speech expressed a sentiment shared by many of the married couples that the stroke had disrupted their plans for the future together (their joint biography, see Bury, 1982) and that this was somehow not fair:

To feel that Jack's like this. I get upset to think we've worked hard together to enjoy this time of life and now this has happened. You feel there's no justice sometimes.

Among the different ways in which the stroke affects the lives of carers, the restrictions on their social life and free use of time were frequently upsetting, mentioned by one in seven of the carers at both the second and third interviews. Occasionally, social activities were lost because they had previously been joint activities with the patient; as a wife said:

I do miss going out together like we used to, I do get a bit depressed over that.

And the husband of a woman who had become housebound said he was most upset because:

There's quite a lot of things that we can't do together like holidays, going for walks together, all of them little things, where we used to have a rave-up.

More commonly, though, supporters had opportunities for independent social activity but were not able to use them. Some were unable to pursue previous interests, as one woman reported:

The fact that I can't socialize, go to classes, mix with people. I used to do that when I was at work.

Others were distressed because they felt themselves to be trapped by the stroke, tied to the patient's needs and to the home in which the patient lived. A son described the most distressing aspect of his father's stroke as:

Being tied to the house itself, because that's where he is.

And, echoing the woman who described the illness as unjust, another wife said the main upset was:

Just that you can't get out really. You've come to an age when you could have a bit of enjoyment in life and you can't, you're stopped.

Altogether the wives of stroke patients appeared to have reduced their social activities (contact with family and friends, visits to pubs, clubs, church, theatre and other events) no more than other carers, but they were more likely to report that their social life had changed. Sixty-three per cent of wives felt that their social life had changed since the stroke compared with 35 per cent of other supporters. In part, this probably reflects a decline in shared social involvement with their husbands, but their comments frequently referred to independent activities outside their home. The wife of a man with mild disability said:

I'm getting an awful bore. I can't get out and do anything.

However, many wives and other supporters appeared to accept the limitations with equanimity, remarking that:

I've got the telephone and that makes a lot of difference.

Or as the husband of a woman with 'severe' disability said:

I just take it as it comes. I've got no intent to go out and leave her.

One-fifth of all supporters described their social activities as 'severely' restricted by the stroke, but 47 per cent of wives said this compared with 11 per cent of other supporters. Nearly three-quarters of the spouses at eighteen months after the stroke were wives so that, in total, 38 per cent of spouses of the patient described their social activities as 'severely' restricted – a high proportion compared with, for example, the 26 per cent of bereaved spouses who said this about their lives during the period of their deceased's last illness (Bowling and Cartwright, 1982). It was not, however, the physical disability caused by stroke that led directly to a restricted social life for carers. The severity of the patient's disability at one month and eighteen months after the stroke was not clearly related to the carer's reporting of social restrictions. The experience of living together with the patient appeared to be an important consideration: in general, 41 per cent of supporters who shared their home with the patient viewed their lives as 'severely' restricted compared with only 6 per cent of the supporters of patients who were living in their own homes. But among supporters who lived with the patient, 50 per cent of women felt their social life was 'severely' restricted compared with 20 per cent of men. Although this difference was not statistically significant, it reflects a fairly consistent difference in the carers' experience of stroke.

Assessments of Quality of Life

The feeling that social life was restricted by the stroke appeared to contribute strongly to the supporter's view that life was less enjoyable since the stroke. In the interviews eighteen months after the stroke, 27 per cent of supporters described life as 'much less' enjoyable and 25 per cent reported that it was 'slightly less' so. However, the proportion of supporters who felt life was (either 'much' or 'slightly') less enjoyable increased from 24 per cent of those who felt their life

Table 1.6   *Supporters' View that Life Is Less Enjoyable and Whether Lives with the Patient*

	Proportion enjoying life less					
	Lives with patient					
	Yes		*No*		*All*	
Supporter's sex: male	60%	(10)	17%	(12)	36%	(22)
female	91%	(22)	35%	(31)	58%	(53)
Patient's sex male	85%	(20)	36%	(11)	68%	(31)
female	75%	(12)	28%	(32)	41%	(44)
All supporters	81%	(32)	30%	(43)	52%	(75)

Figures in parentheses are the numbers on which percentages are based.

was 'not at all' restricted to 93 per cent of those who felt that the stroke had made their social life 'severely' restricted. The carers' comments about their loss of enjoyment frequently referred to the problem of being tied to the patient, if only to give social support. So even the supporters of patients who were in hospital might report a loss of independence; the wife of a man in long-term care described life as 'slightly less' enjoyable:

It wasn't any too convivial before, but I could go out.

And the devoted sister of a bachelor in his early sixties said she enjoyed life 'slightly less' because:

My whole life seems to be wrapped up in hospital now.

In the longer term, only one in eight of the patients lived in a hospital or a residential or nursing home. So, most stroke survivors were supported in the community by their family and friends. The key general condition influencing change in the carers' enjoyment of life appeared to be whether the patient and supporter were living together at the time of the third interview. This is shown in Table 1.6, which also presents differences by sex of the supporter and patient. Supporters who lived with the patient were considerably more likely than others to report that they enjoyed life less, but sex differences between supporters who did or did not live with the patient were not consistently significant.

A further important variable appears to be the quality of the relationship between the supporter and patient before the stroke, as reported by the supporter at the first interview one month after the stroke. While only 42 per cent of supporters who described the relationship before the stroke as 'very happy' were enjoying life less, this proportion was 69 per cent among supporters who said the relationship had been only 'fairly happy' or 'not happy'. However, among supporters who were living with the patient the quality of the relationship before the stroke could not protect their enjoyment of life. It was among the supporters of patients who lived in their own homes that the quality of the relationship before the stroke was a decisive factor: only 10 per cent of those who had enjoyed a 'very happy' relationship reported that, at eighteen months after stroke, they enjoyed life less, compared with 57 per cent of the rest.

Changes in the supporters' enjoyment of life appeared to be influenced more by changes in the person with the stroke than by the physical impairment or the severity of the disability, even though the proportion of supporters who were distressed by the patient's physical dependency had risen sharply between nine and eighteen months after the stroke (see Table 1.5). Among the supporters who described changes in the patient as a person 62 per cent felt they were enjoying life less compared with 27 per cent of the supporters who believed the patient was much the same person as they had been before the stroke. It is possible that the supporter's perception of changes in the patient's mood and behaviour is exaggerated by their favourable reconstruction of the patient as she was before the stroke, or by their greater sensitivity to the patient's mental state following the stroke. As some control for this, supporters were asked in all three interviews a series of specific questions about the frequency of positive and negative moods in the patient and their responses were scored (see Appendix). Changes in the patient's mood were clearly associated with changes in the supporter's enjoyment of life: so, the proportion of supporters who described themselves as enjoying life less increased from 40 per cent for supporters whose ratings indicated improved mood to 77 per cent for supporters whose scores for the patient's 'positive mood' fell by three or more points; and the proportion of supporters who enjoyed life less increased from 27 per cent of the supporters of patients whose score on 'negative mood' had fallen since the stroke to 62 per cent of the supporters of patients whose 'negative mood' score had increased by three or more points.

In general, the supporters of patients who were, eighteen months after stroke, more disabled than they had been before it, were enjoying life less – 65 per cent of these supporters reported they were enjoying life less compared with 32 per cent of the supporters of patients whose level of dependency was not greater than before the stroke. However, the extent of increase in the patient's dependency was not associated with change in the supporter's enjoyment of life.

Clearly many factors mediate the effects of the disability on the life of the supporter. Living with the patient, as well as changes in the personality of the patient and in the supporter's opportunities to maintain their social life appear to be major considerations here.

It might be supposed that the patient's view about change in her enjoyment of life would relate fairly closely to changes in physical disability. However, patients' reports about changes in their enjoyment of life were not associated with changes in Barthel scores since the stroke, and, in comparison with life before the stroke, the only significant distinction was between those patients whose disability had increased (89 per cent of them said they were enjoying life less) and those patients who had returned at least to 'normal' (43 per cent of whom said they were enjoying life less).

Changes in enjoyment of life reported by patients appeared to reflect their attitudes to their life before the stroke and their expectation of what they should be doing or able to do at the current stage of their life. For example, one 80-year-old woman who had been independent but who, following the stroke, needed help to bath and did not walk outdoors, described life as 'slightly' less enjoyable, because:

Well, I always led a quiet life.

And a 76-year-old man, who had moved from living independently with family to living in a residential home and getting about in a wheelchair, also described life after the stroke as only 'slightly' less enjoyable:

But I take no notice of it. You've got to be satisfied as you are, I think.

The patients' feelings about changes in enjoyment in their lives were not related to their age or social class, but men were considerably more likely to report that they enjoyed life 'much less' – 52 per cent of them said this, compared with 26 per cent of women. In their comments, several of the men who enjoyed life 'much less' referred to a loss of freedom or independence – themes which hardly cropped up in the responses of women. A bachelor in his seventies reported that:

I was a free person before the stroke, I could go anywhere I liked and do anything . . . if anything goes wrong I like to put it right.

And a married man who had given up his part-time business following the stroke said he enjoyed life 'much less' because:

We [patient and wife] used to get out more, didn't we? If we wanted a day down the coast we had a day down the coast . . . I can't go away like this. My foot has to be done every day. And with this stroke on me, how can I scrape about like this? My people offered me a wheelchair, but no way would I do that and my wife have to push.

There was no statistically significant difference between male and female patients in the extent of the change in their social activities following the stroke; nor, in general, were men more likely than women to view their social life following the stroke as a problem. Perhaps the feeling of loss of freedom draws upon a more general sense of restriction in the lives of men who, in the years before the stroke, had been used to involvement in work and contacts outside the home.

Satisfaction with Life

To illuminate their general feelings about life eighteen months after stroke, patients and their supporters were invited in the final interview to describe their general satisfaction with life. There have been no previous reports of 'global' life satisfaction among stroke patients or their carers; and the choice of an appropriate question was limited by communication and visuospatial problems among patients. After trying various approaches in the pre-pilot study the 'Faces' scale was selected as a method of assessing general satisfaction with life. The approach appeared easy to understand, acceptable and practical for most of the speech-impaired patients. Respondents were asked to indicate which of seven faces came closest to expressing how they felt about their life as a whole; their responses are shown in Table 1.7.

This approach, using a single-item measure, is common in survey research. The faces are not presented with any definition of the constituents of 'life satisfaction', so the respondent can frame a response within her own interpretation of the meaning and constituents of the construct. This does not mean though that the responses are arbitrary, and the measure has demonstrated good validity and reliability (Andrews and Withey, 1976). One question, however, is whether this assessment amounts to anything more than another measure of affective state. Among both patients and supporters ratings of 'life satisfaction' were highly correlated with levels of 'emotional distress' ($r=-0.6$ in both cases); but only a third of the patients and supporters who reported 'no distress' also rated their life satisfaction with the most positive face (A). This indicates that the

Table 1.7   *Satisfaction with Current 'Life as a Whole' for Patients and Supporters*

Face which came closest to expressing feelings	Patients (%)	Supporters (%)
A	12	20
B	27	26
C	26	24
D	16	16
E	8	10
F	3	1
G	8	3
Number of patients/ supporters (=100%)	74	70

questions are tapping two different, but related, constructs (see George and Bearon, 1980).

These responses of patients and supporters are more negative than those reported for a sample of people aged 70 and over living in the same community – 63 per cent of whom identified their life satisfaction with the smiling faces A or B (Tester, 1986). Although in the stroke study the distribution of responses among patients and supporters is similar (as seen in Table 1.7) there was no significant relationship between the attitudes of the individual patient and their carer (the correlation coefficient was only 0.14). So, patients and supporters take somewhat different views of the general satisfaction in their daily lives following stroke (and probably this would also be the case in, for example, a study comparing the subjective life satisfaction of marital partners).

Spouses and other carers living with the patient appeared less likely than other carers to describe their satisfaction with life by faces A or B. Table 1.8 shows that, in particular, the wives of stroke patients were unlikely to be satisfied with life – only 18 per cent indicated that face A or B represented their feelings. This dissatisfaction with life among wives is a major reason for the marked sex difference in satisfaction among supporters and more so the major difference between the carers of male and female patients. The carers of male patients were markedly less satisfied with life. These differences were not associated with the severity of the patient's disability, but with the quality of the relationship between the patient and the carer. The lack of association between disability and the supporter's quality of life may be due in some part to insensitivity of the measurements; but the greater importance of the supporter's assessment of her relationship with the patient is not unexpected since many of the main difficulties identified by supporters as being caused by the stroke were not due to coping with the physical disability, but to coping with the patient who had that disability.

Satisfaction with life was not associated with the supporter's social class, but younger supporters were more likely to feel that faces A and B represented their feelings: the proportion doing so fell from 60 per cent of supporters aged 25–44, to 28 per cent of those aged 65 or over. This difference is probably due, in part at least, to the relatively small proportion of younger supporters who were either the spouse of, or lived with, the patient. One variable consistently related to subjective assessments of life quality is the respondent's assessment of her health (Brown *et al.*, 1981). Among supporters in Greenwich, 56 per cent of those who rated their health as excellent or good described their satisfaction with life by faces A or B, compared with 32 per cent of carers who said their health was only fair or poor. But the rating by

Table 1.8 *Some Factors Influencing the Supporters' Satisfaction with Life*

Proportion of supporters who indicated that faces A or B represented their feelings about 'life as a whole'

Barthel rating of patient's disability			
at 18 months after stroke:	severe/moderate	52% (25)	
	mild/normal	41% (44)	
Relationship of supporter to			
patient	wife	18% (17)	} 25% (24)
	husband	43% (7)	
	other	58% (40)	
Supporter's sex	female	38% (48)	
	male	64% (22)	
Patient's sex	male	19% (27)	
	female	63% (43)	
Supporter lives with patient		33% (30)	
Patient lives elsewhere		57% (35)	
(excluding hospital)			
Quality of relationship with			
patient at third interview:	very happy	71% (28)	
	fairly happy	36% (33)	
	not happy	0% (8)	

Figures in parentheses are the numbers on which percentages are based.

carers of the patient's health was not associated with their satisfaction with life. Surprisingly, the patient's disability (Barthel score) was not an important factor related to assessments by either the patient or supporter of their satisfaction with life.

The proportion of patients who identified their life satisfaction with faces A or B was 29 per cent among those who were severely or moderately disabled compared with 43 per cent of patients who had mild or no disability, but this difference was not statistically significant. Nor was life satisfaction related to functional improvement following the stroke. The only significant difference was that patients who returned to or improved upon their performance of activities of daily living from before the stroke were more likely to describe their satisfaction with life as a whole by face A; 23 per cent of them did this compared with only 5 per cent of patients who had deteriorated in their performance of ADL (activities of daily living). Physical disability, then, appears to have a relatively small, though not insignificant, influence on the patients' attitudes to life as a whole. In part this may be because physical disability is a common and accepted element in older age – something which generally does not cause unemployment, or have serious financial consequences for the patients; and which may not disrupt the main social activity of visits to and from family and friends. In part this relatively low impact of disability may be having an effect on levels of life satisfaction which were not very high before the stroke; and, in part, it may be that the disability scale is a measure of dependency, and therefore looks at fairly gross capacities. The finer detail of disability – the time it takes to button a shirt, the ability to cut and butter a slice of bread – may be overlooked, although these are meaningful limitations in the lives of patients who are classified as 'independent' in activities of daily living.

The major difference in the patients' life satisfaction was related to their social class: only 13 per cent of patients who were classified as middle-class represented their satisfaction with life by faces A or B compared with 46 per cent of working-class patients. This is opposite to what was found in a survey of the general population of older people (cf. Taylor and Ford, 1983), but may reflect the capacity of working-class people to cope better with fewer resources and options. Possibly working-class patients are more 'fatalistic' about the future and have fewer 'shattered dreams' following stroke: they may feel less need to maintain appearances and have lower expectations of what life will or should offer, though, again, it is important to avoid stereotyping in this regard.

Summary and Implications

The focus of this chapter has been upon the experiences of the carers of the stroke patients rather than upon the patients themselves. In part this emphasis is intended to focus on the reality of caring, especially by the family, and in part the aim has been to consider the experience of stroke from the carer's perspective. Both patients and their carers face assaults upon their functioning at various levels – physical, social, economic, mental. Among these diverse problems, patients and their carers often appear to have different anxieties and priorities. While patients are preoccupied with physical performance and improving their walking, their carers often seem more concerned about the patient's mental state and about restrictions on their own social lives. The data on perceptions of personality change among the patients indicate that carers identify considerably more than patients do. And the main concerns of the carers change over time following the stroke – an understanding of this process of change is critical for timely and effective communication by service providers. At their final interview most of the carers in Greenwich (72 per cent) felt they had not been well prepared with advice and information for the problems they had had to face as a result of the stroke.

The dominant professional view of stroke and its consequences is bound up with physical disability and rehabilitation. For patients, their physical condition must generally impose constraints upon their everyday activities, and this is a major concern for them; but it was striking that the extent of physical disability bore little relationship to their statements about quality of life. This seems an unlikely finding, but, in the extensive research on cardiac disability, it is similarly the case that little association is found between cardiological measures of severity, social handicaps and mental state (Badura and Waltz, 1984; Mayou, 1986). In their study of life satisfaction among people with coronary artery disease Brown and colleagues (1981) report that the more disabled patients tended to be more satisfied; they suggest that more disabled patients may experience some secondary gain through legitimation of the sick role, and through alleviation of their guilt over failure to perform everyday roles. The theory underlying these hypotheses about accommodation to different severities of disability remains underdeveloped.

The experience of caring for stroke patients with varying gradations of dependency appears remarkably similar; it is the division between patients who were and were not assessed as independent that discriminated more clearly between carers who felt that their social life was restricted and between their assessments of change in enjoyment of life. The quality of life of carers who lived with the patient, particularly female carers, diminished almost regardless of the severity of the patient's disability. Perhaps women, who are more likely to be socialized into 'expressive' roles are both more sensitive to changes in the patient as a person, and more distressed by the effects of the illness on personal relationships.

Relatively few carers expressed distress over the physical help they gave to the patient. Tiredness is a problem for many carers caused by giving more practical help, but generally the practical and physical tasks were not a major cause of upset. Carers sometimes received help with practical care for the patient, and, for a variety of reasons, few carers considered that providing help with practical tasks was something to complain about. Nearly a quarter of all carers described social isolation or restriction as the most distressing problem, and the greater significance of social life over practical tasks as a cause of stress has also been reported in a large study of carers in South Wales (Jones and Vetter, 1985). The high proportion of carers who were upset mainly by changes in the patient's mood is a further indication that carers had different 'limits of tolerance' for different problems. For many carers there is an important 'double loss' – of their social and domestic companion, and of the person they knew before the stroke – which may explain some of the greater distress experienced by carers living with the patient. Altogether, the results from this study underline general findings from other research on caring (Anderson, 1987), which point to the poor quality of relationships and social life as prime causes of stress among carers.

George and Bearon (1980) note that the concept of life satisfaction refers to a cognitive comparison between aspirations and achievements. Among the stroke patients and their carers, it appeared that some of the differences in life satisfaction between different groups might be understood in relation to different expectations of the future. This seems to apply particularly to supporters who before the stroke were looking forward to some 'enjoyment in life' (for example, wives of recently retired men) and to patients who were used to making choices or organizing their lives. So, for example, several male patients referred to loss of their freedom or ability to control their lives; and some of the men were probably suffering the uncertainties caused by a reversal of domestic power relations as they had become unable to dictate aspects of their everyday life. The disparity between previous expectations and current experience of daily life may also illuminate the dilemma of middle-class patients whose life satisfaction was, surprisingly, lower than for patients classified as working-class; possibly, following the stroke, these patients found it harder to adjust and to accept lower expectations of life.

The concepts of quality of life and life satisfaction have been useful for describing some differences in the general experience of stroke patients and their carers. The social patterning of this response to stroke indicates some groups at particular risk for reduced quality of life and suggests some factors influencing the relationship between the stroke and the quality of everyday life. However, the global concept of quality of life is relatively uninformative about the conditions of life that give rise to lowered satisfaction. The theoretical underpinning of research on quality of life is insecure, making the interpretation of results difficult. Nevertheless, in another study of patients with chronic illness (Brown *et al.*, 1981), changes in the patients' social activity emerged as the single best predictor of their life satisfaction. The relationship between onset of disability and changes in the social life of both patients and carers is an obvious area for further investigation. However, both variables, disability and social life, need to be measured in ways that are more sensitive to the meaning of illness for patients and their supporters. Measurement of changes in social life, for example, should cover elements of activity that patients and carers value, but should extend to incorporate aspects of the subjective assessment of the quality of significant social relationships.

Although studies of community populations indicate aspects, or domains, of life which appeared to contribute most to its quality, it is not clear that the values attached to the different aspects of life are the same among stroke patients or others with chronic illness. Possibly, for example, the importance of maintaining general social contacts is diminished, while the quality of family life or marriage becomes more important. Conversely, carers may seek compensations in the general social contacts for their less rewarding relationships within the home. The identification of the main causes of satisfaction and distress for patients and carers (and these are likely to be different) is an urgent consideration with implications for practice. Much previous research has been dominated by a perspective which assumes that physical disability is the main influence on the quality of life – a view that appears to neglect major determinants identified in studies of the experience of illness.

The concept of global life satisfaction is flourishing in a climate in which care of the 'whole' person has become the catch-phrase of a progressive orientation. However, the direct effect on life satisfaction of most current practice is probably small. In part, this is because global satisfaction is an insensitive reflection of the impact of specific interventions.

These should be evaluated in their own terms, although it seems reasonable to incorporate some assessment of what patients and carers feel about these interventions. But the problem is also in part because most current interventions are not directed at the social and psychological aspects of physical disability which constitute so much of the patients' and carers' appreciation of the illness. These psychosocial sequelae of stroke appear to be common; supportive care may be enhanced through greater professional awareness of the range of specific problems that patients and carers face in living with stroke. The results of this study suggest that some patients and carers find adjustment more difficult – for example, carers who live with the patients and, especially, those who were less happy in their relationships before the stroke. Information appears to be transferred relatively unsuccessfully to prepare patients and their carers for the problems that arise after stroke; and these problems and priorities change over time demanding some continuity of care and interest. Among the service providers there is a lack of co-ordination of support (Royal College of Physicians, 1986), but the remedy may lie less in the domain of disability specialists than in the strengthening of familiar support from primary health care. If services are going to improve quality of life after stroke they must attend to the aspirations of patients and their supporters – and respond to the constraints in their lives that are most important to them. Help and advice from services needs to be more relevant to the issues – changes in social, particularly marital, relationships and in mood or personality – which appear to exert a profound influence on the quality of life of patients and their carers.

Notes

1　Unless otherwise stated, attention has not been drawn to differences that might have occurred by chance five or more times in a hundred.

Appendix – Patient's Mood

Discussion of changes in the patient's 'personality' or 'mood' following stroke are commonplace, but there has never been an attempt to systematically document these changes in everyday, rather than psychotic, behaviour. Other studies of changes in the mood of patients with senile dementia and with heart disease were used to identify items, and these were investigated in the pilot study. In the main study, supporters were asked at all three interviews how often the patient was:

(1)　warm and affectionate towards you,
(2)　complaining and critical,
(3)　aggressive or bad-tempered,
(4)　cheerful,
(5)　demanding attention,
(6)　alert and interested,
(7)　irritable and easily upset,
(8)　appreciative of things you did,
(9)　depressed.

The responses were coded and scored: never – 0; sometimes – 1; often – 2. These nine items were placed into two groups for scoring: positive (items 1, 4, 6 and 8); and negative (items 2, 3, 5, 7 and 9). The total score for positive mood is from 0 to 8, and for negative mood from 0 to 10.

References

Aho, K., Harmsen, P., Hatano, S., Marquardsen, J., Smirnov, V. E., and Strasser, T. (1980), 'Cerebrovascular disease in the community: results of a WHO collaborative study', *Bulletin of the World Health Organisation*, vol. 58, no. 1, 113–30.

Allen, I., Wicks, M., Finch, J., and Leat, D. (1987), *Informal Care Tomorrow* (London: Policy Studies Institute).

Anderson, R. (1987), 'The unremitting burden on carers', *British Medical Journal*, vol. 294, pp. 73–4.

Andrews, F. M., and Withey, S. B. (1976), *Social Indicators of Well Being* (New York: Plenum Press).

Badura, B., and Waltz, M. (1984), 'Social support and quality of life following myocardial infarction', *Social Indicators Research*, vol. 14, 295–311.

Bowling, A., and Cartwright, A. (1982), *Life after a Death* (London: Tavistock).

British Medical Journal (1974), Editorial: 'Stroke and the family', *British Medical Journal*, vol. 4, p. 122.

Brocklehurst, J. C., Andrews, K., Morris, P. E., Richards, B. and Laycock, P. (1978), *Medical, Social and Psychological Aspects of Stroke*, Final report to the DHSS.

Brocklehurst, J. C., Morris, P., Andrews, K., Richards, B. and Laycock, P. (1981), 'Social effects of stroke', *Social Science and Medicine*, vol. 15A, pp. 35–9.

Brown, J. S., Rawlinson, M. E., and Hilles, N. C. (1981), 'Life satisfaction and chronic disease: exploration of a theoretical model', *Medical Care*, vol. 19, no. 2, pp. 1136–46.

Bury, M. (1982), 'Chronic illness as biographical disruption', *Sociology of Health and Illness*, vol. 4, no. 2, pp. 167–82.

Carstairs, V. (1976), 'Stroke: resource consumption and the cost to the community', in F. J. Gillingham, C. Mawdsley, and A. E. Williams (eds), *Stroke* (Edinburgh: Churchill Livingstone).

Coughlan, A. K., and Humphrey, M. (1982), 'Presenile stroke: long term outcome for patients and their families', *Rheumatology and Rehabilitation*, vol. 21, pp. 115–22.

De Haes, J. C. J. M., and van Knippenberg, F. C. E. (1985), 'The quality of life of cancer patients: a review of the literature', *Social Science and Medicine*, vol. 20, no. 8, pp. 809–17.

Dickens, C. (1841), *Barnaby Rudge* (London: Chapman & Hall).

Garraway, W. M., Akhtar, A. J., Hockey, L., and Prescott, R. J. (1980), 'Management of acute stroke in the elderly: follow up of a controlled trial', *British Medical Journal*, vol. 281, pp. 827–9.

George, L. K., and Bearon, L. B. (1980), *Quality of Life in Older Persons: Meaning and Measurement* (New York: Human Sciences Press).

Harris, A. I., Cox, E., and Smith, C. R. W. (1971), *Handicapped and Impaired in Great Britain. Part 1*, OPCS Social Survey Division (London: HMSO).

Hunt, A. (1978), *The Elderly at Home: A Study of People aged Sixty and*

Over Living in the Community in England in 1976, OPCS Social Survey Division (London: HMSO).

Isaacs, B., Neville, Y., and Rushford, I. (1976), 'The stricken: the social consequences of stroke', *Age and Ageing*, vol. 5, pp. 188–92.

Johnson, E. (1979), *Charles Dickens: His Tragedy and Triumph* (London: Penguin).

Jones, D. A., and Vetter, N. J. (1985), 'Formal and informal support received by carers of elderly dependants', *British Medical Journal*, vol. 291, pp. 643–5.

Mackay, A., and Nias, B. C. (1979), 'Strokes in the young and middle-aged: consequences to the family and to society', *Journal of the Royal College of Physicians of London*, vol. 13, no. 2, pp. 106–12.

Mahoney, F. I., and Barthel, D. W. (1965), 'Functional evaluations: the Barthel index', *Maryland State Medical Journal*, vol. 14, pp. 61–5.

Mayou, R. (1986), 'The psychiatric and social consequences of coronary artery surgery', *Journal of Psychosomatic Research*, vol. 30, pp. 255–71.

Murray, S. K., Garraway, W. M., Akhtar, A. J., and Prescott, R. J. (1982), 'Communication between home and hospital in the management of acute stroke in the elderly', *Health Bulletin*, vol. 40, pp. 214–19.

Najman, J. M., and Levine, S. (1981), 'Evaluating the impact of medical care and technologies on the quality of life: a review and critique', *Social Science and Medicine*, vol. 15F, pp. 107–15.

Office of Population Censuses and Surveys (1985), 'Deaths: selected causes and sex', *Population Trends*, vol. 41, pp. 50–1.

Oxfordshire Community Stroke Project (1983), 'Incidence of stroke in Oxfordshire: first year's experience of a community stroke register', *British Medical Journal*, vol. 287, pp. 713–17.

Pearlin, L. I., and Schooler, C. (1978), 'The structure of coping', *Journal of Health and Social Behaviour*, vol. 19, pp. 2–21.

Royal College of Physicians (1986), 'Physical disability in 1986 and beyond', *Journal of the Royal College of Physicians of London*, vol. 20, pp. 161–94.

Stevens, R. S., and Ambler, W. R. (1982), 'The incidence and survival of stroke patients in a defined community', *Age and Ageing*, vol. 11, pp. 266–74.

Taylor, R., and Ford, G. (1983), 'Inequalities in old age: an examination of age, sex and class differences in a sample of community elderly', *Ageing and Society*, vol. 3, pp. 183–208.

Tester, S., and Meredith, B. (1987), 'Ill informed? A study of information and support for elderly people in the inner-city', *PSI Report* 664, Policy Studies Institute, London.

Wade, D. T., Langton-Hewer, R., Skilbeck, C. E., Bainton, D., and Burns-Cox, C. (1985), 'Controlled trial of a home-care service for acute stroke patients', *Lancet*, vol. 1, pp. 323–6.

Wade, D. T., Legh-Smith, J., and Langton-Hewer, R. (1986), 'Effects of living with and looking after survivors of stroke', *British Medical Journal*, vol. 293, pp. 418–20.

Warlow, C., Wade, D., Sandercock, P., Muir, J., House, A., Bamford, J., Anderson, R., and Allen, C. (1987), *Strokes* (Lancaster: MTP Press).

Weddell, J. M., and Beresford, S. A. A. (1979), *Planning for Stroke Patients* (London: HMSO).

2 Reconstructing Lives: Negotiating the Meaning of Multiple Sclerosis

IAN ROBINSON

Would I be a different person? Would I be of any use to anyone? What function would I be able to perform? Would I be able to hold down a job? How was it all going to turn out? . . . Would any disability stop at my legs or would my arms become useless too? What were the chances of discovering a cure before it was too late? How could I cope for the next 40 years?

(Tom age 30, on discovering his diagnosis of multiple sclerosis)

I was absolutely shattered. I wondered how we were going to cope, and what the future would hold for us. Could David keep his job going? How were we going to manage financially? The worst thing seems to be the unpredictability. I wasn't sure how long his health would last, or mine to look after him.

(Margaret, age 25, on discovering her husband had
multiple sclerosis)

Multiple sclerosis is, in many respects, a medical mystery. It is a chronic neurological disease of unknown aetiology, complex symptomatology, problematic diagnosis, ineffective therapy, and unpredictable prognosis. It affects more women than men; has its onset primarily between the ages of 20 and 50 and variably affects motor and sensory functions (Smith and Scheinberg, 1985). The disease may lead rapidly to wheelchair-bound impairment and an early death, but far more usually has a lengthy course characterized by relapses and remissions with gradually increasing functional difficulties. There are also relatively benign forms of the disease. There are no accurate means at present of predicting the course in those individuals who have multiple sclerosis. It is estimated that there are probably 50,000 cases in Great Britain (Acheson, 1985) and 250,000 in the United States (Baum and Rothschild, 1981).

In this setting the reconstruction and maintenance of a viable personal and social life after the onset of the condition involves managing, and making sense of the management of as many of these potentially disconcerting features as possible. As Strauss (1984, p. 79) indicates: 'The chief business of chronically ill persons is not just to stay alive or keep their symptoms under control, but to live as normally as possible despite the symptoms and disease.'

Living as normally as possible, as for those not affected by chronic disease, is a task woven into the fabric of social life. The immediate social environment of family, friends, helpers, supporters and carers is as instrumental in conditioning the management of multiple sclerosis, as are personal aims, ambitions and objectives of those with the disease. As Burnfield (1985, p. 95) states it: 'MS is not a disease which affects people in isolation. When one person in the family has MS then the whole family "has MS" as well.'

In this discussion the family context, and particularly the relationship between husband and wife is considered in the light of the onset, and development of multiple sclerosis. Some of the changes that occur in this setting are substantial and, in certain cases present major difficulties for the marital relationship.

Investigating the Social Context of Managing of Multiple Sclerosis

Both the process of managing multiple sclerosis, and the ways that people make sense of that social process have been generally under-researched. It appears that the word 'social' has generally been interpreted in a narrow and limited sense in 'psychosocial' research – which has come to constitute a major theme of investigation into the disease. Such research has concentrated on psychopathological features associated with multiple sclerosis (Marsh, Ellison and Strite, 1983), or on questions of the relationship of self-image to the developing disease (Matson and Brooks, 1977). In epidemiological terms the idea of 'the social' has been limited to the demographic correlates of multiple sclerosis (Kurtzke, 1980). What has been under-researched is the idea of disease as developing, and being experienced, in a social context.

The respondents for the study of family, and particularly marital relationships considered here were drawn from a Research Register of people with multiple sclerosis from the British charity ARMS

(Action for Research into Multiple Sclerosis). The Register consists of a national population of members of ARMS who have given written permission for their involvement in research, and is held at, and administered through Brunel, The University of West London. ARMS is one of two major charities working exclusively for people with multiple sclerosis in Britain. It differs from the second major charity, the Multiple Sclerosis Society, in that, amongst other features, its membership is almost exclusively those with the disease, or those who are immediately caring for them. ARMS not only funds major research projects, but – unlike the Multiple Sclerosis Society – is directly involved in its own right with the espousal, organization and support of particular modes of therapeutic intervention in the disease – through nutritional and physiotherapeutic advice and other facilities in local therapy centres.

The specific data on which this study is based are two mail questionnaire surveys of 850 members of the Research Register, the first, about their discovery of the diagnosis of multiple sclerosis, and the second on their demographic characteristics; a random sub-sample of 100 Register members and their spouses from a mail questionnaire survey of members' and their helpers' and supporters' problems; and autobiographies received from members of the Research Register and their spouses. In this study all the quotations are taken from the survey of Register members and their helpers and supporters unless otherwise indicated. The names of those individual husbands and wives who are quoted have been changed to preserve anonymity.

The data, and the subsequent analyses are not claimed to be formally representative of the total population of those with multiple sclerosis. However, such representativeness is indeed particularly difficult, perhaps an impossible goal to achieve given certain features associated with the disease. It is likely that the various modes of onset of multiple sclerosis; the differential initial contact with the health-care system; varied medical referral and diagnostic practices, and the post-diagnostic behaviour of both patients and physicians, will lead to significant problems of representation. This is certainly true of hospital populations – the conventional sampling frame for research studies (Detels *et al.*, 1982).

As an alternative population for research there has been relatively little use of the records of the major charities associated with the disease, although some studies have indicated its viability (for example, Matson and Brooks, 1977). However, becoming a member of such organizations may involve a particular set of values. One study, based on a small sample, has suggested that those who join such organizations are less likely to attempt 'passing' for normal, and

Table 2.1   *Difference in Years between Age at First Suspected Symptom and the Age at Discovery of the Diagnosis of MS*

	All (%)	Men (%)	Women (%)
0–4 years	43.2	51.8	39.9
5–9 years	25.2	23.6	25.9
10–14 years	13.9	14.1	13.9
15+ years	17.7	10.5	20.3
No. of patients (=100%)	826	245	581

Source: ARMS Research Register – Survey on the Discovery of the Diagnosis of Multiple Sclerosis, 1983.

are reconciled to a higher public profile for their status as having a chronic disease (Miles, 1979). It is still not clear whether this observation is generally applicable, and how membership of such an organization affects, or is affected by, the general uncertainties and ambiguities surrounding the disease. In this study of the relationship of families, and particularly husbands and wives, the data and the observations based on them, must be treated as indicative rather than definitive.

Entering the Health-Care System: from Symptoms to Diagnosis

Unlike some acute conditions, or other chronic conditions with a generally acute onset, the time lag can be substantial between perceived first symptoms and the discovery of the diagnosis of multiple sclerosis. This frequently lengthy period is one which places emphasis on informal relationships as well as formal health-care mechanisms for resolving the personal and social ambiguities generated by the symptoms. Table 2.1 indicates the range of the lag. The table indicates there is a substantial delay from first suspected symptoms to the discovery of the diagnosis in many cases. Based on medical studies of the onset of multiple sclerosis (Paty and Poser, 1984) there is no evidence that retrospective inaccuracy in recollecting first symptoms accounts solely for the length of the delay, nor that clinical uncertainty about a definitive diagnosis lasts as long as the delays demonstrated in the table – despite the variability of the early course of multiple sclerosis. The unfolding and subsequent resolution of this frequently lengthy pre-diagnostic process therefore appears to rest on other factors.

Table 2.2 *Being Formally Told and Discovering the Diagnosis of MS*

	All (%)	Men (%)	Women (%)
Discovered prior to being formally told	34.4	29.4	36.9
Did not discover prior to being formally told	60.1	65.7	57.3
Were never formally told	5.5	4.9	5.8
No. of patients (=100%)	826	245	581

Source: ARMS Research Register – Survey on the Discovery of the Diagnosis of Multiple Sclerosis, 1983.

Stewart and Sullivan (1982) suggest that the critical factor is the nature of the continuing negotiations between doctor and patient over the meaning and significance of symptoms, set in a broader social context. Their research is the most sophisticated attempt to place the early experience of multiple sclerosis in a sociological context. Their contribution was to recognize that previous research on the patient's role was inappropriate when considering patient pre-diagnostic behaviour in the case of multiple sclerosis. This previous research had indicated that 'sick' patients passively accepted the authoritative role of doctors, and that doctor–patient relationships were traditional and asymmetrical (Parsons, 1951). The 'sick role', it had been argued, was legitimated by doctors through their powerful professional position, and not actively negotiated by patients. According to Stewart and Sullivan's study of the onset of multiple sclerosis, however, patients were engaged in far more *active* negotiation with their doctors over a long period of time, rather than passively accepting the doctor's judgement on the initial, and often inaccurate diagnosis of the patient's symptoms. Patients, with what was subsequently diagnosed as multiple sclerosis, pursued a vigorous campaign to eliminate the frequent discrepancy between their own perception of what they felt was happening to them, and the doctor's perception. The culmination of this process was a reduction in ambiguity and uncertainty about the disease for the patient. Patients made sense of their symptoms through a sustained and continuous process of negotiation which eventually resulted in their doctor's legitimating their symptoms as those of multiple sclerosis.

As is shown in Table 2.2 more than one-third of the ARMS survey group had discovered their diagnosis before they were formally told, compared, for example, to a fifth of Scambler's population of epileptics who had 'anticipated' their diagnosis (Scambler, 1984, p. 212). It appears that the substantially greater 'anticipation' of the diagnosis in multiple sclerosis was influenced by the diagnostically abortive but lengthy process of interaction with doctors, but also by that diagnosis being a less personally stigmatizing one than that of epilepsy – making it relatively more acceptable to the person with a symptomatology of multiple sclerosis (Scambler, 1984).

The larger proportion of women than men who indicated they had discovered their diagnosis before being formally told may reflect the relative longevity of their symptoms, or more speculatively may reflect other factors – such as a greater reluctance to inform women of their diagnosis. None the less there is evidence to suggest that uncertainties about the diagnosis had prompted the acquisition of this information in a number of ways. This process of information gathering on diagnostic status must not be seen as one which just hinges on the relationship between patient and physician. Patients may discover their diagnosis through diligent detective work; by comparisons with others known to have the disease; through extrapolation from information in the media, including books; by interpretation of overheard conversations; through research on medical records left unattended, or through inadvertent disclosures by paramedical staff (Brunel ARMS Research Unit, 1983; Elian and Dean, 1985). Family members are frequently substantially involved (Scheinberg *et al.*, 1984, p. 209). The cross-cutting network of relationships between patients, their families and their physicians at the point of the revelation of the diagnosis creates a framework through which the past and future experience of multiple sclerosis is mediated.

The patient may be initially excluded from knowledge of the diagnosis, whereas others, family, friends, physicians and paramedical staff are all privy to it (Elian and Dean, 1985). Some physicians may delay the revelation of a diagnosis of multiple sclerosis, or first tell the diagnosis to a family member (Scheinberg *et al.*, 1984, pp. 208–11). Others may engage in what has been called 'managed discovery' of the diagnosis, whereby the attempt is made to engineer discovery at some propitious time in the future by a variety of strategies. Women with multiple sclerosis seem particularly prone to being treated in this way (Brunel ARMS Research Unit, 1983, p. 9). The way in which the diagnosis is discovered may thus involve an array of strategies which present potentially difficult hurdles for family and marital relationships to overcome.

The complexity and number of these strategies, together with the frequently lengthy period of time when symptoms have not been medically explained to the individual's satisfaction, appears to give rise to some surprisingly positive views of the diagnosis. It might be

Table 2.3 *Feelings of Relief on Discovering the Diagnosis of MS*

	All (%)	Men (%)	Women (%)
Experienced a lot	17.0	13.9	18.5
Experienced quite a lot	17.2	15.4	18.1
Experienced a little	18.8	15.9	20.6
Experienced none at all	31.1	38.8	25.8
No response/don't know	16.9	16.0	17.0
No. of patients (=100%)	826	245	581

Source: ARMS Research Register – Survey on the Discovery of the Diagnosis of Multiple Sclerosis, 1983.

expected that being told of the diagnosis of an incurable and disabling chronic disease, the reactions of those so diagnosed would be universally negative and pessimistic. Yet for many, the diagnosis occasions some relief, as is shown in Table 2.3.

This pattern of response to the giving of the diagnosis should not be seen as unusual. An autobiographical account by Susan indicates why some experience the discovery of the diagnosis in a positive way:

[I felt] great relief at knowing at last that my symptoms were no longer a mystery . . . I felt if only I had known earlier I wouldn't have had to struggle as I had done at times, because people – including my family – would have understood and been able to help or make allowances. As it was even my own family thought I was 'putting it on'. I felt hurt deep down inside me that no one had believed me when I told them I didn't feel well.

Susan felt her mystery condition had lasted for 24 years and not only her family, but many doctors she consulted over that period had dismissed her complaints as neurotic. Therefore the relief she experienced on discovering a medically and, just as important, socially legitimate reason for her symptoms was understandable. The revelation of the diagnosis of multiple sclerosis appears to be paradoxically, for many, a basis on which 'normal' social relationships can be re-established after a period of strain and tension.

However, as Table 2.3 shows, relief at the 'successful' culmination of negotiations over previously mysterious symptoms is not felt by approximately one-third of the respondents to the questionnaire. Even where it is felt it may be qualified by shock or anxiety, or be short-lived, when a strategic view is taken of how best to manage the future. In addition, findings from the sample of spouses suggests that

Table 2.4   *Spouses' Knowledge of Diagnosis and Whether Experienced Relief on Discovery of the Diagnosis*

	Percentage	Percentage experiencing any relief
Diagnosis known before partner	39	5
Diagnosis known same time/after partner	61	8

Source: ARMS Research Register – Random Sub-Sample of 100 Members and their Spouses from Survey on Members and their Helpers and Supporters, 1984.

feelings of relief, on the discovery of the diagnosis, are not shared by them. Table 2.4 shows the number of spouses who knew the diagnosis before their respective wives and husbands, and whether they experienced feelings of relief at that knowledge.

These findings, shown in Tables 2.3 and 2.4, tend to suggest that the immediate impact of a diagnosis may be generally more negative for the spouses of those with multiple sclerosis than for those with the disease themselves. However, the responses vary. For spouses, Simons argues, the quality of the relationship with their partner prior to the onset of symptoms determines their response to the diagnosis (Simons, 1984b, p. 7). Spouses dissatisfied with their marriages before onset were likely to readily accept the diagnosis as a means of distancing themselves from their partners, whereas those highly satisfied with their marriages were likely to resist the attribution of the diagnosis. However, no data is supplied to support this argument. None the less, one of the common strategies of physicians – to first relay a diagnosis to a spouse rather than to the person with the disease (indicated in Scheinberg *et al.*, 1984) – seems misplaced. This is especially so if it is based on the assumption that the person to whom the diagnosis relates is likely to be more distressed and to view the revelation of the diagnosis more negatively than their spouse.

The experience of the pre-diagnostic phase of the disease, to the point of discovery of the diagnosis is thus a significant one. The frequently lengthy process, both within and outside the family circle, indicates a quest by many of those with puzzling symptoms to reassert their personal and social credibility in the face of a sceptical response to their claim to sickness. The point of diagnosis can thus be a point where that credibility is established. At the same time, for a spouse or more generally for family members it can be a time when alternative – and perhaps less painful – explanations of the symptoms and behaviour of those diagnosed are demolished.

Table 2.5 *Marital Status of ARMS Research Register Members Aged 21 or over Compared to OPCS Estimates for England and Wales, 1980*

| | ARMS Research Register | | OPCS | |
	Men (%)	Women (%)	Men (%)	Women (%)
Married	81.3	77.3	67.2	62.2
Single	14.3	10.5	26.2	19.5
Divorced/separated	4.4	8.4	2.9	3.6
Widowed	—	3.8	3.7	14.7
Total (=100%)	245	581	18,328,400	19,854,800

Sources: ARMS Research Register – Survey on Demographic Characteristics, 1981. Register General's Annual Report for 1980 OPCS, HMSO, 1981.

The Marital Context of Multiple Sclerosis – Experience Following the Diagnosis

The ARMS Research Register provides the possibility of exploring a number of issues associated with the marital context of the disease following the discovery of the diagnosis. A high proportion of the members of the ARMS Research Register are married – as shown in Table 2.5 – far higher than estimates of the national population. Thus for the Research Register members the problems and issues generated by the functional, personal and social consequences following the discovery of the diagnosis are largely played out in the context of a marital relationship.

It is also clear that there is a higher proportion of those currently divorced and separated amongst Register members. Such a situation has been indicated in two other studies (Lilius *et al.*, 1976; Simons, 1984c, p. 117). Both of these studies point to a variety of factors embedded in the marital relationship which were associated with marital breakdown. However, the analysis in each case is suggestive rather than fully documented. In order to explore further aspects of the marital relationship a random subsample of 100 members of the Research Register and their spouses has been drawn from the mail questionnaire survey of members and their helpers and supporters indicated earlier.

As a basis for the analysis it is important first of all to address the question of the *perceived* levels of functional disability in this subsample. For it is not the existence of clinically measured impairment

Table 2.6 *Perceptions of Functional Disability by Those with MS and their Spouses*

	All		Women with MS and their husbands		Men with MS and their wives	
	Those with MS (%)	Spouses (%)	Those with MS (%)	Spouses (%)	Those with MS (%)	Spouses (%)
Perceive need help with						
Washing	29	43	22	37	46	57
Drinking	21	26	13	17	43	50
Eating	16	20	8	12	36	39
Dressing	35	39	25	29	61	64
Perceive need wheelchair	56	63	50	60	71	71
Perceive some problems with incontinence	64	78	60	75	75	86
Total (n=)	100		72		28	

Source: Arms Research Register – Random Sub-Sample of 100 members and their Spouses from Survey on Members and their Helpers and Supporters, 1984.
N.B. The sex ratio of people with multiple sclerosis shown in this table is broadly equivalent to that found in other studies (Robinson *et al.*, 1983).

that, of itself, indicates either the impact, or the significance, of the disease for everyday life. It is the ways in which those impairments are interpreted by those concerned which are crucial.

The levels of functional disability in this research population, revealed through the responses of members and their spouses, vary considerably on a number of criteria. One of the notable features of these findings, as shown in Table 2.6, is the generally higher level of functional disability in those with the disease as perceived by spouses, compared to that reported by those with multiple sclerosis themselves. The second feature is the higher level of disability perceived by, and about husbands with the disease. The latter finding was also reported in Matson and Brooks's study (1977, p. 246), which used members of a self-help organization for the research. It is not clear whether this finding is an artefact of the population used in this kind of research, for studies based on other populations with multiple sclerosis have not found a higher level of self- or other assessed male functional disability (Confavereux *et al.*, 1980; Clark *et al.*, 1982). It could reflect a reluctance amongst more mildly affected men with the disease to join self-help organizations, or it may be contingent on the way that men and their wives perceive the nature and impact of their disability.

The relatively consistent perception of a higher level of functional disability by spouses of those with multiple sclerosis, shown in Table 2.6, has been found elsewhere (Lincoln, 1981). Lincoln implies that the explanation of the discrepancy between the perceptions of people with the disease and their relatives, lies in an association she found between that discrepancy and the intellectual impairment of people with multiple sclerosis (1981, p. 87). However, no rationale, apart from the statistical association, is given for this view. It seems just as plausible, following the line of argument of Matson and Brooks (1977), that the discrepancy lies in the process of making sense of the disease, and its broader impact on the life-style, expectations and adjustment of both the person with the condition and their relatives.

This point may be considered by analysing a further series of observations offered by husbands and wives on their life with multiple sclerosis. Table 2.7 displays the perceptions of husbands and wives about family happiness; about how the person with multiple sclerosis is coping with the disease; and about others' ability to understand the situation of someone with multiple sclerosis. Despite the generally more optimistic view of their specific functional capacities by people with the disease compared to their spouses, this does not imply that their perception of their general ability to cope is more optimistic. Indeed this perception is, overall, substantially more pessimistic than the view of their spouses. This difference is

Table 2.7   *Perceptions of Coping, Family Happiness, and Ability to Understand the Situation of Those with MS*

	All	Women with MS and their husbands	Men with MS and their wives
Percentage perceiving person with MS coping very well or quite well			
Those with MS	49	44	61
Spouses	73	78	61
Percentage perceiving family relationship always happy			
Those with MS	20	21	18
Spouses	14	17	7
Percentage perceiving others understand situation of person with MS very well or quite well			
Those with MS	19	14	32
Spouses	28	29	25
Total (n =)	100	72	28

Source: ARMS Research Register – Random Sub-Sample of 100 Members and their Spouses from Survey on Members and their Helpers and Supporters, 1984.

accounted for by the substantial discrepancy between the views of women with multiple sclerosis and their husbands. Women with the disease in this research feel they are less able to cope than men, even when the perceived level of disability of the latter is higher. It is thus not surprising that such women are less likely than men with the disease, or their husbands, to feel others understand their situation. On the other hand husbands rate their wives' ability to cope highly. Conversely the congruence between the views of men with the disease and their wives in this setting appears particularly striking.

These findings suggest that it can too easily be assumed that there is a linear relationship between the duration, and degree of physical disability, and the extent of perceived inability to cope. Matson and Brooks's research on people with multiple sclerosis indicates conversely that their self-concept – for both sexes – actually improves with the duration of the disease, despite some mediation with the degree of disability that they experience (1977, p. 247). However, having undermined an assumed positive relationship between duration of disease and maladjustment, they then resurrect a series of psychological stages through which that self-concept increases – denial, resistance, affirmation and ultimately integration – while reporting (p. 148) that 'No clear patterns are suggested [from their research] for coping strategies on the basis of the amount of time people have the disease or on the basis of impairment.'

Therefore it remains speculative to suggest that there is a standard personal adjustment process through which individuals, or indeed families, pass. This may not only be because of different psychological parameters at work in individuals, but also because of the availability and use of different social resources in making sense of, and adapting to the disease which Matson and Brooks do not consider. It is particularly important to seek to explain, through the availability and use of social resources, why there is such a discrepancy between the views of women with multiple sclerosis, and their husbands, as to how they are coping.

Making Sense of Multiple Sclerosis

Making sense of the disease is a process mediated through a complex series of social interactions, as has already been indicated. One of the most potent of these interactions is that between husband and wife. The views of spouses about the strategies of their partners with the disease, and the latter's personal culpability for, and capacity to challenge the disease, is particularly crucial. These views may be associated with the onus which is placed on the person with multiple sclerosis to be 'responsible for' their own condition, especially when there is no demonstrable medical cause, treatment, or indeed responsibility for it. In Table 2.8 some of these views are reported. It can be seen that although a large majority of spouses do not believe that their partners could have avoided the disease, more husbands than wives believed that avoidance was possible. Fighting the disease is the strategy perceived by the majority of spouses as that on which their partners are currently engaged. However, husbands perceived their wives fighting the disease more, and accepting it less than wives who have husbands with multiple sclerosis. The concepts of 'fighting' and 'accepting' the disease say little about the precise behaviours engaged in, but they do indicate the general nature of personal tactics towards multiple sclerosis which are perceived in the marital relationship. Marjorie, for example, gives an indication of how personally 'fighting the disease' has now become integrated into her life – it is a daily battle between her and this alien intruder. In her autobiographical account she writes:

I am going to fight you [the disease]; I try to do a little of everything. We have now moved into a bungalow which saves me going up stairs. I can still drive the car short distances, I can then feel independent. I used to love gardening. You should see me balancing my sticks watering the plants, or lying down I can plant and weed, I can't go on my knees for I can't get up, but when I lie I can drag myself up. I manage to hang the washing out by holding on to the line. I have a wheelchair which I will go in only if we go to an exhibition, or for long walks.

In her autobiography the fight has become personalized for Jane too:

After having time to think about the implications of having MS, my reactions were to fight it, and not let it beat me. I intend to carry on and live as normally as possible . . . I did not want people to treat me any differently than they had done before. I was adamant I was going to win through.

This view may not only be reinforced by the actions and beliefs of their husbands, but also by the negative consequences of being seen to 'accept the disease' or, even worse 'give up'. If the disease is seen to have a psychological aetiology, or is only held at bay, once contracted, by particular personal traits, then the results of a 'failure to fight' are profound. They place the person with MS in double jeopardy, from the disease itself, and from the personal and social stigma arising from complacency or 'not trying' to help themselves. More women than men seem liable to this pressure which may be associated with the more general scepticism about women's symptoms of illness (Nathanson, 1975), than with any specific feature associated with multiple sclerosis. It may be partly a fear of this double failure which conditions the generally pessimistic view of women with multiple sclerosis, about their overall capacity to cope, despite their greater perceived functional competence than men with the disease.

The pressure which can be put on wives with the disease by their husbands to fight the disease and not 'give in' is indicated by Colin's account of his wife Rachel's illness:

I was worried, but not unduly so [on being told the diagnosis] because she did not seem too ill. When the illness was explained to me I didn't really believe it. She got better after a few weeks and things went on as before. When she had another attack she got better as she had done previously – this happened with several attacks over a period of eight years.

However, Rachel then had an attack with a different resolution:

Table 2.8 *Spouses' Views on the Avoidance of MS, and Partners' Strategies Currently Pursued*

	All	Husbands	Wives
Percentage believing partner could have avoided disease	14	17	7
Perceived current strategy of partner:			
Fighting disease	59	63	50
Accepting disease	28	24	39
Ignoring disease	2	2	4
Total (n =)	100	72	28

Source: ARMS Research Register – Random Sub-Sample of 100 Members and their Spouses from Survey on Members and their Helpers and Supporters, 1984.

within a space of a week she could hardly walk at all. I was concerned but expected this to run the same course as the earlier attacks. But it didn't. Some friends, to whom we went on holiday, had borrowed a wheelchair just in case! I didn't want to see her in a wheelchair, although it made things easier for her. I told her on the way home from the holiday that she was not to have a wheelchair at home. A few weeks later I came home from work to find my teenaged daughter had borrowed a wheelchair from the Red Cross . . . I was cross and upset about this but I knew it had to be. Family life then changed quite a bit.

Outside, as well as inside the family circle, there is often a continuing problem related to the legitimacy of the disease, as well as the perceived attitudes towards it. This is despite the sense of relief felt by many on the conferring of medical validation at the point of discovery of the diagnosis. The credibility of the diagnosis in everyday life appears to be undermined for those who are relatively mildly affected or who may have remissions, by the low social visibility of the disease. The relatively low proportion of people with multiple sclerosis who feel that others understand them well – shown in Table 2.7 – can be largely attributed to this factor. Contrary to the views of Stewart and Sullivan (1982), whose analysis is only developed to the point of discovery of the diagnosis, social uncertainties continue. One respondent in the present study, Karen, indicates why this is so:

Unless a person is closely related to you and sees the daily effects of MS on everyday life then it must be extremely difficult to imagine feelings in a person's body that they have never experienced, especially in my case where there is little obvious sign of MS. For the greater part of the time it is not apparent that I have MS. It is only when I am having an MS attack that anyone would know there is anything wrong with me. When one sees badly affected MS people then perhaps there is a greater degree of comprehension. I know amongst my friends and family that they think, at the times I am not obviously suffering from MS, then I am symptom free and therefore able to lead a normal life i.e. late nights and dancing etc. It has to be told to them that this is not the case.

Even Karen's supposition that being 'badly affected' would clarify a person's status as having a socially legitimate sickness is not necessarily true. Joy writes:

Some people can't understand why I'm in a wheelchair sometimes and not other times . . . with some, as long as I look cheerful and say I'm feeling fine they can cope with me but if I say I don't feel well they ignore the remark, or say I *look* well! I feel that some of them think I'm being lazy or giving up if I'm in a wheelchair, and they are inclined to talk right over my head to my pusher. (original emphasis)

Making sense of the disease in a social context is thus a complex and continuing task. Both inside and outside the family circle there is not only a struggle to understand the clinical trajectory of the condition, but to make the symptoms understood in a way that is socially credible and which allow a 'proper' and accepted sick role. Women with the disease seem to have a specially hard task to obtain this status. It may be successfully, although perhaps only temporarily, achieved by the strategy of fighting the disease, widely recognized as a plausible personal strategy, and rather less easily by 'accepting' the disease. The mediation of the meaning of multiple sclerosis has, in this process, been largely transferred from the world of medicine to the lay world of family, friends and acquaintances, and their assumptions about appropriate behaviour in the face of MS.

Managing Marital Relationships

The reconstruction of a viable life with the disease involves a multiplicity of negotiations both about social relationships – some of them considered above – and about the practicalities of care. Cunningham (1977, pp. 59–71) places particular emphasis on the role changes, within the family, likely to accompany living with the disease, which she argues become more marked with increasing functional disability. Role changes might be anticipated. However it is unwise to see those changes as related solely, in a linear way, to functional disability – especially in mild forms or the early stages of the disease. Nor must it be assumed that there is a clear and universal set of roles which emerge in a family setting with multiple sclerosis.

None the less, one of the changes that does appear to occur with the intervention of the disease, is a rethinking of family roles, especially those of husband and wife. The latitude for a variety of outcomes to the negotiation may be higher in situations where the course of the disease is relatively benign, or where there are substantial periods of remission – perhaps 50 per cent of cases (Kraft *et al.*, 1981). One of the marital strategies in this situation may be to attempt to continue roles as before – to seek to keep the potential social changes which might be wrought by the disease at bay. There is a pact between husband and wife to diminish the social, if not the physical consequences of multiple sclerosis. Andrew says:

> My wife treats me as a normal person who may just find it difficult to walk. Our relationship could not be improved . . . we carry on as we did before we knew it was multiple sclerosis, and we are not going to let it affect us.

Alison, his wife, argues that:

> It is the attitude of the person with MS, and who they live with which makes life what it is . . . [Andrew's illness] limits in some ways what we do, but it does not affect the quality of our life or shall I say we are doing our damnedest to make sure it doesn't.

Such a strategy is congruent with the idea of 'fighting the disease'. This may be mutually acceptable where both partners have a compatible and agreed view of the disease, and their complementary roles, but is fragile when that view fractures, as in the case of Colin and Rachel above.

Other husbands and wives, also living with milder forms of the disease, indicate the enhanced quality of life brought by the knowledge of multiple sclerosis, which they argue has led them to appreciate each other in ways that they could not have done before. This approach to their lives may also be reinforced by placing their experience in a religious context. For example, May indicates that:

My family accept me as I am. I believe we now have a better life than we did before, that may sound strange, but we appreciate each other more. With God's help we have gained from the MS. God has never let me down when I have confided in Him.

Her husband George says:

The quality of our lives is better than it has ever been. We merely have to make adjustments to maintain that quality. God has brought us closer than ever before. We have overcome some of the things that have hindered us growing together . . . our relationship is based on the fact that God loves us.

Such strategies seem inherently easier to adopt when the disease is in a relatively mild form. As functional problems become severe, and involve continuous practical care, options become more limited, particularly those which sustain roles in the marriage as they were before. In these circumstances there may be an exclusion of the person with multiple sclerosis from key managerial decisions in the relationship. This is particularly associated with a situation where severe functional incapacities dominate daily life. The degree of physical dependence appears to be easily translated into a perception of generalized personal incompetence, by both husband and wife. For example, John feels that his physical incapacity is a major problem, especially when difficulties with his son arise. He says:

My wife and daughter accept my situation sadly and reluctantly, but my son, aged 15, is very disturbed and upset emotionally . . . I feel left out of discipline over the children because I am static in an armchair and cannot even phone the school. I have lost the ability to be a real father and husband.

His wife (Jean's) view of his situation is that it is inevitable given the fact that:

My husband is 100% totally dependent on me for *all needs*, physical, psychological, business, pleasure, health and safety 24 hours a day. (original emphasis)

Another wheelchair-bound man, Jeff, felt irritated by his wife who, after being described as loving, he considers is

a bit short tempered due, she says, to the extra work she has to do . . . she tries to encourage me to do things, or more often not to do them, usually at the wrong time . . . my wife thinks that things will go wrong if I do simple things, so she says she prefers to do for me, rather than clear up the mess afterwards.

Jeff's wife, Anna, is weighed down with both the practicalities of coping with him, and the recent complete loss of hope following what she describes as 'the complete failure of long exhaustive treatment'. She also resents the way that life, her life, is dominated by his condition, as is also implied in Jean's comments above. She indicates that:

Sharing life with someone who is disabled is a burden because basic things essential for normal life have been taken away and one has to conform and adapt to this abnormal condition. Our life has been affected in every way – we are unable to go for walks, or concerts etc., because my husband has weak legs. We can only eat what he can eat. The furniture and the stairs had to be modified to suit him . . . [Yet] sometimes I have a quarrel with my husband when he answers me in a bad way, when I make an innocent remark.

Paradoxically, despite the evident difficulties and tensions underlying their interaction, both John and Jean, and Jeff and Anna describe their family relationships as generally happy. It may be that in admitting to, discussing and dealing with the substantial problems involved in practical managerial tasks – however unsatisfactorily – attention can be deflected from stark questions about future options for the relationship as a whole, which may themselves be partly contingent on the death of the person with multiple sclerosis. Traditionally for women such options have been more limited than those for men.

The pressures of major daily practical care, especially in marriages where people with multiple sclerosis are severely disabled, take their toll on the relationship itself. Table 2.9 illustrates spouses' perceptions of their own health status, and some aspects of the relationship with the person with the disease. In general it appears that wives perceive themselves to be more affected than husbands in their relationships with their spouse with multiple sclerosis. Emotionally, such relationships appear to be more volatile, and the perceived health effects greater. This may be partly conditioned by the greater functional incapacity of the men with multiple sclerosis in this study.

The substantial problems which women perceive in caring for their husbands are further confirmed by the findings shown in Table 2.10. Such women are more likely to perceive their helping role as being a burden, to perceive their social activities being affected a great deal,

Table 2.9   *Spouses' Perceptions of their Health and Aspects of Relationship with Person with MS*

	All	Husbands	Wives
	%	%	%
Own health perceived as very good	43	42	46
Symptoms of illness in last 4 weeks	30	28	36
Perceive own health or well-being not at all affected by role as helper	66	76	39
Person with MS demands a great deal, or quite a lot of attention	22	15	39
Person with MS felt cross a great deal, or quite a lot	17	11	32
Self and spouse with MS laughed a great deal, or quite a lot together	43	39	54
Total (n =)	100	72	28

Source: ARMS Research Register – Random Sub-Sample of 100 Members and their Spouses from Survey on Members and their Helpers and Supporters, 1984.

and perceive they need more help and support. This is despite the fact that they generally have rather more close friends than men in the same position. One further feature of Table 2.10 may provide a partial explanation for some of these findings. There is a substantially higher proportion of male carers in full-time employment than women. This is not unexpected, but even where the functional and practical problems of partners are similiar, it may allow men a different and compensating domain of action and control over their lives. Such a compensating domain is less likely to be available, or used by women carers.

In summary, the flexibility of strategies which may be used to renegotiate marital relationships affected by the course of multiple sclerosis, is substantially influenced by the social intrusiveness of increasing functional incapacity, or disability. This does not imply that there is a direct, linear and unequivocal association between those relationships and functional problems. It is more that the range of *possible* options appears more limited than in the early stages of the disease or in mild cases. The possibility of conventional social roles in marriage – even considering their breadth and variety – appears less easy in these circumstances. The renegotiation of the relationship to the satisfaction of both partners appears, from the evidence of this research, to be more problematic for marriages where wives live with husbands with multiple sclerosis, than for husbands with wives with the disease.

Table 2.10   *The Context of Caring*

	All	Husbands	Wives
	%	%	%
Perceiving helping role 'no burden'	48	50	43
Perceiving social ac;tivities affected a great deal	43	36	61
Having more than 4 close friends	56	51	68
Feels need additional help and support by others	60	53	79
Known person with MS ill for more than 10 years	44	46	43
In full-time employment	60	71	25
Total (n =)	100	72	28

Source: ARMS Research Register – Random Sub-Sample of 100 Members and their Spouses from Survey on Members and their Helpers and Supporters, 1984.

Reconstructing Life with Multiple Sclerosis

In this study some issues relating to the perception and management of multiple sclerosis have been discussed in the context of marital relationships. The process of managing the disease is a complex one. The dynamics of normal' individual and marital relationships are overladen by the complex course of the disease and its interpretation. Strategies for managing this process which may seem appropriate at one stage, are not at another. However, the simplistic imposition of a series of stages through which people, and their relationships pass, does not do justice to the complicated nature of the issues involved – and in any case cannot easily be shown to occur.

This research has indicated two further features, in addition to the general complexity of managerial strategies within the marital relationship. The first of these is that there are frequently differences in attitudes and perceptions between spouses over what is happening to that relationship. It cannot be assumed that both partners have an identical view of the present and how the future should be managed. In medical rehabilitation interventions may take place on the mistaken assumption that such a common set of interests universally exists (see Power, 1985). The second feature is that the perceived ability to cope of women both with the disease, and looking after husbands with multiple sclerosis, seem less than for men in similar situations. This perceived ability to cope appears to be largely independent of perceived functional difficulties and whether women themselves have the disease or are spouses of men with MS. In general, women's perceptions of their problems and how to deal with them are more pessimistic than the perceptions of men. Such a finding is generally consonant with other analyses which stress the onus on women both in a caring situation, and when they themselves are ill (see for example Graham, 1985). This issue deserves further and more specific exploration.

Finally, the research reported here has emphasized the importance of the social context of the disease and particularly one central social relationship in which the drama of the disease is played out. It has indicated the importance of the 'social' in studying the experience of illness. Research based solely on the functional disabilities of people with the disease on the one hand, or on their individual psychological status on the other hand, cannot document the complexity and effects of social interactions on how people with MS, their spouses, and their families experience and manage their lives.

References

Acheson, E. D. (1985), 'The epidemiology of multiple sclerosis', in W. B. Mathews, E. D. Acheson, J. R. Batchelor and R. O. Weller (eds), *McAlpine's Multiple Sclerosis* (London: Churchill Livingstone).

Baum, H. M., and Rothschild, B. B. (1981), 'The incidence and prevalence of reported multiple sclerosis', *Annals of Neurology*, vol. 10, pp. 420–8.

Brunel ARMS Research Unit (1983), *Discovering the Diagnosis of MS*, General Report No. 3, Brunel ARMS Research Unit, Dept. of Human Sciences, Brunel, The University of West London.

Burnfield, A. (1985), *Multiple Sclerosis: A Personal Exploration* (London: Souvenir Press).

Clark, V. A., Detels, R., Visscher, B. R., Valdiviezo, N. L., Malmgren, R. M., and Dudley, J. P. (1982), 'Factors associated with a malignant course of multiple sclerosis', *Journal of the American Medical Association*, 20 August, pp. 856–60.

Confavereux, C., Aimard, G., and Devic, M. (1980), 'Course and prognosis of multiple sclerosis assessed by computerised data processing of 349 patients', *Brain*, vol. 103, pp. 281–300.

Cunningham, D. J. (1977), *Stigma and Social Isolation: Self Perceived Problems of a Group of Multiple Sclerosis Sufferers*, Report no. 27, Health Services Research Unit, Centre for Research in the Social Sciences, University of Kent, Canterbury.

Detels, R., Clark, V. A., Valdiviezo, N. L., Visscher, B. R., Malmgren, R. M., and Dudley, J. P. (1982), 'Factors associated with a rapid course of multiple sclerosis', *Archives of Neurology*, vol. 39, pp. 337–41.

Elian, M. and Dean, G. (1985), 'To tell or not to tell the diagnosis of multiple sclerosis', *Lancet*, 6 July, pp. 27–8.

Graham, H. (1985), 'Providers, negotiators, and mediators: women as the hidden carers', in E. Lewin and V. Olesen (eds), *Women, Health and Healing* (London: Tavistock), pp. 25–52.

Kraft, G. H., Freal, J. E., Coryell, J. K., Hanan, C. L., and Chitnis, N. (1981), 'Multiple sclerosis: early prognostic guidelines', *Archives of Physical Medicine and Rehabilitation*, vol. 62, pp. 54–8.

Kurtzke, J. F. (1980), Multiple sclerosis: an overview' in F. C. Rose (ed.) *Clinical Neuroepidemiology* (London: Pitman), pp. 170–95.

Lilius, H. E., Valtonen, E. J., and Wikstrom, J. (1976), 'Sexual problems in patients suffering from multiple sclerosis', *Scandinavian Journal of Social Medicine*, vol. 4, p. 41.

Lincoln, N. B. (1981), 'Discrepancies between capabilities and performance of activities of daily living in multiple sclerosis patients', *International Rehabilitation Medicine*, vol. 3, pp. 84–8.

Marsh, G. G., Ellison, G. W., and Strite, C. (1983), 'Psychosocial and rehabilitation approaches to multiple sclerosis', *Annual Review of Rehabilitation*, pp. 242–67

Matson, R. R., and Brooks, N. A. (1977), 'Adjusting to multiple sclerosis – an exploratory study', *Social Science and Medicine*, vol. 11, pp. 245–50.

Miles, A. (1979), 'Some psycho-social consequences of multiple sclerosis: problems of social interaction and group identity', *British Journal of Medical Psychology*, vol. 52, pp. 321–31.

Nathanson, C. A. (1975), 'Illness and the feminine role: a theoretical review', *Social Science and Medicine*, vol. 9, pp. 57–62.

Parsons, T. (1951), *The Social System* (Glencoe, Ill.: The Free Press).

Paty, D. W., and Poser, C. (1984), 'Clinical signs and symptoms of multiple sclerosis' in D. Paty, W. I. McDonald, L. Scheinberg and G. C. Ebers, *The Diagnosis of Multiple Sclerosis* (New York: Thieme-Stratton), pp. 27–43.

Power, P. W. (1985), 'Family coping behaviours in chronic illness: a rehabilitation perspective', *Rehabilitation Literature*, vol. 46, pp. 78–83.

Robinson, I., Bakes, C., and Lawson, A. (1983), 'Questioning the facts: the sex ratio in multiple sclerosis', Academic Working Paper, Brunel ARMS Research Unit, Dept. of Human Sciences, Brunel, The University of West London

Scambler, G. (1984), 'Perceiving and coping with stigmatizing illness', in R. Fitzpatrick, J. Hinton, S. Newman, G. Scambler and J. Thompson, *The Experience of Illness* (London: Tavistock), pp. 203–26.

Scheinberg, L. C., Kalb, R. C., Larocca, N. G., Geisser, B. S., Slater, R. J., and Poser, C. M. (1984), 'The doctor–patient relationship in multiple sclerosis', in C. M Poser, D. W. Paty, L. C. Scheinberg, W. I. McDonald and G. C. Ebers, *The Diagnosis of Multiple Sclerosis* (New York: Thieme-Stratton), pp. 205–15.

Simons, A. (ed.) (1984a), *Multiple Sclerosis: Psychological and Social Aspects* (London: Heinemann Medical).

Simons, A. (1984b), 'Problems of providing support for people with multiple sclerosis and their families', in A. Simons (ed.) (1984a), pp. 1–20.

Simons, A. (1984c), 'Perceptions of health care', in A. Simons (ed.) (1984a), pp. 115–32.

Smith, C. R. and Scheinberg, L. C. (1985), 'Clinical features of multiple sclerosis', *Seminars in Neurology*, vol. 5, no. 2, pp. 85–93.

Stewart, D. C., and Sullivan, T. J. (1982), 'Illness behaviour and the sick role: the case of multiple sclerosis', *Social Science and Medicine*, vol. 16, pp. 1397–1404.

Strauss, A. (1984), *Chronic Illness and the Quality of Life*, 2nd. ed. (Chicago: Mosby).

3 Striking Balances: Living with Parkinson's Disease

RUTH PINDER

The Patient's Perspective: A Neglected Topic?

Ever since the publication of James Parkinson's seminal work 'Essay on the shaking palsy' in 1817, writing about Parkinson's disease (PD) has remained the prerogative of doctors and scientists – and only latterly epidemiologists and paramedics. The few texts available to the layman, though sympathetic, are heavily normative and prescriptive.

Socio-psychological aspects of PD have received relatively little attention in the literature. One of the few autobiographical accounts which exists (Dorros, 1981) gives an insightful and moving picture of what it is like to live with the illness, but such reports are rare and other excursions (Todes, 1983) give only brief and tantalizing glimpses into a world which still remains largely unexplored. Sacks's (1973) study describing his work with post-encephalitic Parkinson patients has now become a minor classic and is a further honourable exception to the general picture.

Attempts to explore some of the social implications of PD have also been sparse. The contributions of Singer (1973, 1974) have provided us with a theory of premature social ageing, by comparing the social and economic functioning of a sample of PD patients with a sample of comparably aged people in the general population. By analyzing patients' attitudes towards themselves and their outlook on life she found that the chief impact of impairment was on current work and family role performances, and that the effects of the illness impinged disproportionately on those contracting PD atypically early in life.

All of the above contributions, except that of Todes, are American. The first important British contribution was that of Oxtoby (1982) who explored the social needs of PD patients by means of a postal questionnaire administered to a random sample of patients in touch with the Parkinson's Disease Society. Questions were aimed at eliciting basic socio-demographic data on patients, their perceptions of health and impairment, their evaluation of medical and social services, perceptions about social life, and the role of the Society.

Oxtoby's study works well as the sample was fairly homogeneous and the survey is a good example of what may be achieved by this method. Its socio-demographic data provide a framework and identify departure points for further analysis. Where this approach requires extension, as Oxtoby readily acknowledges, is in the attempt to elicit subjective feelings and attitudes.

Neither the Oxtoby survey nor the analyses by Singer have been able to penetrate the life experience of those who have PD. The way people deal with the daily contingencies and demands of living with the illness has been virtually ignored. Yet to understand this is an essential *pre*condition to the many prescriptive statements of need which often characterize health care delivery writing. As Strauss *et al.* (1985, p. x) note: 'reform without prior understanding can only lead to ineffectual reform, or even to measures that will make matters worse'. It is in an attempt to redress this imbalance and obtain access to such meanings that this chapter has been conceived.[1] It also represents a personal attempt to make wider social sense of my own experience of living with a husband who has multiple sclerosis.

THEORETICAL APPROACH

I have adopted a symbolic interactionist perspective as this seems most clearly illustrative of the processes at work in managing chronic illness. Handling encounters with others is an interpretative process. We define each other's utterances and actively respond on the basis of such interpretations. As Blumer (1962, p. 183) suggests, an individual's behaviour 'is not a result of such things as environmental pressures, stimuli, motives, attitudes and ideas, but arises instead from how he interprets and handles these things in the action which he is constructing'.

A number of concepts emerged from the writings of the early interactionists which I have used here, such as strategy management, and the notions of illness career[2] and trajectory.[3] However, I have focused on what I consider to be a more fundamental concept which analytically cuts across constructs such as strategy management: that of balancing.

It is derived from the work of Fagerhaugh and Strauss (1977) on pain management. It is concerned above all with interpretation and choice. In managing any discomfiting symptom, people are actively engaged in making decisions about what, when and how to accomplish certain goals and tasks, and defining the considerations which have to be taken into account to achieve these. In making such calculations, various options are negotiated – or 'traded off' – in search of the most viable outcome at any one point in time. Balancing is both a personal and, more importantly, a social process. It involves bargaining with others as well as oneself.

Thus the possibility of conflict is always present. Being caught 'off-balance' – a situation of *dis*equilibrium – may readily be appreciated. This may arise when people are balancing different dimensions at the same time, when there is disagreement over priorities, when the social environment or the way family members define salient issues change, or when the appearance of new symptoms requires new calculations to be made and a new equilibrium negotiated.

Balancing is, of course, an activity in which we are all engaged. Where the chronically ill differ is in the nature of the considerations which are traded off. Most people predicate their lives on the notion of an orderly, predictable and inherently stable world. Plans are made in the reasonably confident expectation of their materializing. This is essentially a survival device, protecting us from experiencing the world as intolerably anarchic.

Predictability, however, is precisely what most chronically ill people cannot assume. The trade-offs and strategies which those with PD make in their lives represent, I suggest, attempts to restore some semblance of this taken-for-granted aspect of the world.

The two major aspects of balancing I shall deal with here are the control of symptoms (both illness- and drug-related), and the management of a complex drug regimen, Levodopa and its derivatives. These in turn will be set against the many other considerations involved in managing PD: subjects' perceptions of disability and handicap, difficulties in sustaining tasks and family roles, preserving an acceptable self-image, the role of self-help, and the crucial need for medical information as a resource.

Research Strategy

My theoretical stance complements my methodological position. In order to understand these interpretative processes and the calculations which flow from them, the researcher must take the 'standpoint of the acting unit' (Blumer, 1962).

Conceptual framework and methodology are, in turn, interwoven with the aims of this intentionally exploratory study. It is not designed to establish generalizations about all those with PD but to penetrate as closely as possible what the experience of living with PD means to those involved. The success with which anyone can claim to achieve such 'privileged access to shared meanings' (Platt, 1982) is, of course, open to question. Perhaps what may legitimately be claimed are approximations to other people's realities.

Thus the objective of the research was to focus on *subjects'* definitions of the problem rather than those of the researcher. As it transpired, the wish to enter the field *tabula rasa* was slightly misconceived: it was simply not possible to jettison entirely my own experience. This had both advantages and disadvantages. It enabled me to be aware of, and sensitive to, the needs and vulnerabilities of my subjects. I knew where to stop, where not to intrude. Perhaps precisely because I *did* know what living with chronic illness meant, experientially as well as cognitively, I was allowed to explore where others might not have been able to. My experience of living with a husband who has MS often arose in the context of queries such as 'Why us? Why Parkinson sufferers?' In response to my explanation Mrs U, for example, said 'You know what it's all about, then'.

On the other hand, the temptation to translate 'PD reality' into my own framework of 'MS reality' may have led initially to my seeing connections where they did not exist. With time I believe this has been corrected and both the commonalities and differences of the PD and MS experience are better appreciated as a result.

RESEARCH DESIGN

The decision to focus on a small number of subjects and to concentrate on multiple in-depth interviews was a logical extension of my aims. Though I did some participant observation by attending the Parkinson's Disease Society's local branch meetings, the difficulties of doing true participant observation made the interview the obvious tool and home interviewing the natural location.

Early familiarization with how two couples experienced and coped with PD was gained through referral from my family doctor. A totally unstructured approach was found to be inhibiting and was abandoned in favour of providing broad topics around which to talk, accompanied by the use of an Interview Guide. Despite my general unwillingness to impose definitions, there were certain areas I *did* want to cover, such as what areas caused people difficulties, how problems were dealt with, what hindered and what helped.

A total of thirty-nine interviews, with ten people suffering from PD, was conducted over ten months, people being seen on average four times. Talks lasted on average 1½ hours, and time spent with patients added a further hour or more to each session.

Conversations were tape-recorded and unedited transcripts returned to subjects for amendment and correction. This was one of the most valuable exercises of the study. Subjects *did* alert me at subsequent talks to passages they wanted to alter or felt misrepresented what they wanted to say. Part of a paper I had written, for example, was completely revised in the light of Mrs Q's comments about the previous transcript when we met again: 'I hadn't wanted to give the impression that . . .', she commented.

The returned transcripts were not at all what Mr and Mrs J had expected: 'We thought you'd have put us with others and sort of *explained*, not just this'. This alerted me to the necessity of consulting patients with anything I subsequently wrote. Drafts of this chapter were sent to the group for their comments and criticisms. The general reaction was one of immense pleasure. Of course much of this may be attributed to the fact of their being consulted at all. As a result, some modifications, chiefly ones of emphasis, were made in the text.

Any concern that writing about what is a painful subject might have been depressing was dispelled by Mrs Q: 'You've done it very nicely. You've not made it horrible. It's like someone really understanding the illness which is nice. You've taken the trouble to get to know people'. Additionally Mr I provided some feedback concerning the appropriateness of my conceptual tools. He was particularly pleased with the idea of normalizing and confirmed 'You've got it absolutely right'. Perhaps the most pertinent comment in terms of the goals of this chapter came from Mr C. He wrote: 'Your chapter might help to inform people of the realities of PD and if it does only this then it will, to my mind, have served its purpose.'

Other research tools   The extent to which one sees oneself as disabled and handicapped is one of the major factors in calculating options. Subjects were therefore asked to rate themselves along two five-point scales of disability and handicap, using the criteria outlined by Bury (1979) (Table 3.1). Cards describing both concepts were given to patients to tick. Although care was taken to ensure patients understood the distinction the exercise was still problematic. In using any such scales, the underlying assumption is that health/ill-health is a continuum on which people can place themselves 'once and for all'. In fact responses vary situationally and over time. Moreover, the way one perceives disability and handicap is itself a coping strategy. Thus Mrs Q was reluctant to classify herself on the disability scale at all, eventually opting for two categories, 'moderate' and 'severe'. When

Table 3.1   *Subjects' Age, Perceived Feelings of Disability and Handicap, and Duration of Illness since Formal Diagnosis*

Subject	Age	Perceived feelings of disability[a]	Perceived feelings of handicap[b]	Duration of illness since diagnosis (years)
Mr C	59	Mild	Quite severe	1
Mr R	72	Severe	Quite severe	2½
Mr Y	75	Mild	Quite severe	4
Mrs P	61	Moderate	Moderate	4
Mr J	65	Moderate	Moderate	5½
Mrs F	54	Moderate	Slight to moderate	7
Mrs Q	74	Moderate to severe	Very severe	10
Mr U	74	Severe	Quite severe	11
Mr I	63	Severe	Very severe	12
Miss N	60	Quite severe	Quite severe	25

[a]*Disability:* the restriction on, or inability to perform activities in a way considered normal for one's age/sex.

[b]*Handicap:* the social, economic, or environmental feelings of disadvantage arising from the illness.

Source: Bury, 1979.

not incapacitated by severe muscle spasm, she feels tolerably well. Similarly Mrs F, defining herself as 'otherwise healthy', wished to classify her handicap as 'slight to moderate'. It may readily be seen from the table that duration of illness is not a good predictor of such evaluations.

Finally subjects were asked to complete a 'Fact Sheet' of questions to provide very basic socio-demographic data for comparative purposes.

The subjects   As membership of the Parkinson's Disease Society is known to over-represent the non-manual classes, I compiled a wide-ranging list of possible sources of subjects and systematically worked through it. The criteria for selection were also broad in order to embrace as many social types as possible.

The ten subjects were recruited as follows: three from three general practices; two from two day centres; three were 'snowballers' (friends of subjects already seen); and two subjects were referred to me by the Society. They were included in the study as the problems they presented coincided with the broader remit of the project when I was searching for subjects.

Despite my intentions, nine subjects turned out to be members of the Society. Seven lived with their spouse at home (Mr and Mrs U having recently transferred to sheltered accommodation), and three lived alone. All were retired except Mrs F who worked full-time. Other characteristics of the group included a preponderance of consultant-only managed patients, under-representation from Classes IV and V (semi-skilled and unskilled manual workers), and an emphasis on those more severely impaired.

OBTAINING 'ACCOUNTS'

I had created a setting where the project, in a sense, belonged both to the subjects and to myself. I find that where people are actively encouraged to share in responsibility for the talk they create, not only is it a mutually pleasurable experience, but it is the way people come to know one another and feel able to share in each others' lives.

Things happen when one embarks on unconventional interviewing. I will discuss only two of the many practical and epistemological issues which are raised and which troubled me. I cannot claim to have resolved them.

First, the issue of involvement. Not only do the theoretical imperatives of interactionism demand involvement with one's subjects, but the preservation of a detached persona is also counter-productive, if not almost offensive. It is quite impossible to spend over ten hours in someone's house and remain aloof. So I gave of myself and shared my experiences where these were asked.

People responded, with questions about my own situation, about the project and the setting of the talks – questions which I readily answered. Much more difficult were questions about the nature and implications of PD and its drug regimen.[4] Mr and Mrs R, for instance, when first interviewed, had deliberately chosen not to know about the illness. However, over a period of five months, I was both witness, and to an unknown extent, party to, a radical shift in their perspective. Dealing honestly and responsibly with a question in our last talk about side-effects was extremely difficult. However well or inadequately I dealt with it, I was none the less *there*, a reference point for them to use and a possible channel of referral to others.[5]

This is not a dilemma which can be resolved by the 'safer' procedure of questionnaires. Particularly for PD, where writing is so difficult, any questions about symptoms or side-effects may include a list for subjects to tick where appropriate. The survey researcher is, of necessity, ignorant of any consternation reading such a list may cause.

Similar problems are posed by spouses talking together when an emotive issue or incident is raised of which one spouse is unaware. With continued face-to-face contact, however, the incident can be discussed – perhaps ultimately to both partners' advantage. As Mrs J commented:

> This is a wonderful excuse you being here for us to air things we probably wouldn't have discussed . . . I'm very glad you *can* disturb the balance, because there comes a time when one's literally boiling inside, and not to have the outlet to say what one's thinking . . .

This raises the interrelated questions of the researcher's role. It is one which constantly changes and matures in line with the dynamic nature of the interaction itself. Emphatically, however, it was not that of a therapist (a role adopted by Gyllenskold, 1982) in attempting to 'work through' any of the above problems. In most cases I progressed from being an unknown quantity (researcher) to being a friend, but a friend of a 'peculiar kind' (Agar, 1980). This involved me in doing things with subjects, such as drafting letters, teaching relaxation exercises, accompanying one patient to a concert and another to a meal – activities generally considered to breach the rules of 'proper' interviewing. These were simply things I wanted to do. Not to have done them would have meant adopting a stance totally at variance with the spirit of the relationships I developed.

Involvement did not, I believe, become *over*-involvement. I was able, after completing the talks, to detach myself sufficiently to search for the kind of patterns, themes and, above all, *in*consistencies integral to this kind of analysis. Yet contact is still maintained with the group. I do not feel I have abandoned them.

What is important is that one's values, attitudes and beliefs should be explicitly recognized as integral to the encounter (Sherwood, 1980), and that these change cumulatively with each meeting. To assume otherwise is totally to mask the interpretive nature of the encounter (Wynne, 1984). Moreover, not only does the researcher's increased knowledge and awareness act on the data; so do the changing and emergent attitudes of subjects. The very act of paraphrasing often raises issues people had not previously contemplated. Mrs R found the talks aired 'things we hadn't even thought of. It's been very helpful'. In the process, interviews become more truly akin to conversations.

Finally a word on people's use of talk as 'accounts'. The validity of what subjects said is not at issue here. I am more concerned with how patients interpret and give meaning to their lives than with the extent to which these interpretations coincide with any objective state of 'reality'. The talks gave patients the opportunity of reconstructing events in a way that made them appear morally competent, responsible adults (Locker 1981, p. 23).

Ultimately whichever method one uses rests on the kind of information wanted. The data which emerge from the use of this approach is, for my purposes, more interesting and meaningful than that generated by a quantitative analysis. Even more importantly, it also needs to be recognizable to my subjects. It must provide them with the means of identifying themselves in a broader explanatory context to aid them in making wider social sense of their illness experience. The success of my attempts to validate the data indicates that this has been achieved.

Striking Balances: Illness and Drug Therapy Management – the Control of Symptoms

Like other chronic illnesses which are of unknown aetiology, progressive and incurable, the trajectory of PD in any individual is uncertain and unpredictable. Its manifestations vary considerably from person to person. The classic triad of symptoms – tremor, rigidity and slowness of movement – is supplemented by a host of others which may affect some patients but not others. These range from chronic fatigue, early morning immobility, 'mumbly' if not incomprehensible speech, stooping gait, freezing or start/hesitation episodes, to a mask-like facial immobility, all of which may be thoroughly disconcerting socially.

Superimposed on these symptoms – and often difficult to separate – are problems arising from the side-effects of the medication. Whereas the drugs mask some of the illness symptoms some of the time, they can produce other symptoms, such as mood and memory disturbances, involuntary movements, end-of-dose deterioration, and various forms of fluctuations, most dramatically the 'on/off' syndrome, where a patient changes from mobility to total immobility, often many times a day and with startling rapidity. In its extreme form this is known as 'yo-yoing'. Levodopa does not halt the underlying progression of the illness itself and tends ultimately to lose its efficacy. To add to the confusion, some symptoms are both illness- and drug-related and, as the illness progresses, these become increasingly difficult to disentangle. More importantly, *subjects* often have difficulty distinguishing them. For the purposes of analysis I have, therefore, treated them together. Patients must contend with multiple layers of uncertainty and unpredictability.

Even though he saw himself as being only mildly disabled, uncertainty as to just what he could usefully accomplish had led Mr C into a kind of mental paralysis where avoidance of all activities was his temporary mode of adaptation. As he commented:

> You see when I retired I had this plan of campaign . . . I wanted to continue flying which I can't any longer . . . I had visions of joining an organization like the Citizens' Advice Bureau, doing something useful which would occupy my time . . . But I mean I'd have to write notes over the phone, I'd have to speak to people. I get this – like a frog in my throat occasionally – and they'd either take you for an idiot or something wrong with you and your advice wouldn't be accepted as sensible, or you'd have to explain what the matter was and I wouldn't want to. But that was going to be secondary to my main hobby which was flying. The difficulty now is to think of something which I could do which is going to replace that. And also, of course, the will to do it which is difficult . . . I haven't been able to start something else, you see.

It cannot, of course, be assumed that balances are always neatly struck. One of the most handicapping features about such a chronic illness is the precarious nature of the trade-offs which are made and the frequency with which one is caught off-balance. Periods of equilibrium are interspersed with periods of intense *dis*equilibrium while new balancing plateaux are being negotiated – possibly one reason for the discrepancy between Mr C's perception of his sense of disability and handicap.

Covering As with any potentially discrediting condition, questions of visibility and unpredictability constantly have to be juggled with decisions about whether or not to tell, a factor which affected other subjects in various life areas. Covering tactics designed to reject the social significance of disability are generally employed, but the risk of inadvertent disclosure and the incurring of disbelief, or even accusations of malingering, are always present.

Mrs F, however, felt sufficiently stable to be able to calculate within fairly fine limits what she was able to accomplish. With experience she has learnt about the pattern of symptoms, their likely duration and intensity, and their implications for sustaining work and social demands – for the moment. As she explained:

> I arrange things at the office, appointments, when I know I'm going to be in an 'on' situation, which is why I put Thursday night for the interview because I don't work Friday mornings. If there are any repercussions it doesn't matter.

Nevertheless, she, too, is well aware of the ways she can still be 'caught out'. Foot spasms, or as she describes it 'curly toes episodes' occur periodically and may last anything from ten minutes to an hour stretching her covering strategies to the limit. She described one such episode at work:

It happened once when I was taking a property on and I didn't know what to do, because he didn't know and I was trying to carry on a conversation and trying to control it from the inside. I can't talk and control it at the same time. You need to be very careful not to have too long a day and take an outside appointment at the end of the day. It's at the end of the day when it happens.

Strict timetabling is crucial to her work management. It is, however, a price she readily pays for enabling her to lead a reasonably normal and satisfying work-life. Covering is facilitated by the gatekeeping tactics of her secretary who is 'in the know'.

For Mrs Q, new symptoms had precipitated new crises which, despite her years of experience, had left her thoroughly off-balance. She talked about the muscle spasms which periodically incapacitate her and apparently strike without rhyme or reason.

I can't understand it . . . Last week, three days I didn't have them. And yet I've been having two and three a day for the rest. And you try, you think what did I do that I didn't get them? What did I do differently? I've tried putting food, you know, different foods down, I write it down and I think, well, let's see if they make any difference. But they don't. And it's just these last two or three weeks, say two or three days, sometimes I don't get them. Then suddenly they come again . . . They don't have a pattern. If they did you could weave your life around them.

The *handicapping* nature of such unpredictability is readily apparent. It is in anticipation of the spasms occurring that she feels obliged to withdraw from social contacts outside home. New trade-offs have been made, such as relinquishing her role as initiator in social relationships. She now has to wait until people choose to come and see her. Nevertheless she still relies on long-established covering strategies which have served her well to date. Considerable effort and ingenuity are spent in ensuring she is not a 'chore' to her many visitors. Normalizing relationships with her family is her main priority.

Balancing between spouses   Balancing essentially involves other people, particularly patients' immediate families. Any differences in the definition of the illness trajectory *between* spouses may lead to serious difficulties. Although Mr Y defined himself as 'mildly disabled', this was not an interpretation accepted by his wife. Their lives were subject to intense disequilibrium as Mrs Y oscillated back and forth, from minute to minute, hour to hour and day to day over the question of whether to put her husband in a home, trading off the fears of her own loneliness against her perceived inability to manage him.

Differences in definitions also occurred between other spouses, such as for Mrs C and Mrs J. However, it seemed these could be contained within the supportiveness of their respective relationships. For Mrs Y, the perception of her husband's trajectory was not purely a physiologically objective fact. She was also weighing up definitions of her own deteriorating health against her perceived ability to manage her husband's frequent falls. A high price had been paid in terms of social isolation. As Mrs Y said:

> Friends, they don't *come* here very often. They phone me and tell me this and tell me that. But they don't actually *visit* here any more. They don't know how to behave towards him, I suppose.

It was a painful contrast to the rich social life enjoyed by the couple prior to the onset of Mr Y's illness. However, it was compounded by additional loneliness experienced within the confines of their marriage. Mr Y was virtually incapable of speech. With the greatest difficulty he said: 'I have decided not to let the loneliness bother me.'

Social isolation is perhaps one of the more distressing features of chronic illness. It is often both self-imposed – as in the case of Mrs P who withdrew altogether when her face 'froze' and speech was impossible, such was the felt stigma of her impairment – as well as being imposed from outside. Mrs U, like Mrs Y, felt the handicapping effects of illness as the unaffected spouse. As she commented, 'Well, we're both disabled aren't we . . . I can't do what I'd like to do. I can't just go swanning off can I? I'm tied up. My first priority is him.'

Others, however, found ways of circumventing this. Mr I, for instance, had a wide circle of friends who were not deterred if they inadvertently caught him in an 'off'. And Miss N, bereft of speech after brain surgery in the late 1960s, had nevertheless managed to carry on in spite of many years of loneliness and the inability to find a marriage partner. Her courage in 'getting things out of life' was attested to both by the nurse who called and her gentleman friend with whom she has formed a new relationship – and a new equilibrium – in life. She wrote:

> I've got a lot to be thankful for, but there I had it so young and without having the [brain] operation, who can tell what would have happened . . . But I was a fighter and I was determined it should not win . . . And I feel that life is sweet, or so they say.

Over time   The need to accommodate to the increasing severity of symptoms often involves a radical restructuring of life. Some of the themes indicated so far are illustrated in more advanced form by Mr U. Additional considerations also have to be balanced. Mobile for only two hours in the morning, he is dependent on others for help the remainder of the day. The inability to reciprocate was initially felt to be particularly galling but accommodation has been made to this over time. As he commented (not without difficulty): 'I've got used to it now. Having to ask people to come and help you. And *waiting* for 'em to come and help . . . You've got nothing to give in place of it though.' Time is a factor which increasingly dominates life-style. All normal activities, such as having a bath or socializing with the other residents, have to be squeezed into that two hours before his symptoms return.

Temporal considerations are even more complicated when periods of symptom relief are themselves unpredictable (as shown earlier in less severe form by Mrs Q). Mr I's life was characterized by unpredictable and often violent 'yo-yoing'. Arriving one morning to talk I found him glued in frozen immobility in his chair. Enjoined by his wife to tell him a story, it was like watching a butterfly emerge from its chrysalis as he retrieved his speech, loosened up, flexed his muscles, and came to life before my eyes. Within an hour he was conversing animatedly and then performed his 'party trick', running up and down the stairs to his flat. An hour later, darkness descended again and he was reduced to total dependence on his wife. He described this as 'the Lazarus effect':

> I cram in to the periods when I'm flexible all the things I would have liked to have done the rest of the day. It doesn't always work that way though. One day I may be nine-tenths of the day free, although that's very rare, and another much less. There's nothing I can do about it.

Life was structured round these precious intervals during which energies were stretched towards restoring some semblance of normality.

Resources for coping   Implicit so far in what has been said is the use of self-help measures as a strategy. More explicitly, they are also a resource. Mrs Q, for example, practises physiotherapy exercises by marching down the corridor to empty her rubbish. 'There's a fear of taking those little steps I see some people doing. I do think it helps if you march along', she said. Although the total unpredictability of Mr I's swings made attempts to plan life impossible, he took part in yoga classes when possible. As he put it, 'it's a bit less of lack of control really'.

Although seemingly small and insignificant, such attempts indicate the struggle to regain some purchase over the arbitrariness of the illness. To a greater or lesser extent, similar tactics were engaged in by most subjects in the group.

Information about the implications of PD is a crucial resource. To know the implications, as far as they can be known, is also to be 'in control' of the illness, and is, I suggest, part of the broader attempt to restore that sense of taken-for-grantedness enjoyed by others. Subjects, however, can only balance what they understand.

The role of doctors as a source of information was seen as problematic. Subjects rarely felt the implications of PD were discussed with them by their doctors. It must be stressed that the exact prognosis cannot be predicted early on. It is often only after a period of time that a likely pattern can be discerned. Yet certain *general* features of PD *can* be explained. Such bits and pieces as were assembled by patients were often the result of reading. Membership of the Parkinson's Disease Society was an important supplementary source of information. At different stages of their illness careers, therefore, patients had variable amounts of information with which to weigh their ability to carry on.

The complexity of the issue is well illustrated by Mrs P who discussed her changing needs for information:

> I would like to discuss a lot of things with him [Dr X] . . . Well the symptoms really. I've never had the opportunity to discuss the symptoms. And what to expect. I'd like to ask him. It's hard isn't it. The whole thing really. I'd like to discuss how other people cope with the illness on a fuller scale.

The amount of information held profoundly affects the considerations which are taken into account. In the earlier stages of her illness Mrs P was ignorant of the side-effects of drugs. She continued:

> He told me nothing at all. It would have been a help if I'd known because after each appointment I thought it was part of the illness,

the side-effects. I used to spend so much time in bookshops trying to find out. If I'd known that I'd have sorted something out.

The relief Mrs F felt when she did finally acquire and assimilate the information she was searching for demonstrates its central importance:

I found it much easier to come to terms with everything when I knew exactly what was happening, in laymen's terms . . . because I'd read the books I was better able to explain my situation. I could describe it in more accurate terms.

The need for patients to feel in some sort of control over what is going on, yet confronted with a profession apparently reluctant fully to share the information necessary suggests that an inappropriate model for dealing with a chronic condition is being applied (Barnard, 1985). A similar ambiguity will be seen to surround the question of developing expertise in managing the daily drug routine.

Summary – striking balances Patients are engaged in constant revisions as perceptions of disability and handicap change and life options are modified or reduced. New trade-offs are made as symptoms are redefined, but periods of disequilibrium when subjects are off-balance are common. Information plays a crucial role in deciding what is to be assessed. Balancing problems generally become more complex as new symptoms emerge. Yet despite this, a certain continuity of strategy management seems to emerge over time. Strategies of acquiescence, avoidance, covering, combating and accommodation are recurrent themes at different stages in people's illness careers. Where one might have expected a change in direction as the perceived severity of symptoms increased, patients' major concerns were largely geared to preserving some core of normality, even though room for manoeuvre was often radically reduced.

The Drug Regimen

This section will explore some of the group's efforts to balance the additional uncertainties, unpredictabilities and intrusiveness posed by the administration of the drug regimen. Clinically a balance is being sought between minimizing the symptoms of the illness consistent with incurring the lowest possible incidence of side-effects. It is a balance which, as the illness progresses, needs constant renegotiation. Subjects' recourse to lay knowledge, additional timetabling and scheduling strategies, and the development of a degree of expertise in managing the regimen illustrate the complexity of this additional balancing exercise.

Lack of information again appears to be an important consideration. The rationale of drug treatment and the decreasing efficacy of the drugs over time rarely appeared to be adequately explained to patients. Mr C expressed this most forcibly but his remarks were by no means untypical of those made by subjects diagnosed less recently than he.

> I mean there doesn't seem to me even the remotest rationale as yet for the treatment . . . You wonder why one drug is picked rather than the other. I think it just depends which specialist you go to. I mean why use Madopar instead of Sinemet? There must *be* a difference. But no specialist I've met is prepared to say 'Well, I would choose Sinemet for this patient and Madopar for that patient'. And give me a concrete reason for doing so.

Not surprisingly some subjects were often bewildered and confused. Mrs J, for instance, was obliged to rely on familiar recipes of knowledge gained over long experience with her husband's migraine medication to try and explain the apparent lack of efficacy of his current Levodopa regime:

> The basic problem is that a doctor will re-prescribe. And you had these migraine tablets for twenty years constantly churned out and the same thing's happening for Parkinson's . . . It's what I've been saying, isn't there anything else they can do now this is levelling off a bit? I mean if you go for any other complaint and it doesn't seem any better or worse you'd want to say 'Well, let's try this, let's try that'.

In the ensuing vacuum Mr J had evolved a strategy of his own, that of adjusting his drug schedule according to how he feels.

> It's something I've done off my own bat. I believe my body tells me what is required. I say to myself 'I'm getting a bit of the shakes, I need so-and-so.' I'm usually right.

To a limited extent he felt 'in charge', but this was a precarious equilibrium as his wife strongly disapproved, wanting him to stick to the 'rules'.

Although Mr J and Mr C generally felt the current drug regime was not entirely helpful and its clinical administration haphazard, it did not constitute an intrusive element in their lives.

Invasion   For Mrs P, however, the regime management quite dominated her life space and additional strategies were employed to manage it, namely strict timetabling and scheduling of all other activities around the regime. Her medication had recently been altered so she was faced with the problems of balancing all over again. She explained:

> Nothing could interfere with the taking of pills. They structure my life. Pill-taking, if you like, has ruled my life . . . For example this morning [when she slept through the alarm] my first thought was 'I've got to get those tablets down me before you come' . . . I've got to take medicines at different times *to enable me to do things*. It's not a case of 'take one tablet twice a day'. (my emphasis)

Talks with her were punctuated by pauses to consult the clock, calculate to the nearest five minutes the timing of her next dosage and decide what topics we could accomplish in the intervening time. Although defining herself as only moderately disabled and handicapped, the intrusiveness of the regime was the price she was prepared to pay to achieve some of the things she wanted and to sustain some semblance of a normal life-style.

The devastating effects of *mis*timing the pill regime were painfully illustrated in one of the first talks I had with Mr I early in the project. In his interest in the conversation, he had missed his 11.00 a.m. pill and I was insufficiently aware at the time of the necessity of checking people's schedules before embarking on talks. When I left him half an hour later, I found him virtually collapsed outside the door, an image of himself he had rigorously controlled for my benefit. One of the few strategies left open to him, as he explained later, was that of 'putting on a show', no matter what the cost was to him afterwards. Again the struggles to normalize social relationships is a powerful one, even if room for manoeuvre is minimal.

Mr and Mrs R were preoccupied both with the intrusiveness and the unpredictability involved in coming to terms with the drug regime. The need to check and double-check that Mr R was armed with the necessary dosage before embarking on an otherwise simple shopping trip was an added chore. But the apparent impossibility of being able to rely on the efficacy of one tactic over time made nonsense of attempts to plan and control life. Mr R's strategy was one of 'endurance'. As he explained:

I try to do things to overcome the pain. I had a period when I used to take my pills at a set time each day and when the pains came I had to get myself into a position kicking my legs. It didn't help so I dropped that. I now have a system whereby I take one to start with, then I take two, then I take one, then I keep topping up. And that system is working reasonably well at the moment. But at any time it might stop working and then I'd have to find something else.

Patient expertise   The fragility with which Mr R defined his position highlights a facet of PD which often characterizes chronic as opposed to acute illness careers: namely the necessity of developing a degree of expertise in handling both the illness and the drug therapy. However, the transition from patients' early expectations of medical control over their regime to a recognition that some control of drug balancing lies in their hands often comes as a shock. This was vividly expressed by Mr R: 'I wish the specialist would take me by the neck and say "Look, here's a regime, now go away and *stick* to it"', rather than being 'given permission' to adjust his dosage.

Mrs F, however, enjoyed relying on her own expertise. She was able to look back on her own period of disequilibrium when she had been dried out and experienced to the full the extent to which her illness had progressed, with some detachment. Now, with the approval of her doctors, she makes her own small adjustments according to the demands of the day:

What they are nice about, they say in their letter 'This lady is intelligent, she knows what she's doing, will adjust her own dose'. So they just put one of the doses on the bottle, but I don't necessarily follow that.

The dependence of doctors on patients' *own* evaluations of what is going on in their bodies is perhaps one of the more equivocal considerations involved in managing the drug regime. As with other older patients, few subjects had been socialized into expecting to share with their doctors in any decision-making process. Patients such as Mr R were ill-prepared for such a role. It was felt that doctors were rarely explicit in guiding subjects towards a *modus vivendi* where their own daily knowledge and experience would be the linchpin in future illness and drug management.

Thus handling the additional demands of a drug regimen, with its own almost independent career, only serves to accentuate the unpredictability, uncertainty and intrusiveness which already have to be contended with in managing symptoms. Additional strategies have to be adopted in weighing up how best to manage a therapeutic regime which is in itself problematic.

Discussion and Implications

An understanding of the complexity of the considerations which have to be balanced and their relationship with strategy management and resources is pivotal to an understanding of how chronic illness is managed. I have emphasized how the process of weighing up options is essentially socially patterned. The necessity of carrying on, at whatever level of functioning, is related to carrying on *doing* – sustaining family and other relationships, work tasks, and so on. Managing chronic illness cannot be conceptualized as taking place in a social vacuum. It is firmly wedded to the social context in which illness is experienced.

What a sociological perspective – and in particular an interactionist approach – has to offer is to demonstrate the capacity of people purposefully to define and grapple with their environment. People are not passively subject to the play of social forces, external or internal stimuli. Faced with the demands of living with uncertainty, unpredictability and intrusiveness, problems are actively defined and redefined as perceptions of disability and handicap shift and the meaning of symptoms change. Their implications for sustaining other important life areas are continuously assessed. Options chosen are *products* of how subjects define the situation.

What is interesting is that a similar cluster of strategies seems to operate at each balancing point. The struggle appears to be one of carrying on as normally as possible in an attempt, I suggest, to recapture some of that 'taken-for-grantedness' enjoyed by others.

Whereas many of the above features are common to other chronic illnesses – and indeed other life situations which represent loss and threat – some aspects are condition-specific. The use of a replacement therapy brings additional complications, uncertainties and unpredictabilities. The regime is not a constant. Periodically it has to be juggled and readjusted as the illness progresses, and ultimately it tends to cease to be effective. This calls for the adoption and refinement of very particular coping strategies by patients, chief of which are strict timetabling and scheduling of activities around the regime.

The use of Levodopa increases the life-span of those with PD, but this increased longevity brings further social, medical and biographical complications in its wake. Levodopa is a young drug, in use only since 1969, and its implications for end-of-career quality of life have yet to be fully understood. As medical technology increasingly impinges on other, at the moment untreatable, chronic illnesses, the 'Parkinson experience' may well come to dominate the illness scene. As Strauss *et al.* (1985) suggest, such 'halfway technology' is creating a new kind of chronic illness.

Given the broader remit of the project, any practical implications will be addressed to patients' relations with the medical profession. The need for patients to develop some expertise, both in handling the daily demands of living with PD and coping with the exigencies of the drug regime, requires the development of policies more appropriate to the management of long-term illness. Patients need to be helped and guided towards what seems to some an unfamiliar role. Doctors, in effect, must act as facilitators in this process if they are to be of help and relevance to the chronically ill.

This demands new patterns of interaction based on a more truly participatory model of information sharing and decision making. The paradox of expecting patients to acquire some expertise but without sufficient information to do so has been demonstrated. This means a much closer appreciation of the way *patients* define their priorities and needs, and a respect for *their* – perhaps competing – preferences.

Two practical considerations suggest themselves. One is for the current emphasis in medical training on an interventionist approach to be shifted towards one geared to an understanding and supportive role. The second is the use by the medical profession and other health carers of the Parkinson's Disease Society as an educative and enabling resource.

I have scarcely done justice to the many other issues involved. Theoretically I have been concerned with people's definitions of the situation and their capacity to act on those definitions. A more sophisticated analysis of *how* subjects' meaning structures are socially constructed could extend the value of this analysis. Methodologically I have observed the conventions and deleted from subjects' talk those features which might detract from its readability. The implications of using unedited transcripts for analysis are yet to be explored. Finally, a longitudinal study of the same patients would enable a much clearer picture to emerge of the changing nature of patients' definitions, the basis on which such decisions are made, and the reversibility or otherwise of decisions for future illness careers.

What I hope I have achieved is the provision of some insights into what the 'reality' of living with PD means to people. Such an awareness is an essential prerequisite for the development of meaningful policies to help those with PD not only carry on, but carry on with an improved quality of life.

Notes

My grateful thanks are due to Dr Marie Oxtoby, Dr Peter Blatchford, Dr Christopher Ashton and Ms Anna Wynne for their helpful comments on earlier drafts of this chapter.

1   This is part of a wider study, funded by the Parkinson's Disease Society, into 'Patient and Doctor Perceptions of the Management of Parkinson's Disease'. A sample of doctors was being interviewed in 1977 to obtain their perspective.

2   This is used to stress the processual nature of the illness and its management, which is marked by various phases, stages and plateaux.

3   I am employing this term to indicate both the physical unfolding of PD and to stress the impact on others' expectations and definitions. Trajectories for the chronically ill generally move downwards, but their shape is highly variable depending on the condition and variations within that condition.

4   To the best of my knowledge, Oakley (1981) has been one of the few writers successfully to have addressed this problem, although the field of obstetrics and gynaecology is less fraught with questions of incurability and progressiveness than that posed by PD.

5   The unedited transcript gives an accurate account of how I handled this issue. Constraints of space preclude its inclusion here.

References

Agar, M. H. (1980), *The Professional Stranger: An Informal Introduction to Ethnography* (London: Academic Press).

Barnard, D. (1985), 'Unsung questions of medical ethics', *Social Science and Medicine*, vol. 21, pp. 243–9.

Blumer, H. (1962), 'Society as symbolic interaction', in A. M. Rose (ed.), *Human Behavior and Social Processes: An Interactionist Approach* (London: Routledge & Kegan Paul).

Bury, M. (1979), 'Disablement in society: towards an integrated perspective', *International Journal of Rehabilitation Research*, vol. 2, no. 1, pp. 33–40.

Dorros, S. (1981), *Parkinson's: A Patient's View* (Washington, DC: Seven Locks Press).

Fagerhaugh, S. Y. and Strauss, A. L. (1977), *The Politics of Pain Management* (Reading, Mass.: Addison-Wesley).

Gyllenskold, K. (1982), *Breast Cancer: The Psychological Effects of the Disease and its Treatment* (London: Tavistock).

Locker, D (1981), *Symptoms and Illness: The Cognitive Organization of Disorder* (London: Tavistock).

Oakley, A. (1981), 'Interviewing women: a contradiction in terms', in H. Roberts (ed.), *Doing Feminist Research* (London: Routledge & Kegan Paul).

Oxtoby, M. (1982), *Parkinson's Disease Patients and their Social Needs: A*

Survey of Patients in Contact with the Parkinson's Disease Society (London: Parkinson's Disease Society).

Platt, J. (1982), 'The origin myth of "Participant observation"', paper given at the Annual Meeting of the American Sociological Association.

Sacks, O. (1973), *Awakenings* (London: Duckworth).

Sherwood, R. (1980), *The Psychodynamics of Race: Vicious and Benign Spirals* (Brighton: Harvester Press).

Singer, E. (1973), 'Social costs of Parkinson's disease', *Journal of Chronic Disease*, vol. 26, pp. 243–54.

Singer, E. (1974), 'Premature social aging: the social-psychological consequences of a chronic illness', *Social Science and Medicine*, vol. 8, pp. 143–51.

Strauss, A. L., Fagerhaugh, S. Y., Suczek, B., and Wiener,C. (1985), *Social Organization of Medical Work* (Chicago: University of Chicago Press).

Todes, C. (1983), 'Disabilities and how to live with them: inside Parkinsonism – a psychiatrist's personal experience', *Lancet*, 30 April, pp. 977–8.

Wynne, A. (1984), 'Accounting for accounts of multiple sclerosis', paper given at the George Saaton Centennial Communication and Cognition Conference, University of Gent, Belgium, 14–17 November.

4 *Meanings at Risk: The Experience of Arthritis*

MICHAEL BURY

Introduction

Much modern sociology conveys the view that contemporary society is strongly functional, indeed, prescriptive in character, involving multiple roles and a complex division of labour. Whichever version of the modernity thesis one follows one thing is clear: social life today is simultaneously highly organized and precarious. Technical sophistication marches alongside psychological anxiety, not least in the field of medicine (for example, see Comaroff and Maguire, 1981, and, more broadly, Berger *et al.*, 1974). Social support and social control walk hand in hand, and indeed, it is not always easy to tell the difference.

Modern social systems demand (at least of their adult members, the ageing process presenting a further problem) a range of physical and psychological attributes: a set of particular competencies (Hirst and Woolley, 1982). The human body becomes important not only for its instrumental capacities but also as a cultural or symbolic domain. No wonder that numerous volumes have been written about the intricacies of human interaction and such issues as non-verbal communication. Experiencing chronic illness against such a back-cloth creates a host of possible social and emotional uncertainties for the individual, in addition to physical disability. Suffering the onset of symptoms involves changes in the body and in social relationships which are already likely to be complex.

In attempting to understand the nature of chronic illness in contemporary society, therefore, our perspective has to place the individual in a wider context. For example, in a recent paper on arthritis in the family I attempted to describe the varying impact such an illness has on family members (Bury, 1985). The perspective developed was of the family as both supportive and controlling. In illness individuals can turn to their families for help, but they cannot know how appeals that are made will work out. They cannot know precisely what the 'limits of tolerance' are in advance of reaching them (or coming close to them) nor whether one strategy for handling symptoms and disability in the home will be regarded more positively than another.

Requests for recognition and help are tempered by judgements about the effects such requests will have on relationships, both in the present and for the future. Fears of dependency on others, or even rejection, are inevitably caught up in seeking help (Locker, 1983). Family members may well have different views of the situation and of appropriate behaviour in the face of illness, or have similar views but at different stages of the illness trajectory. In particular they may differ in the views they have about the likely future of the illness and its outcome, as well as such matters as the role of professional care.

In developing this approach to chronic illness, and trying to come to grips with its complexity, it has become clear that much of the experience and meaning of illness is *emergent* in character. That this should be so is hardly surprising given the strong cultural emphasis on achievement, action and success in contemporary society and the essentially ambiguous situation this creates for those 'failing' through illness or other misfortune. Chronic illness not only disrupts individual biographies and family relationships but it also cuts across the prescriptive patterns of modern social systems. No clear alternative and valued role is on offer – at best the 'sick role' offers only temporary respite. Thus different responses by those affected carry different costs, with none of them entirely resolving the essential ambiguity at the centre of the experience.

From this viewpoint the emphasis in the sociological literature on the 'strategic management' of illness (Wiener, 1975), on 'narrative reconstruction' (Williams, 1984), on 'trajectories' and adaptation (Strauss and Glaser, 1975), and on the management of uncertainty (Davis, 1963) is surely correct. Yet even here the active and *pragmatic* nature of such coping mechanisms often seems understated, as if the search for stable meanings in the face of suffering were, all things considered, relatively straightforward. Sometimes, in fact, certain stages in response to illness are described (as in other situations of 'misfortune' – unemployment or bereavement, for example) as if deviation from such a staged response might itself be unhealthy or deviant. Our conceptual categories may imply this even if they do not suggest it outright. In contrast, it is the pragmatic, and even performative aspects of meaning (Sahlins, 1976; 1985) which I wish to emphasize in this chapter and a brief clarification of what is meant by this might be helpful at this point. Two aspects are of particular relevance; meaning as consequence and meaning as significance.

MEANING AS CONSEQUENCE

In discussing the meaning of chronic illness much of the literature refers to its consequences for the individual. Although, for example, Blaxter (1976) is concerned with the varying definitions used in the field of chronic illness, especially those used by medical and welfare personnel, her study focuses on the problems which chronic illness and disability create for the individual. Money problems, job problems and problems of personal care and practical daily living are shown to be the consequences of disability. In other words, the meaning of disability is coping with or adapting to a chronic illness and its sequelae. Professional services and their attendant 'definitional processes' are evaluated in this light.

Though the relationships can be complicated, chronic illness is characterized by its disabling and handicapping consequences. The effects of chronic illness create both activity restriction (disability) and social disadvantage (handicap) (Bury, 1979). Conceptualizing the consequences of chronic illness in this way concentrates attention on both practical problems and policy issues. By spelling out what chronic illness means in these respects it is hoped that more sensitive appraisals of need may be developed and a broader recognition of its impact be gained. A recent study of rheumatoid arthritis (Locker, 1983), for example, outlined the disadvantages experienced by individuals in coming to terms with the ravages of chronic illness, the effects of pain and disability, and the regimens necessary to cope with its impact on their lives. Even gaining extra time in order to rest may be a source of disadvantage; time spent in coping with symptoms cannot be given to other valued activities. In this sense the meaning of chronic illness concerns the problems, consequences and costs which it entails.

MEANING AS SIGNIFICANCE

In addition to the social problems which chronic illness creates, there is a second level of meaning involved, namely the significance or connotations that conditions carry. As Zola (1983) has put it, even terms such as 'disability' and 'invalidity' have several meanings not the least of which is the devaluing of individuals and their personal worth. To be an invalid is bad enough but for this to mean that the individual is 'invalid' is another matter altogether. At this level, therefore, we are concerned with what medical conditions and disabilities signify within particular cultures. Conditions vary in their significance, whether it be in terms of specific disabilities,

disfigurement, or future outlook. Fears and anxieties which surround disease onset, and persist in various forms throughout the
experience, concern the perceived character of the condition for both
biological functioning and cultural competence. The experience of
chronic illness always operates simultaneously at these two levels.

Although some perceptions and beliefs about a chronic illness may
be apparent to the individual from the outset, some may not. In the
case of rheumatoid arthritis, 'received wisdom' suggests that it is
crippling and painful. Patients, particularly those in their early
years, may find it hard to square their experience with the common
belief that arthritis is a disease of the elderly. The connotations of
the conditions, in this sense, may create a feeling of 'premature
ageing' in which stages of the individual's biography may be felt to
be lost (Singer, 1974). Individuals and communities have expectations about disabling illnesses available to them from the immediate
cultural environment, and these provide a context for the thoughts
and anxieties as to what the condition will mean. Fears of stigma and
discrimination derive not so much from the disability as from the
significance accorded to the condition by others.

These aspects of meaning in chronic illness are important to an
understanding of the strategies people employ. In essence, the
experience of chronic illness involves testing structures of support
and risking meanings within the practical constraints of home and
work. Relationships do not *guarantee* particular responses, indeed it
is the response that shapes the relationships; meanings change as
they are tested and altered as they are *put at risk*. Individuals and
their families cannot be entirely sure what the event of such an
illness means or will mean for the future; meanings are fashioned in
the flux of change, as events unfold. Guesses and speculation may be
made, in order to inform action, but the meaning of events only
emerges as a product of change and its interaction with the structures of everyday life.

Importantly, there is no guarantee that significant others will
respond in a wholly predictable or supportive manner. The contingencies of family life and the expectations that members have of
relationships are all put under threat. Thus, the essentially ambiguous nature of chronic illness is constantly confirmed in practice.
Relationships are thrown into relief by the occurrence of illness, and
social life becomes more of a 'performance' than hitherto. An
increasing range of actions become quasi-deliberate and more loosely
related to culturally prescribed codes of conduct, a situation in
which meanings must be reconstructed.

It is with these issues in mind, and in an attempt to give them some empirical support, that I now turn directly to the arthritis study.

The Study Design

The study from which the case materials presented here have been taken was carried out by the author in the late 1970s in Greater Manchester. Twenty-five women and five men with rheumatoid arthritis were interviewed using an interview schedule covering the experience of the onset and development of the illness, its impact on work and home life, and the processes of seeking medical help. The thirty respondents had all been referred to an out-patient rheumatology clinic for their arthritis. Some of the respondents were 'new to the disease' but I interviewed all of them at least twice, once before and at least once after their early contact with the hospital.

Although the study was concerned with the early stages of illness, it should be noted that given the insidious nature of such illness, it is not surprising that many respondents had been living with symptoms for a considerable period. Certainly, by the second interview the presence of arthritis had become part of their everyday lives. All the respondents were facing an altered future and were experiencing symptoms (sometimes severe) at the time of the interviews, and were, as we shall see, struggling with the meaning and implications of events, both for themselves and for others. In fact, the arrival of an interviewer reinforced for some the fact that their situation was not normal – why else was someone from the University coming to interview them? For others the interviews were understood simply as part of the research activities of the University and hospital.

The variations in response to the interviews highlights the limitations as well as the strengths of the methods employed in this study. The purpose of the interviewing was to map out the meaning of rheumatoid arthritis and its social impact. The assumption from which this sprang (partly formed by my own observations) was that clinics which patients attended did not systematically attend to such issues, the possible effects they might have on treatments, or the impact the illness might have on those who would be called upon to give support. I also assumed that such issues were important, indeed central, to patients' experiences. I shall return to these assumptions at the end of the chapter.

At the same time I harboured other assumptions about my own activities, the most important of which was that it was possible for me to identify dimensions of experience common to those living with rheumatoid arthritis as well as the particular contingencies of individual circumstances. I assumed that my interviewing technique would be an effective way of doing so. As I have noted, however, distinguishing the impact of the illness from the ordinary uncertainties and problems of meaning is an issue facing both the researcher, and the respondents themselves (Wiener, 1975). Thus my interpretation of the accounts I was given should be viewed in this light.

Although there is a possibility that what is being described as the impact of the illness and disability is only part of the story, I should add that my respondents were themselves well aware of this in providing accounts of their illness experiences. Methodological difficulties of this kind are bound to arise where reliance on respondents' accounts is given priority over direct observation. In their favour, the descriptive and exploratory techniques employed here allow for the views and experiences of those living with the problems to be given pride of place, offsetting the tendency in social science for experience and meaning to be reduced to 'variables' (Blumer, 1969). Even so, much depends on the quality of interpretations offered, though it is fair to add that no method of enquiry can escape the problems of interpretation (Berger and Kellner, 1982).

The Study Group

Given the way hospital out-patient services are organized, it was inevitable that my sample would not be representative of rheumatoid arthritis sufferers, though the number of men and women in the sample roughly reproduce the gender distribution of arthritis. As can be seen in Table 4.1, the study group is relatively young. Generally speaking, rheumatology clinics prefer to be presented with patients who show the early signs of the disease or florid symptoms that can be treated. General practitioners are thus under pressure to detect and refer early cases in a spirit of therapeutic optimism and good husbandry of their community flock. Similarly, the common image of arthritis being part of old age may deter referral of older people for specialist care, both by patients and their families, or their doctors. It is clear that ideas about the disease influence events such as referral and I will touch on this in my discussion.

Twenty-three of the thirty individuals were married, three were separated (not so far as I could detect because of their arthritis), and four of the women had been widowed. The majority, therefore, were living within family settings, often with teenage children at home or partly at home. Most respondents were working, or had been working until very recently including the majority of women, fifteen in all. In order to convey something of the context of the respondents' situation

Table 4.1   *The Study Group – by Age and Sex*

Age	Women	Men
<24	2	—
25–34	7	—
35–44	4	—
45–54	6	3
55–64	3	2
>65	3	—
Total	25	5

Table 4.2 shows that the working women had a variety of occupations; at the time of initial interview two of the full-time working women were 'off sick' with their arthritis. Others had experienced periods of sick leave because of their symptoms. Of the five men, four were of working age, three of whom were self-employed and only one was a manual worker, 'off sick' at the time of initial interview.

This, then, in brief outline, is the context of the study, and of the lives of the respondents. All of the households I visited were facing the usual problems which confront working people, namely, 'getting by' in precarious economic circumstances (Pahl, 1984), though the group varied considerably in terms of job security and income. All were facing the disruptive event of illness in their lives, and were working out what resources they could call on, whether at home, at work, or at the clinic, and how best to do so. I intend to focus first on a single (though not untypical) case in some detail in order to illustrate some of the processes involved. I shall then review a wider range of material from the study in order to examine the relationship between the impact of the illness on immediate social relationships and the decision to seek more formal help.

Legitimation and Chronic Illness – the Case of Mrs M

Mrs M lived in a Manchester suburb with her husband and two children, both of whom were in their late teens. She was 46 years of age at the time of interview and had worked for some years as a telephone operator. From time to time, during the previous five years she told me she had been to her GP with various problems, indicating some form of rheumatism. But these had not been interpreted by her doctor or by herself as meaning that she had a specific or serious

Table 4.2 *The Working Women by Age and Occupation*

Age	Full-time	Part-time
24	Secretary	Shop assistant
25–34	Punch-card operator	School child supervisor
	Secretary	
	Machine operator	
35–44	Wages booking clerk	Barmaid
45–54	School kitchen supervisor	Office cleaner
	Telephonist	Handicapped school helper
		Paid housework
55–64	Bakery worker	Shop cleaner

arthritic complaint. On one occasion she had experienced pain in her feet, especially in her big toe, and had thought she might be suffering from bunions. This was dismissed by her GP although no alternative explanation was offered. Subsequently she reported pains in her knees and had been prescribed four aspirins a day on the general understanding that she might have a touch of rheumatism. None of these symptoms seemed to worsen and Mrs M assumed that they were either a sign of getting older or that she had overdone particular household chores. Within the domestic division of labour she had traditionally been responsible for most of the shopping, including the carrying of heavy bags, and she assumed that this might explain her aching legs and feet. Her early visits to the GP gave her no grounds for further thought about the problem.

But the symptoms did not entirely disappear. As time went on she noticed that her body was beginning to fail her. She said:

> I'd say it started properly about 18 months ago. I noticed that it was awkward to carry bags, shopping bags. I think the very first thing was my knees. I felt as though they were going to give way when I was going up and down stairs. There are three flights at work. Well, I'm on the third floor, so if the lift wasn't working I had to walk up and this is how I noticed it. And also I never used to wait for the lift coming down, I used to always run down. I had to stop because I felt as though I was going to fall.

Even so, Mrs M kept trying to minimize the problem in her mind. When I asked her what she thought was happening she said 'I didn't think anything really, I just never thought anything'. Then her elbows and one of her shoulders began to ache. She found she was knocking herself painfully and couldn't bear carrying a shoulder bag. And this made her think that it was something more than just her previous 'rheumatic' symptoms. Their severity and persistence began to be worrying. Still, she hung on to a view of herself as basically healthy (as most people with chronic illness do). She did not want to see herself crossing the dividing line, even though her healthy self-image was becoming difficult to sustain.

She stated that she consulted her GP again. This time he began to consider that she might have a specific rheumatic condition and indeed the word 'rheumatoid' seems to have been introduced at this point. He put her back on aspirin. Mrs M could not remember exactly what form of words was used, largely because she was only slowly becoming aware of their significance and because she kept hoping the problems would be self-limiting. But she had to face the fact that they might not be. She stated:

By that time I was beginning to think it was a bit more than just a bit of weakness, because I have a friend in London, she's had arthritis since she was about 30. She's had operations on her feet and it did set me thinking a little bit, when I started to feel a bit better with the aspirin I thought Oh, well, its going.

Reverberating in her mind, however, was the doctor's loose references to 'rheumatoid'. Mrs M said she was dismayed to hear him use this term, but because it was couched in such a vague context she hoped that its use signified less than she feared. It was still possible to treat the problem as a diffuse and not too serious, 'rheumatism'.

Then, on a day in March, she suddenly became ill at work, and the situation began to worsen. In retrospect she dated the onset of her rheumatoid arthritis from that point. Again, she stated:

It seemed to come and go a little bit until March, and one day I went out at my lunch hour at work and I did some shopping and I felt really quite ill. One of the girls said, when I got back, was I alright, and I said, well I don't feel too good, because every bone hurt, I don't think there was a bone that didn't hurt. But I just thought it was, maybe, flu coming on or something, but with every bone hurting.

Before this event she had allowed her aspirin to cease and had adopted a frame of mind that perhaps nothing more would come of her aches and pains. Now she had to revise her views in line with the possibility of a more serious rheumatic complaint, unbelievable though this still seemed. By the early summer her GP decided to undertake blood tests, which proved to be positive. This meant that she probably had rheumatoid arthritis, although her GP continued to dissimulate in confronting Mrs M directly with the diagnosis and its implications. From Mrs M's point of view this situation developed partly because the GP wished to 'ease her mind' about the possibility of her having a crippling disease, and partly, of course, because the GP could not be sure about the diagnosis or the severity of the condition. At this stage he prescribed aspirin once more and suggested she attend a rheumatological out-patient clinic.

One of the central features of these early experiences for Mrs M was that they were largely hers alone. Although one or two visits to the GP during this time were known to her husband and children little significance was placed on them. The following extract from my interview with Mrs M illustrates this point. This is taken from an early part of the interview when Mrs M had begun to discuss how she had realized that there might be something more to consider than just 'a bit of rheumatism'. Though Mr M was aware that his wife was facing difficulties he felt he had no reason to take any special interest:

Interviewer: Did your husband know at the time?
Mrs M: No, I didn't say much to you did I, really?
Mr M: I thought it was rheumatism, something like that you know, didn't pay much attention. I didn't personally, because she doesn't tell me much you see, we are getting older and we expect these aches and pains.

As the interview progressed and the details of her story emerged more fully, Mr M began to realize, perhaps for the first time, that his wife was facing a serious situation. The fears which were at the back of her mind were threatening to disrupt normal family relationships, but the actual symptoms remained close enough to everyday aches and pains for them to be ignored by the rest of the family. At one level this is precisely what Mrs M wanted, but was unable to maintain. As time went on she felt the need to see her problems openly recognized but being anxious about what this would mean she sought ways to put this off. She vacillated between disguising her symptoms and attempts to have them regarded as real and legitimate by those around her. This became particularly apparent when the interview turned to discuss the way the signs of Mrs M's illness had become visible. At one point I asked whether she was becoming aware of visible signs of her illness. She said she was, especially with her hands.

Again a sequence from the interview reveals what was going on.

Mrs M:	My hands bother me quite a bit really.
Interviewer:	What's happened to them, can you describe it to me?
Mrs M:	Well, this joint that's swollen, that one, my fingers are quite sore.
Interviewer:	That shape has come about recently has it?
Mrs M:	Yes.
Interviewer:	And your little finger, swollen here?
Mrs M:	Yes, the joints, in fact all of them are swollen, but that one is the worst, my knuckles here. That one, I'm a telephonist, I do quite a bit of writing so I have to keep changing my pencil, writing different, trying not to get knocked, because it's really quite painful because there's six of us . . . yes I can't grip like I did. Fell down the stairs last week didn't I, and I was trying to grip the bannister?
Mr M:	Well . . .
Mrs M:	Not fell, I slipped, it was my own fault because I had no slippers on but I was gripping the bannister, but it didn't grip properly, which means I went down about five stairs.
Mr M:	Mind you, it's a broad bannister, it takes me all my time to grip it.
Mrs M:	Yes, but I find out that I'm dropping things that I could kind of get hold of.

At this point it was clear that a tension was developing between Mr and Mrs M. During most of the interview Mr M sat with his wife, quietly listening to what was being said. But from time to time he could not but be drawn in. This was particularly true when we touched on the recognition of the illness by others around Mrs M. Let me continue by picking up the interview when Mrs M returned to the way her hands were changing shape. At this time Mrs M's daughter had also come into the room

Mrs M:	I thought for a while that it was with crocheting, a bit of rheumatism with the crocheting, or something like that. Anyway, I've not done any for a long time. I could only do some for a short period. I find the joints tend to burn inside.
Interviewer:	Does it worry you that you can see the problem, that it's becoming visible?
Mrs M:	Yes, well I do tend to look at it, and of course you see I'm sat like this with my hands in front of me all day so you do tend to look a bit.

Interviewer: Has your family noticed?

Mrs M: I don't think they've seen my hands, really.

Daughter: I noticed it, I noticed her hands.

Interviewer: You did? How long ago?

Daughter: Three or four months ago.

Mr M: Can't say I've noticed much difference. You've always had, you know, your fingers . . .

Mrs M: I don't think you know what I mean do you?

Mr M: You can't see them bigger, no, I haven't noticed it that bad until you pointed it out.

Mrs M: You've not seen them really. I don't go around crying on your shoulder a lot, do I?

Mr M: She doesn't tell me much. I have to dig and I think she's got the doctor on the hook. He doesn't tell me much. But I'm going to pin him down next time I go. I'll ask him the questions I want to know.

Mr M became more defensive as this exchange developed. What seemed to him a reasonable definition of what his wife was facing, namely no more than would normally be expected with the passing years, was emerging as something more serious. This was complicated by the fact that, three or four years previously, Mr M had suffered a heart attack. Two processes, therefore, were at work. First, Mrs M had a great deal of difficulty knowing whether and how to disclose her thoughts and feelings about her difficulties. Second, Mr M's illness seemed more obviously serious, warranting considerable attention by the rest of the family. Mrs M felt inclined to underplay her own worries as much as she could. Thus past events and their 'pre-illness' relationship exerted an influence over events.

Even so, Mrs M expressed resentment about her husband's indifference to her symptoms. Later in the interview she described how at Christmas, before the March onset date, she had spent a long period with her friend from London, discussing the 'ins and outs' of her friend's arthritis, and her own experiences. When she disclosed this to me her husband and daughter then began to exchange comments to the effect that they had wondered what had been going on at the time. Mrs M sat quietly, letting these rather defensive exchanges take their course. Unwittingly, the interview was partly becoming an exercise for Mrs M to pursue the legitimacy of her illness. The appearance of an interviewer had signalled to her and her family that her illness was becoming more disruptive than had hitherto been recognized. In Mrs M's case the confirmation of the diagnosis by the hospital consultant was almost a formality. By that time the illness was already established and playing a major part in her daily life, and, as we have seen, was affecting her family situation, at least, from her own viewpoint.

My second interview with Mrs M confirmed this picture, though the pain from her arthritis had been brought under a degree of control through a new regimen of drugs. Small changes in household tasks and the physical environment had been instituted: taps had been changed in the kitchen and some help was on offer to help with routine tasks. But these changes were being instituted with caution and mixed feelings. They were brought about, more often than not, without any discussion or open decision-making among family members. Mrs M continued to view with some anxiety placing demands on her husband and of reaching the 'limits of tolerance' within the home.

Just as doctors frequently employ a 'gradual dawning' approach to conveying serious information to patients, so patients may employ a similar strategy with regard to significant others. This is not simply a mechanism for avoiding unpleasant reaction, it is part and parcel of not knowing quite what the reaction will be. It is part of the problem of discovering meaning both in terms of practical consequences and in terms of the wider significance of the disease as a 'crippling' condition. I return here to the notion of 'risking meanings' against situations and events. Mrs M could discuss the situation more openly with a close friend because she was able to judge more fully what the illness would mean to the friend, and what her reaction would be. Friends, after all, are functional in that they can offer sympathy without having to take full responsibility for the consequences. Their possible constraining role is limited (though avoidance and even rejection is well within their power) and their support less qualified and beset by anxiety.

In the home, however, the degree of uncertainty and anxiety is greater. The reordering of even small aspects of daily life can prove difficult. For example, as with so many suffering with chronic illness, Mrs M found herself wanting to conserve her energy by resting more during the day. Yet even taking periods of rest needed careful thought. She discovered that resting involves making demands on others, not only for the peace and quiet in which to do it, but also for an acceptance that the rest is necessary. As with many others in this study the absence of a clear response by spouse or family created a persistent feeling of uncertainty about adopting particular strategies or calling for help. As Locker (1983) points out such deliberations are as much a part of the 'disadvantage' created by chronic illness as are the more tangible effects such as loss of income.

What is also involved here is that individuals and their spouses are viewing present circumstances in terms of the future. Demands or expectations of recognition and help may well involve setting precedents, not all of them welcome. When Mrs M let it be known that she could not turn the taps on or off in the kitchen, she was risking that her husband and daughter might precipitately decide that she would *no longer* do so, and that the future would be affected as well as the present. In other words, she was concerned about how present difficulties would be interpreted by family members in terms of the wider significance of arthritis as a disabling illness. In Mrs M's case small issues such as this multiplied to create a situation of some anxiety for the family, each member with their own prior views about arthritis, its occurrence and course and appropriate behaviour in its wake. Thus, how Mrs M conducted herself in the home (and to a lesser degree at work), and what kind of 'performance' came to be involved were intimately bound up with her experience of its apparent meaning for others. However much particular problems were resolved in practice a concern with the future constantly snapped at the heels of her efforts to bring events under control. By the same token, Mrs M's views of medical care involved a mixture of hope and anxiety, in particular that of getting specialist help. Mrs M, like many patients in this study, had already seen her GP, but the decision to attend an out-patient clinic marked a new stage in her 'career'.

Seeking Help from the Clinic

In considering case material in this connection I think it useful to invoke Zola's well-known work on 'from person to patient' (Zola, 1973). Though the 'triggers' Zola describes have often been reiterated in medical sociology textbooks they have received little empirical exploration and I use them here as a means of organizing my data and developing the argument presented so far. I am less concerned here with the referral process as such, than with what going to a specialist tells us about decision-making in the course of an illness – in particular, how social factors rather than symptoms alone influence action. Patients in this study were already in contact with their GPs before any interviewing took place. However, a new stage in the unfolding illness occurred with the decision to seek specialist advice. I am therefore using Zola's approach to explore aspects of the course of illness rather than the process of 'coming into care'. The triggers involved in seeking professional help according to Zola are as follows: (1) the occurrence of an interpersonal crisis in the person's life, (2) the *perceived* interference of the illness with social or personal relations, (3) 'sanctioning', (4) the *perceived* interference with vocational or physical activity, and (5) the 'temporalizing of symptomatology'. Let me take each of these in turn.

(1) THE OCCURRENCE OF AN INTERPERSONAL CRISIS

In Zola's discussion this referred to seeking help where symptoms themselves were not worsening but where 'a crisis called attention to the symptoms, causing the patient to dwell on them and finally to do something about them'. Given what I have already said about the uncertainty of disguising symptoms and the hidden nature of the disease in its early stages, together with the difficulty in involving others, it was unlikely that many patients would have been contemplating referral against a background of interpersonal *crisis*, though it is clear from Mrs M's case amongst others that considerable strain was involved. Although interpersonal crises may be involved in the development of disability through rheumatoid arthritis they were not prominent in triggering referral. Most situations were managed below the crisis point. But a few cases did involve this element.

At the extreme of the spectrum Mrs B, for example, one of the few older patients in the sample, had been suffering symptoms for many years. Indeed, she was the only person referred to the clinic as a 'new case' who turned out to be a lapsed old case. The decision to offer her a new referral came about as a result of a crisis at home. It was not that Mrs B's symptoms had worsened but Mr B had demanded that the GP 'relieve the pressure' on the home. A crisis had developed, following the separation and subsequent divorce of their only son. He had not long been married and had apparently given up good career prospects as an architect (long worked for by his parents) in order to 'go off wandering' as Mr B put it.

Since that time, some six months prior to any initial contact, their disappointment with their son's behaviour had turned to a more persistent unhappiness, especially for Mr B. He told me that referral had been sought because there were no signs of improvement in Mrs B's rheumatoid arthritis and, therefore, she might benefit from new treatment. Mr B needed a break from the role of constant carer. In other words, it was the meaning of the illness for the carer rather than the patient which was critical. Although Mrs B had managed to retain some degree of mobility this was very limited, especially outside the home. Mr B had maintained a car in order that they should be able to get out, but such journeys had become so infrequent that the car had turned into a useless symbol of isolation. Thus, Mr B had openly asked their GP for referral. Finally, Mrs B was taken into a long-stay hospital in Derbyshire, for bed-rest and treatment even though she did not institute or have high expectations of the referral. In the referral from GP to clinic and from clinic to long-stay hospital, the doctors were very much divided over her case. Her symptoms, chronic though they were, did not warrant urgent clinical intervention, but the crisis in the home demanded that some action be taken. Mrs B herself was unhappy about the referral, but acted passively in the face of the definition of the situation being pursued by her husband. To do otherwise would have run the risk of a much more damaging crisis.

In another case, the occurrence of an interpersonal crisis coincided with the disruption of an occupational role and general functioning (see section (4) below) and both played a part in referral to the specialist clinic. In fact, Mrs S experienced what can only be called a continual crisis existence. Living in a poor district of Manchester she had faced a variety of problems, both in her marriage and in trying to secure permanent and satisfactory employment. The onset of arthritis came as the 'last straw'. For many weeks both her husband and her GP were inclined to see her medical problems as minor ones, even though the onset had included periods when her knees were so swollen that she was unable to walk and had to take to her bed. Yet again she experienced considerable anxiety concerning the reactions of others as well as the symptoms of her illness. Finally, following a particular crisis in which she had failed to get a job locally, she left her two young children with a neighbour and presented herself one evening at a local chemical works where office cleaning was available. On his returning home her husband stormed off to the factory, and, she stated, more or less dragged her back home. A violent fight ensued, from which she was finally able to retreat to bed. Though her symptoms had not worsened, a visit from her GP the next day led to referral.

(2) THE PERCEIVED INTERFERENCE OF THE ILLNESS WITH SOCIAL AND PERSONAL RELATIONS

In contrast with the above source of referral this deals less with a personal *crisis* than the effects of symptoms on social and personal relations in the sense I have discussed them in this chapter. An inability to maintain friendships, go to the cinema or pub without discomfort and embarrassment, or the growing worry about the response by significant others can mean that the individual feels that the time has come to 'do something' about the arthritis. Particular cases show that this process did play an observable part in help-seeking in the present study.

Mrs G for example, a woman in her early twenties, had experienced fluctuating symptoms over a number of years dating back to her teens. These had been seen as 'a touch of rheumatism', but had faded prior to her marriage, and the birth of her child. Eighteen months after the birth her back and knees began to ache persistently, particularly in the early morning, and it became clear that her 'rheumatism' had not disappeared. Her symptoms became more severe as time went on and the impact of the illness on her and her young marriage were quickly picked up by her GP, a woman doctor. Although her symptoms were worsening she resisted suggestions for referral because of her attempts to maintain her marital and maternal roles. In other words, she wished to avoid the perceived interference which her symptoms were creating in her interpersonal relations by resisting referral. In addition, she received little help from those around her and the idea of referral to the clinic raised insurmountable practical problems, for example, in arranging a baby minder. Finally, it was precisely these problems of baby care and her relationship with her husband that persuaded her to accept referral. Her symptoms were relatively stable, after the initial onset period, but the maintenance of her everyday life was coming more problematic to her. Her baby was becoming more demanding and her illness more restrictive. In addition, she felt that unless she sought further help her relationship with her husband would become critical. The uncertainty involved in deciding between two unfavourable courses of action, seeking help or not seeking it, was strongly demonstrated.

For some individuals the process of referral itself involved a crisis in legitimacy, concerning the precise meaning or the significance of symptoms themselves. The insidious onset and the fluctuating nature of symptoms created an ambivalence about agreeing to attend a specialist clinic. Symptoms often seemed to be stabilizing after an initial period, or were such that the individual had difficulty in telling whether they were worsening or not. When such ambivalence was combined with particular social difficulties there was a reluctance to agree to suggestions for a further referral. Mrs C, for example, had delayed attending the clinic, even though her GP felt that she should, because her husband had had an accident. She said:

> I should have gone [to the clinic] before but my husband got run over 12 months last October. Had a very bad accident and he was in the hospital, and, er, so I didn't want to get involved myself, you see. He was in plaster up to here for seven months. Fractured, five fractures in his leg. So I let it ride. I don't know whether I should have gone before.

In fact, just prior to my first contact, Mrs C's symptoms had worsened, though her husband's medical state, though still worrying, had improved. Both these changes prompted her to pursue referral. Only when it did not interfere with other areas of her personal life, in particular her husband's involvement with the hospital, did she feel justified in taking action on her own behalf. Zola's discussion suggested that referral under this heading reflected the perceived interference of symptoms with the individual's activities; mine suggests that decisions about referral also involve the individual assessing the impact of using services on other family members.

(3) SANCTIONING

By this Zola means that a decision to seek help can require someone else sanctioning their behaviour. It is not that the individual is necessarily stoical, simply that he or she is unwilling to take the responsibility for the decision alone. This, again, is likely to be relevant in situations where insidious and chronic symptoms occur, for, as I have noted, people are often unsure about what steps to take. Zola states that in his sample 'sanctioning' behaviour, as a direct source of referral was rare, even though he could see a more indirect involvement of others in the referral process. This holds true for the present study as well. What is of interest here is that sanctioning seemed particularly important in the case of male respondents living with a spouse. Clearly, the numbers are not large enough for me to do more than suggest a possible trend, but it is clear that for three out of the five men 'sanctioning' was important. I would like to illustrate the point in some detail.

Mr B, who was in his early fifties at the time of interview, lived with his wife in a suburb of Manchester. Their three children had grown up and moved away from home. He owned a small engineering works and had been experiencing 'rheumaticky' symptoms on and off for three years. His GP had initially sent him to an orthopaedic surgeon, after he had complained about painful feet, but little ensued from this consultation. Then, some nine months prior to my contact, his pains had worsened in his feet and ankles, and one had begun to swell. But, still he and his wife (a nurse) had treated the situation 'realistically' as he put it, as no more than a nuisance. The new symptoms were taken back to the GP who then referred him to a 'medical man' (presumably a general physician) at a local hospital. This turned out to be a very different experience. His main problem at that time was with a swollen finger on one hand. He told me:

> The second finger, here; anyway it became swollen, extremely painful, very very swollen, like a Palethorpe sausage, hot and shiny instead of cold. He said he could relieve the pain and swelling with cortisone injections, which were painful. I've had shrapnel in my leg and a bullet through my hand, and one or two other things like that, that have given me pain, but this injection! It was a course of

five injections into five different points of the joint. The first two
were bearable, relatively bearable. The third one – my feet came
up, my head went down – Jesus wept!

After this, however, his symptoms did abate; the painful injections
seemed to work. While he was far from happy with the situation, he
felt unjustified in taking any further action. He didn't want to risk
being seen to exaggerate his problems so he simply decided to put up
with them. But, according to his own account, his wife could see his
illness worsening. A common-sense approach was not enough. She
encouraged and finally badgered him to return once again to his GP to
ask for further help. In the end he did so, and was referred to the
rheumatology clinic. This account was also confirmed by Mr B's wife,
who was present for part of the first interview.

Mr G lived a mile from Mr B. Mr G who also had a long history of
vague rheumatic symptoms, without ever thinking of them as arthritis, had for many years been a plasterer. Recently he had given this up
and bought a fish and chip shop which he ran with his wife. He had
suffered from what he took to be fibrositis and had always maintained
an attitude of being able to 'work it off'. Some two years before I met
him he had decided to seek further help, because his wrists and
knuckles began to swell. He had visited a private doctor, who put him
on a twelve months course of steroid-based tablets. Again, in the
initial months they seemed to work, and then two months before the
course was due to finish, his symptoms returned. The doctor then
told him that he could do no more.

During the next year he tried to carry on as normal, and although
some mention of arthritis had cropped up in his recent contacts with
the medical services he still preferred to think of it as a less
threatening 'rheumatic' problem. But his work and social life were
becoming more difficult to sustain. Suggestions from his wife that he
should seek further help were rejected, even though he admitted that
he wanted to He said he did not want to 'make a fuss', and that he felt
there was little more that could be done. But his wife persisted. The
following extract from my first interview with Mr G summarizes what
happened:

Mr G: Well that's about the position . . . we decided we'd just
                 have to leave it. They [his private doctor] couldn't do
                 very much. Nothing further known about this. I
                 couldn't take another course, because I was at my
                 limit. So that was it.
Interviewer: That led you to go back to your GP?
Mr G: Well, my wife did this on her own, yes. I said 'Oh blow

it, I can live with it'. You see poor old people hobbling around. It's not quite so bad, it's just sometimes worse than others. It's affected me much more, because I used to like walking miles. I loved walking, especially on holiday . . . up very early in the morning. Now I find it quite difficult sometimes, shopping with my wife I say 'oh go on, I'll follow you up'. This distresses you after being so active.

Interviewer: Your wife actually arranged your appointment at the hospital with your doctor?

Mr G: Oh well, yes, she said 'I'm going to see the doctor about going for another opinion'. That's the position of things, because we've heard about this Professor gentleman at the University . . . well I may not see him . . . my point, my idea of not going down there wasn't being a martyr, but saying, well other people, some of them are much worse off than me.

From the context of this exchange I assumed that the hesitant comments in the last paragraph reflected a discussion that had been going on between Mr G and his wife for several months. Mr G did not want to take the responsibility for seeking further help and waited until his wife took the initiative.

As I have said, I am reluctant to draw general conclusions from such cases, but I did not observe this kind of 'sanctioning' among the women respondents. This is not to say that women patients do not mobilize resources of various kinds in order to deal with problems, including attempts to 'legitimize' the illness, but there appears to be a role open to men to 'resist' seeking help, and thus not being seen as weak, yet gaining sanction for help-seeking through a wife's pressure (Maclean, 1981). In Mr G's case direct action by his wife was involved. Men combine 'not making a fuss' with having the responsibility for referral accepted by others. There is an interesting contrast, and link, between this kind of sanctioning and the behaviour of men once they do occupy the sick role. Parsons (1951) seemed to have men in mind when he described the 'regression' involved in being ill – a return to a child-like state of dependency. Intuitively, many women might testify to this interpretation of the behaviour of their sick menfolk! Before the sick role is sanctioned men appear stubbornly stoical; once ill they show exaggerated weakness, a more open display of dependency being less structured in the case of women. But, in relation to referral practices in general, it was the last two of Zola's headings in conjunction with (2) above which were more representative among the sample, especially among the female patients.

(4) PERCEIVED INTERFERENCE WITH WORK OR PHYSICAL ACTIVITY

In the early stages of rheumatoid arthritis a typical description of its practical effects was as a worrisome 'nuisance'. When asked what this 'nuisance' referred to it was often the disruption of routines at home and work. The inability to open a can or dust a shelf were seen as disruptions of physical functions which seemed trivial and yet grew in importance as a source of anxiety as symptoms persisted. They meant that the preparation of food, the carrying out of daily tasks, were not just temporarily disrupted but, as the illness progressed, were becoming permanent features of everyday life auguring ill for the future. The fluctuating nature of the symptoms made functional problems worse. One day a woman might ask a family member for help with household tasks only to find on the next day that she could do it herself. This inevitably created problems of persuading others that quite severe pains could 'come and go', the boundaries of which were not easy to establish.

Zola emphasizes 'perceived' interference in order to account for the wide range of tolerance individuals will show in facing symptoms. Some individuals will find disruptions intolerable even if they have not happened very frequently whereas others will go on performing painful actions until they are literally unable to turn a tap, hold a pen, or stand up straight in the morning. Let me take two cases to illustrate what approximates to a midpoint between these two extremes. I want to suggest that these incidents occurred frequently among the majority of the sample and that they were uppermost in respondents' minds when accounting for why referral to the specialist clinic had occurred at the time it did.

Mrs G aged 47, lived with her husband, another man who had recently had a heart attack and was still off work, in a poor district on the outskirts of Manchester. She also had one daughter in her teens, living at home. Mrs G had a job as a domestic cleaner in a private house. During the early stages of her illness she had experienced what was diagnosed as a 'frozen shoulder'. This term is used in rheumatology to refer to a specific rheumatic condition, requiring specific treatments. But it is also recognized that it is used loosely to refer to a range of shoulder problems, especially by general practitioners. Again, Mrs G just felt this was a localized rheumatism, though her own family's history of arthritis did lead her to speculate further, and worry about it.

This worry persisted, especially when she began to notice changes in her hands and pain in one of her hips, though this latter trouble was fleeting. But the situation with her husband meant that she kept putting off seeking help. Mrs G described the situation in the following way:

Well, it was only just there [her shoulder]. It wasn't in my hand. Then it got so bad on the Friday it moved from there completely and it was in this arm, in my wrist. I couldn't even comb my hair or do anything with this hand. It is worrying me, and I thought, well if I'm going to be crippled . . . because my husband, you know, he's got a bad heart and he's not worked for two and a half years. I'm the only one that's kind of working and doing the housework. I do domestic work. I only go in the morning, but I mean they are very good where I go to work, I can sit down and rest if I want. But now getting up in the morning, and getting dressed, I'm finding difficulty when I go to bed at night and get up in the morning. Even my hands are stiff . . . my daughter, she's very good really. She keeps saying, 'Oh you won't be crippled, you know,' but I keep saying, well you will have to pull your weight now you know because she doesn't do a lot, but she does when I'm poorly. She'll have to.

Clearly, a number of problems were running together in Mrs G's comments. Her symptoms were assessed in terms of their impact on her relationships with her husband and daughter. In this sense we can see help-seeking behaviour influenced by this factor, described in (2) above. The prime mover, however, was that she had increasing difficulty in carrying out personal, household and work tasks. Her growing inability to function in these areas meant that she had to reassess her responsibilities to her family. While her symptoms were perceived to involve only mild functional difficulties, she struggled on as wage earner, wife and mother. But the more her symptoms limited how far she could carry out these tasks the more it was necessary for her to rethink her situation and seek help. Mrs G had to develop new tactics and arguments in ensuring her daughter's practical help in the house. In addition, she was constantly exercised by the implications of what these changes might mean for the future and how best to face up to them.

Mrs J showed that 'sanctioning' (this time by the GP) and perceptions of functional difficulties can also run together, although it was the severity of the latter that really provided the grounds for referral. For Mrs J the situation had developed very rapidly. As a wages clerk at a local factory Mrs J, a married woman of 37, with three children, was extremely busy and relied on the use of her hands, especially at work. She said:

Well, it was between Christmas and New Year, you know, the holidays. I woke up one morning and my finger was bent and very swollen and I went to work. I think it was the third of January, and

I went to see the doctor there at work and he seemed to think I'd knocked it, you know, he made a joke saying I'd been drunk and knocked it up. So it got strapped up. I got up one morning and it was alright, so I was pleased about that and then a couple of weeks later it was in both index fingers and I knew then I hadn't knocked it up. We were on the list to change family doctors . . . so I phoned the new doctor and when I went she sent me straight away for blood tests and X-rays . . . She said I hadn't to go to work just to rest them [her fingers] and not to do any housework, because they were very aggravated, and I wrote all day at work, nothing else, which she said wasn't helping.

Certainly from Mrs J's point of view, it was this last factor which was critical though she was also increasingly experiencing a more systemic illness. She was torn between working on, and possibly making her arthritis worse, and stopping, with the probability of jeopardizing her job. Her GP's strictures about work and housework helped her to make the decision to stop work and seek specialist help. In fact, Mrs J went further by asking the GP to telephone her husband the same evening, to tell him that these functional difficulties were real and serious and that housework in particular should be kept to a minimum. The GP agreed, and Mrs J so arranged things at home with her children to ensure that Mr J answered the telephone when it rang. Later, in an interview with me, Mr J stated that this 'subterfuge' had been unnecessary as he would have agreed that housework routines needed changing, but Mrs J was taking no chances. This ploy was an extreme and rare case of using an outside agency to directly sanction a change in an individual's situation, and of meeting the likely meaning of events for others head on. In agreement with Zola, we can see that such functional problems and the practical difficulties occasioned by the illness are not simply objective facts, but are contingent on the individual's perception of the situation, and the contexts in which she has to carry out her daily tasks.

(5)   THE TEMPORALIZING OF SYMPTOMATOLOGY

This last referral process can be treated as a parallel feature of the general situation described so far. What Zola has in mind is that referral processes often rely on 'the setting of external time criteria'. This 'temporal standard' overlaps many of the processes discussed above. As Zola states, it is a very familiar device, which we all use: 'If it isn't better in 3 days, or one week, or 7 hours or 6 months than I'll take care of it'.

This is particularly important in chronic illnesses, with their characteristic insidious onset and long duration. As will be clear by now individuals face uncertainty about taking action about their symptoms, or, indeed what interpretations to place on bodily changes. Also, they cannot be sure if their own definitions are the same as others' in their immediate network. They are reluctant to define themselves as seriously ill or suffering with a potentially disabling condition. Only a rapid onset of symptoms or a sudden exacerbation of problems that have been 'grumbling' for months or even years can alter this situation. Otherwise it is preferable to wait and see if it will pass off.

Though it was not possible to see a clear example of such 'temporalizing' playing an independent part in the referral process it ran through each case in one way or another. In Mrs J's case, discussed above, the virtual disappearance of her initial symptoms made her feel 'pleased'. Then, two weeks later they came back and she knew she simply could not dismiss them as a temporary nuisance. She waited a further week, to see if they would disappear again. Once this time limit was reached she went back to her doctor. Mr G's case illustrated that the time-scale could extend over a number of years. Even when the symptoms returned in a more persistent form, Mr G was still inclined to 'work them off' in the hope that they would eventually go away. The instituting of a drug regimen by his GP allowed a further postponement of further investigation or treatment. Finally, as we saw, his wife provided an open recognition that his 'time was up' by contacting the GP in order to arrange another specialist opinion of his troubles.

By definition, the temporal aspects of chronic illness are central to its development and experience. The monitoring of symptoms and functional limitations over time play an important part in living with a chronic condition like rheumatoid arthritis. The important point to grasp is that the temporal dimension marks out changes and shifts in the definition of what is going on by all of the actors involved, how it is to be understood and expressed and what action needs to be taken. To know whether an illness is getting better or worse, whether it is to be treated lightly or not, or whether various kinds of action are needed requires paying attention to the time-scale on which the events are taking place. To take a step too 'early' or too 'late' in reacting to the illness might mean that the individual is out of step with others' expectations, be they over the right time to seek help, to report the ineffectiveness of treatment, or express the need for other forms of practical or emotional help. The threat of such disjunctions, both between doctors (or other professionals) and patients' definitions and more importantly between individuals and their informal carers is a major theme in living with chronic illness.

Conclusion

The aim of this chapter has been to chart some of the territory of the meaning of living with rheumatoid arthritis, particularly its impact on social relationships. Rather than testing fixed and pre-formed hypotheses, the research reported here was designed to be exploratory in character, in an attempt to build up a picture of the illness and its consequences. The data presented reinforce the general observation that the onset and development of arthritis is simultaneously an assault on the body and a disruption of social life. Sufferers and those with whom they must interact (especially in the family) have to attend to both levels of reality. However, the chapter has also tried to show that the meaning of chronic illness only emerges over time as specific aspects of the condition make themselves felt. The sufferer and 'significant others' are pitched into a situation of considerable insecurity where past, present and future meanings, are placed 'at risk'. Images of self, of others and of the disease are tested against the constraints of practical social life and of the expectations governing behaviour in the wider culture.

Working in a situation of considerable uncertainty, then, individuals, families and others frequently test the limits of the strength of their relationships, particularly the amount of support and care they are able or willing to afford each other. Although stable meanings can be re-established in the face of rheumatoid arthritis such stability is at best precarious and contingent: transformations of meaning are always a potential threat. Help-seeking may turn into dependence, reciprocal social interaction may transform itself into embarrassment and awkwardness. At worst, demands for sympathy and understanding may create conflict and even cause rejection. No simple 'role prescription' exists in our society for the chronically ill, or for those with whom they have contact, to guide social interaction.

Not surprisingly, therefore, the experience of rheumatoid arthritis is characterized by anxiety. The present chapter has sought to show that cultural constraints rather than psychological disposition are at the heart of the problem, and are an important way of understanding the strain and worry patients and their carers face. To be sure, psychological factors may well be involved, but the source of the problems stems not so much from the individual's personality or intelligence, or the 'coping skills' they have at their disposal, but from the clash between loss of confidence in the body and the implications this has for maintaining culturally ordered meanings.

It is clear, then, that the response to rheumatoid arthritis, though contingent or emergent in character is also socially patterned. The present chapter points to variations in experience, for example, gender differences in help-seeking behaviour, but the limitations of the present study forestall anything but tentative suggestions in this direction. Further research should pay greater attention to such matters; class, gender and age in relation to chronic illness are obvious dimensions to be explored in a more systematic form. In this way the distribution of meanings surrounding the experience of chronic illness may be further clarified. Again, it is not so much a question of researching the 'attributes' of individuals from different class, sex, or age groups which is at issue, but how such a chronic illness as rheumatoid arthritis relates to, and is shaped by, specific segments of the cultural order.

In addition to these sociological research issues there are, I think, some policy implications to be drawn from the present discussion. First, is the question of the responsiveness of services. It is clear from this study that health services play an important part for many living with a chronic illness, and that considerable skill is needed in developing services in a situation where meanings are uncertain and ambiguous. Evidence from this study, as well as from others (for example, Fitzpatrick and Hopkins, 1983) underlines the fact that patients wish medical knowledge and treatments to be applied to the circumstances of their particular case. In other words they wish the *particular configuration* of their illness and its consequences to be assessed and appreciated (a matter which recent legislation on disability in Britain has attempted to codify). All too often generalized reassurance is all that is offered; those with rheumatoid arthritis, for example, may be told that their fears of being crippled are unfounded and that only a small proportion of sufferers end up severely disabled. Such reassurance is rarely effective as patients and their families wish to know (and frequently take steps to find out) how these generalities relate to *their* disease and *their* circumstances. Thus, in addition to facing up to the reactions of loved ones, a further layer of meanings is added, namely those of the professionals with whom the sufferer comes into contact. These, too, have to be examined and tested against practical circumstances – a matter which professionals only concerned with 'compliance' are likely to find it hard to understand. Put another way, variations in response between patients and their families need closer appreciation by service providers. The potential gap between patients' perceptions and those of professionals is open to both systematic scrutiny and improvement. The improvement of care lies, in part, along this route (Bury, 1986).

Second, and as an aspect of professional–provider relationships, is the issue of 'shared care'. The present study emphasizes the *active* role of patients and their families in coming to terms with rheumatoid arthritis. Patients are not simply 'recipients' of services. As the evidence on help-seeking shows, people approach health services against a social backdrop of some complexity. Whereas health services are generally well regarded in contemporary societies, a level of ambiguity exists in their use. Patients in the present study, for example, expressed considerable concern about the appropriateness of referral to specialist out-patients departments and uncertainty about the relevance of a rheumatological clinic to their problems. In order to allay such apprehension a greater recognition of patients' views of treatment and its effects is needed. Not only this, but it is clear that providers need to be far more involved in helping to support families of patients: of caring for carers. Indeed, providers have the potential for playing a more conscious mediating role between patients and their families.

Finally, the present study lends weight to the view that a condition such as rheumatoid arthritis cannot be viewed in terms of physical functioning alone. The experience of arthritis most certainly involves pain and discomfort, and even disfigurement, and effective treatment for these will obviously be a major priority for patients. But patients must also live with what the illness means; with its consequences for daily life and an altered future. Service providers are often aware of these realities but the problem lies in fashioning a professional role which enables them to intervene appropriately. At the least, providers need to let patients and their families know that the problems they face, and the efforts they make to live with them, are appreciated. More than this, providers have the potential to give long-term support to patients and their families, of mediating between carers and the cared for, and of placing the experience of illness at the centre of health-care provision.

References

Berger, P., and Kellner, H. (1982), *Sociology Reinterpreted* (London: Penguin).

Berger, P., Berger, B., and Kellner, H. (1974), *The Homeless Mind* (London: Penguin).

Blaxter, M. (1976), *The Meaning of Disability* (London: Heinemann).

Blumer, H. (1969), 'Sociological analysis and the "variable"', in *Symbolic Interactionism: Perspective and Method* (Englewood Cliffs, NJ: Prentice Hall).

Bury, M. R. (1979), 'Disablement in society: towards an integrated perspective', *International Journal on Rehabilitation Research*, vol. 2, no. 1, pp. 33–40.

Bury, M. R. (1982), 'Chronic illness as biographical disruption', *Sociology of Health and Illness*, vol. 4, no. 2, pp. 167–82.

Bury, M. R. (1985), 'Arthritis in the family: problems in adaptation and self-care', in N. M. Hadler and D. B. Gillings, *Arthritis and Society: The Impact of Musculoskeletal Diseases* (London: Butterworth).

Bury, M. R. (1986), 'Social constructionism and the development of medical sociology', *Sociology of Health and Illness*, vol. 8, no. 2, pp. 137–69.

Comaroff, J., and Maguire, P. (1981), 'Ambiguity and the search for meaning: childhood leukemia in the modern clinical context', *Social Science and Medicine*, vol. 15B, pp. 115–23.

Davis, F. (1963), *Passage through Crisis* (Indianapolis: Bobbs-Merrill).

Fitzpatrick, R., and Hopkins, A. P. (1983), 'Problems in the conceptual framework of patient satisfaction research: an empirical exploration', *Sociology of Health and Illness*, vol. 5, no. 3, pp. 297–311.

Hirst, P., and Woolley, P. (1982), *Human Attributes and Social Relations* (London: Tavistock).

Locker, D. (1983), *Disability and Disadvantage: The Consequences of Chronic Illness* (London: Tavistock).

Maclean, U. (1981), *Heart Attack: Survival, Recovery, Prevention* (London: Granada).

Pahl, R. E. (1984), *Divisions of Labour* (Oxford: Basil Blackwell).

Parsons, T. (1951), *The Social System* (London: Routledge & Kegan Paul).

Sahlins, M. (1976), *Culture and Practical Reason* (Chicago: University of Chicago Press).

Sahlins, M. (1985), *Islands of History* (Chicago: University of Chicago Press).

Singer, E. (1974), 'Premature social ageing: the social–psychological consequences of a chronic illness', *Social Science and Medicine*, vol. 18, pp. 143–51.

Strauss, A., and Glaser, B. (1975), *Chronic Illness and the Quality of Life* (St. Louis: Mosby).

Wiener, C. (1975), 'The burden of rheumatoid arthritis: tolerating the uncertainty', *Social Science and Medicine*, vol. 9, pp. 97–104.

Williams, G. (1984), 'The genesis of chronic illness: narrative reconstruction', *Sociology of Health and Illness*, vol. 6, no. 2, pp. 175–200.

Zola, I. K. (1973), 'Pathways to the doctor – from person to patient', *Social Science and Medicine*, vol. 7, pp. 677–89.

5 Wives of Heart Attack Patients: The Stress of Caring

THOMAS SCHOTT and BERNHARD BADURA*

As a life-threatening illness, heart disease causes serious damage which is not only physical, but is also generally reflected in severe mental stress for both patients and their next of kin. On the basis of existing research two factors appear to be of decisive significance for successful recovery and quality of life after a heart attack: first, appropriate medical treatment; but also, secondly, social support present in the encouragement, reassurance and counselling of doctors and nurses, and above all of friends and relatives, particularly the patient's spouse.

The results reported here, from a longitudinal study of almost one thousand men with a first myocardial infarction, confirm this general picture. The first part of the chapter presents the background, theoretical model and methodology of the Oldenburg longitudinal study. In the second part we turn to consider the relatively uninvestigated problems of the spouses of the heart patients and how they cope with being a main source of support for the patients. Drawing upon data from questionnaires to wives one year after their husbands' infarction, the following two questions are addressed: how stressful is the life-event, a heart attack, for the patient's wife; and what conditions alleviate or aggravate the 'stress of caring'?

Background

The link between the family and health has, since the days of Freud, been subject to many different interpretations. From the perspective

* This chapter was prepared in conjuction with Gary Kaufhold, Harald Lohmann, Holger Pfaff and Millard Waltz.

of psychoanalysis, family relationships were viewed mainly as causes or triggers of mental disturbances and psychosomatic illnesses. More recently, research in social epidemiology and quality of life, as well as the changing panorama of illness, has directed greater attention to the role of the family in promoting health or protecting from illness (Bradburn, 1969; Campbell, 1981; Badura and Waltz, 1984).

Nearly a century ago, the French sociologist Durkheim referred in his classic study of suicide to the positive influence of family relationships on health (Durkheim, 1973). His research indicated that, alongside the spiritual force of (above all Catholic) religion, social relationships established in the family protected against mental anguish and the corresponding inclination to suicide. He concluded that 'When marriage and family are intact' they are 'better able to endure a crisis' (1973, p. 217). In recent times this thesis has been impressively supported by Gove's analyses of American mortality statistics (Gove, 1973). He argues that unmarried people are more likely to be socially isolated and that their lives are short of gratifying personal ties. Moreover, this lack of personal relationships tends to foster a health-damaging life-style with, for example, increased cigarette or alcohol consumption. Ultimately, so Gove argues, people who live alone suffer following the onset of serious illness from a lack of informal support and from inadequate domestic care. A series of studies have, in recent years, documented the positive significance of social relationships, particularly marriage, for health and life expectancy (Bradburn, 1969; Pearlin and Johnson, 1977; Berkman and Syme, 1979; Campbell, 1981).

The main focus of aetiological research has been to explain either illness-specific mortality rates or total mortality. However, an American study (Ruberman *et al.*, 1984) has also indicated that a lack of available social support (social isolation) may increase the risk of death among survivors of a first myocardial infarction. In addition, research in rehabilitation has sought for many years to identify determinants of the quality of life of people with chronic illness. The narrow medical perspective – that the extent of physical impairment, caused, for example by a heart attack will be the single most important predictor of life quality – has not been confirmed (Croog *et al.*, 1968; Doehrman, 1977; Monteiro, 1979). It must be presumed that the critical determinants of the quality of life of people with chronic illness are also located in their social context and their personality. Thus the family and social support represent important *contexts* within which health problems are experienced as well as acting as *causal* factors in this occurrence. In brief summary, this approach marked the state of research at the time when we began the Oldenburg longitudinal study (for a detailed overview see Badura,

1981). Since heart disease is overwhelmingly the main contributor to premature death among men (although the rate of deaths due to infarction is also increasing among women), the main interest of the study was in the consequences of a heart attack for the lives and recovery of male survivors. The principal research question was about how living conditions – marriage and family circumstances, work and, of course, medical care – affected the process of coping with the illness.

In this study, the experience of, and coping with, a serious chronic illness are conceptualized as a stress process (cf. Pearlin *et al.*, 1981). The heart attack has a range of consequences at different levels (Badura *et al.*, 1987): it tears the sufferer, often without warning, out of his daily life; causes severe pains and unfamiliar symptoms; releases fears about further complications and premature death; generates dependency and new needs for practical help; removes feelings of control over oneself and one's life; disrupts plans for the future; puts doubts against valued pastimes and habits; raises or strengthens worries about family life, employment and financial situation; and, not least, generates or increases self-doubt about the appropriateness of previous activities, goals and ways of life. A heart attack, therefore, causes not only serious physical damage, but it also makes, in most cases severe psychological demands on both the individuals and the 'significant others' with whom they live. The burden of the event and experience of a heart attack, expressed, for example, in fear of early retirement, together with strains existing before the illness, and possibly contributing to it, such as problems at home or at work, all create a stress process for the individual patient. The management of these specific stressors depends upon the quality of personal resources (for example, self-confidence, coping style) and social resources (for example, social support from doctors, nurses, or the informal network), as well as material resources (for example, money, housing) available to patients.

The main variables in the Oldenburg study and some relationships between them are presented in Figure 5.1. In diagrammatic form this shows that social support from either the informal network or from experts – in the shape of affection, recognition, information, and practical or material help – can reduce the effects of stressors on the patient and his spouse, or can help them to avoid these stressors or make them more easily tolerated (arrows 1 and 2). On the other hand, the stress of a serious illness may have a negative impact on the social network and its capacities: for example, if the illness results in the worsening of existing marital difficulties (arrow 3). A life-threatening chronic illness is generally experienced as a severe stress, regardless of the social support received, and, in the patient's spouse, it often

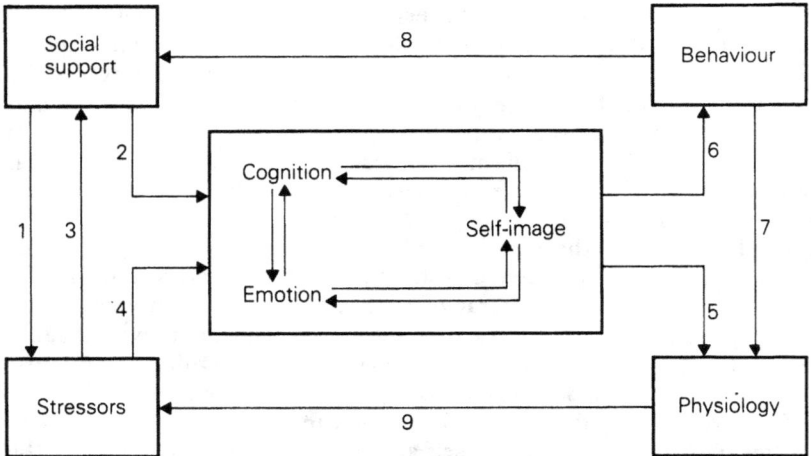

Figure 5.1 Relationships in the Oldenburg study

releases feelings of fear, uncertainty and hopelessness (arrow 4). We hypothesized that health-relevant physiological responses and behavioural changes (for example, smoking or diet) depended upon coping (the different patterns of processing of the illness and its consequences related to the individual's cognition, emotion and self-image) and upon the scale and quality of the social support that was experienced (arrows 5, 6 and 7). However, behaviour may also influence the level of social support (arrow 8); for example, a patient who has become depressed following the illness may have a considerable negative effect on his marriage if he increasingly withdraws from social contact or if his spouse feels herself overworked by either his condition or his behaviour. Finally a deterioration in the patient's health may reinforce existing fears and uncertainties, and thereby further increase the stress triggered by the illness (arrow 9).

The Spouses

A grave life-event, such as a heart attack, clearly effects not only the patients themselves, but usually has an impact on the lives of the immediate family, particularly that of the patient's spouse. The contribution of wives as a main source of social support to seriously ill spouses is a comparatively well researched issue (see DiMatteo and Hays, 1981; Gottlieb, 1981), but very little is known systematically about what it means for a woman to be the wife of a chronically ill heart patient. (A notable start in this area has been made by Maclean,

1981.) How stressful for the patient's wife is the life-event of a heart attack, and how serious are the effects of this event on her physical, mental and social well-being? Above all, what are the circumstances which make it more or less difficult for the spouse to handle the stress caused by a serious illness, the 'stress of caring'? (Belle, 1982).

On the basis of the available studies about the family and heart attack tentative conclusions can be drawn; most generally, that the man's heart attack places considerable demands for adjustment on the whole family, and especially the spouse, who seek to respond in various ways with varying degrees of success (Speedling, 1982). For wives, their husband's heart attack signals the start of a relatively long period of stress. Above all the studies reveal considerable psychological distress, and show clear symptoms of worry and tension, as well as uncertainty and despondency (Skelton and Dominan, 1973; Croog and Fitzgerald, 1978; Mayou *et al.*, 1978). While these symptoms are ubiquitous in the first days after the infarction, they generally diminish in the later phases of adjustment and mastery; however, for some women, there is a feeling of persistent stress, associated with markedly reduced feelings of psychological and social well-being. Thus, for example, Skelton and Dominan (1973) report that, a year after the infarction, a high proportion of wives continued to suffer anxiety and other symptoms of distress; similar observations are made in the report of Mayou and colleagues (1978).

As we have noted, the process of coming to terms with a chronic illness and the patients' approaches to overcoming the illness may be described as a stress process. This perspective can also be employed to describe the situation of the patients' wives, since they also find themselves in a process of stress and adjustment, triggered by their husband's heart attack. Within these processes of dealing with stressors are some problems resulting from the illness; but the everyday burdens, independent of the illness, as well as the personal and social resources of the women, are important determinants of the success of coping with the stresses of the illness. The sudden onset of the illness puts pressure on the wives in several respects. In the first place, the spouses must deal with the shock of the infarction, then with anxieties and uncertainties about the patient's survival and the further worries about his health.

In the Federal Republic of Germany the first phase is almost invariably experienced while the patient is in hospital. On average the period of in-patient care lasts for more than two months, if time in the acute hospital and rehabilitation clinic are included together. Often, there are only a few days with the family at home between the patient's stay in the acute hospital and the following in-patient period of rehabilitative treatment. For about a quarter of all patients this second phase of in-patient care follows on directly from the acute treatment, and contact between husband and wife is reduced to hospital visits. This relatively long period of separation from the family was experienced as a stress by about half of the men in our study; a similar proportion of women are probably equally troubled. In addition to the social support of children, friends and kin, the spouse's involvement in medical treatment and care is vital for her psychological stability in this early phase, and for her understanding of the patient's recovery process. Generous visiting hours and friendly contact with staff are only one aspect of this involvement. It is probably more decisive in this report to consider the advice and information received by the patient's wife, especially from the doctor treating her husband. These aspects are likely to be linked so that good relationships with staff are conducive to good communication.

The process of coping with the illness in the family is entirely different when the patient returns home, and the illness must be incorporated back into daily life. The patient's self-image and mental state are primary concerns for the spouse. She will first orient her efforts to shield her husband from stress and irritations, will seek to cheer him up, and will support him in regaining his mental equilibrium and self-confidence. Unfortunately, it appears that during this phase many wives tend to be cautious and 'overprotective' with negative consequences for the patient (Halhuber, 1980; Speedling, 1982). Of course, the meaning of the condition to the spouse must be taken into account. Behaviour which may be overprotective to a professional may be a sign of care and concern to the spouse.

Important aspects of dail, life, as well as relations between the marital partners, are prone to change following a heart attack. Although a majority of men return, after a relatively short time, to their usual work, a large proportion remain on sick leave up to one year after the infarction or else take early retirement. (In the Oldenburg study this proportion was 40 per cent.) Financial losses and a changed daily routine are just two of the possible consequences for both marital partners. This may lead to friction in the marriage and to shifts and changes in roles; and both partners may need to work out new daily relationships to each other.

Having set the scene we now go on to consider our own research in some detail.

The Oldenburg Longitudinal Study: Design and Methods

The experiences of about one thousand men with a first myocardial infarction have been investigated in this study. So far three postal questionnaires have been administered: the first shortly before discharge from the acute hospital (T1); a second about six months after the onset of the illness (T2); and a third questionnaire six months later (T3). In addition, the hospital doctor was asked to complete a questionnaire (T1), as was the patient's general practitioner (T3) and, most relevantly for the following reflections, the patient's wife (T3). The patients were identified through notifications from 213 hospitals, selected to be representative of all acute hospitals in West Germany. The first phase of the study was completed in May 1983; response rates to the second and third questionnaires were 85 and 72 per cent respectively, so that altogether completed questionnaires for the first year after the heart attack are available for nearly 600 patients (Details of the study design and results are presented in Badura, 1984; Badura and Waltz, 1984; Badura *et al.*, 1987.) At one year after the infarction questionnaires were sent to the wives of the patients and almost 70 per cent returned a completed questionnaire, providing data for 519 wives, on which the current analyses are based. These data have been collected at only one point in time and our analyses therefore have the limitations of all cross-sectional designs. Our interpretation of causal links derives from the theoretical model, but our conclusions about the meaning of the interrelationships between variables must be tentative.

The average age of patients in this study is 53 (58 per cent are aged 50 or over); their partners are, on average, 6 years younger. Somewhat fewer than half the wives were employed at the time of the investigation, and two-thirds of these were working part-time. Nearly all the women, 90 per cent, had children.

THE EXPERIENCE OF THE WIVES

The following data on the consequences for wives of the heart patients is organized in two main sections. The first part describes the situation of the women, and the 'stress of caring' that they experienced. The thesis is presented that, for these women, the heart attack is also a major life-event, with serious psychological and social ramifications, that may have a long-term impact on their psychological health and their quality of life. The second part builds upon these results and examines the interplay of factors leading to chronic stress and its psychosocial consequences.

The 'stress of caring' It is hardly surprising that a sudden and life-threatening illness should cause distress, not only to the sufferer, but also shock, fear, uncertainty and existential threat to his family. This is the experience of most wives following the heart attack. It is followed by a phase of accommodation, adjustment, reflection and analysis of the situation, regarding both the spouse's life and the patient's illness. Although this is the typical pattern it is clearly one that is achieved with considerable effort and under favourable circumstances. Understandably, some patients and their spouses face anxiety or depression which develop into chronic problems, colouring and disrupting the entire life of the patient and his wife. The process of initial shock, ebbing threat and precarious return towards normal is illustrated in the following results. The 'stress of caring' is conceived in terms of the spouse's general life stress, her worries about the patient's health, and the extent of changes in daily life caused by the heart attack.

General stress over the year after heart attack   The wives were asked, retrospectively, to characterize the extent of the stress at different stages after the infarction. Their responses shown in Figure 5.2 are among the most unequivocal in the study, showing that the first few days after the infarction were viewed by nearly all the women as the period during which they felt most under stress. Altogether 83 per cent of the wives described the period as one of very severe stress and a further 13 per cent identified severe stress; only 4 per cent of the respondents said that they suffered little or no stress during the first days after the heart attack. The proportion of women who classified the stress as severe or very severe declined continuously over the year following the illness. Nevertheless, a substantial minority of wives (26 per cent) rated their stress as severe or very severe a year after their husband's heart attack. Considering the relatively long period since the onset of the illness, it seems reasonable to speak of these women as suffering from chronic stress. Not surprisingly, this self-rating of chronic stress was clearly related to assessments of psychological well-being, such as anxiety (correlation coefficient, $r = 0.25$) and depression ($r = 0.38$). Furthermore, the women who felt severely stressed a year after the illness rated their husband's health more negatively ($r = 0.34$) and they were more worried about their spouse's state of health ($r = 0.37$).

The centrality of the heart attack for the woman's life and the consequential distress is also revealed in other findings. It may be supposed, for example, that her husband's illness had an effect on the woman's own health since more than 80 per cent of the women described their health as either fairly good or poor during the period shortly after the infarction. About a year later, following a period of adjustment and reorientation, this proportion had fallen to 26 per cent – similar to that in the general population. Further evidence of the shock incurred after the heart attack is manifested in the wives' assessment of change in their health over the year after the event:

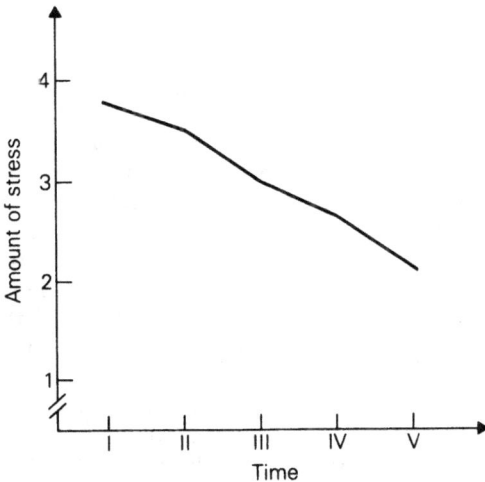

I   In the first days after the heart attack, $\bar{x} = 3.8$, $s = 0.5$
II During patient's hospital stay, $\bar{x} = 3.5$, $s = 0.83$
III In the first weeks after discharge, $\bar{x} = 3.0$, $s = 0.89$
IV During the period of rehabilitation, $\bar{x} = 2.7$, $s = 0.89$
V   In the last few weeks, $\bar{x} = 2.18$, $s = 0.78$

Figure 5.2 Perceived stress of spouse in the year after heart attack (averages)

73 per cent described themselves as feeling better, 23 per cent unchanged and 4 per cent worse than they had been shortly after the infarction.

Worries and anxieties about the patient's health   Twelve months after the heart attack only 9 per cent of the wives described the patient's health as poor, 46 per cent as fair, 43 per cent as good, and 2 per cent as very good. Welcome as this result sounds, it gives a misleading impression of the actual threat and psychological stress which parallel the illness. For it is not only the physical condition of her husband which determines the woman's level of stress, rather it is anxiety about a second infarction and uncertainty about dealing with the illness – concerns about 'is the patient behaving appropriately?' and 'am I doing the right things?' – which dominate the woman's daily life and play a critical role in her response. This concern is indicated by the high proportion of wives, 90 per cent, who, twelve months after the infarction, described themselves as often or very often worried about their spouses' health. This worry is much more common among the wives than other urgent concerns about, for example, their own health, financial problems, children, or their marital relationship. It has been reported that spouses often feel themselves in some way to blame for the patient's heart attack (Skelton and Dominan, 1973) and therefore see themselves as responsible to a large extent for their spouses' health; but they also feel uncertain and helpless, with comments such as, 'I don't know how to deal with him. What ever I do is wrong.' (Monteiro, 1979, p. 114). These comments made by the wife of a heart patient appear to be symptomatic of the situation of many women following their husband's infarction. In the current study one-third of the women felt that they were partly to blame for their husband's illness. And these women who felt in some way responsible were more likely to be dissatisfied with their husband's health or recovery behaviour ($r = -0.15$). They were also in poorer psychological health than other women, presenting with higher levels of both anxiety ($r = 0.14$) and symptoms of depression ($r = 0.23$).

Effects of the illness on marriage and family life   The heart attack heralds changes not only in physical and mental well-being, but in a reorganization of normal family and marital roles. More than half, 52 per cent, of the wives reported that they shouldered more responsibility within the family after the infarction. This finding supports the earlier research of Finlayson and McEwen (1977), in which a similar proportion of women felt that their daily family role had changed. In our study, 35 per cent of the wives described themselves as more burdened at home and 37 per cent felt that their husband was more demanding since his illness. As a consequence of this burden and strain 32 per cent of the wives felt they had less time for themselves, and some felt that they were becoming socially isolated, since 17 per cent considered that since the illness they had hardly mixed in the company of other people.

In many marriages the illness leads not only to a reorganization of family life, but to a crisis in the relationship. This crisis need not necessarily develop into a long-term deterioration in the relationship, since the challenge posed by the illness may also encourage closer feeling between the partners. Speedling (1982) has suggested that relationships in some families are in a better condition after the crisis of illness than they were previously, although it is difficult to document such an assertion. However, in relation only to the quality of married life, the Oldenburg study confirms this general proposition: 46 per cent of women expressed the opinion that, since the heart attack their marital relationship had become closer, 48 per cent described their relationship as unchanged, and only 6 per cent of the

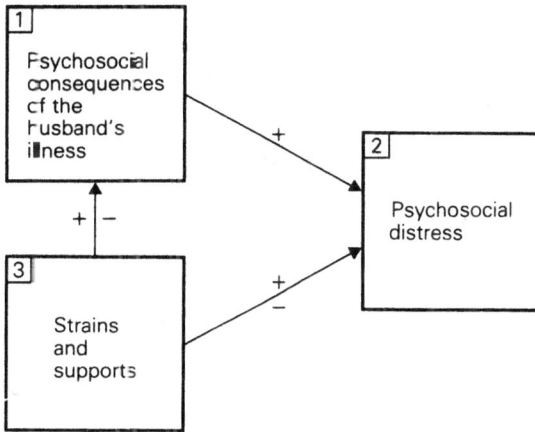

Figure 5.3 The stress process

women reported a deterioration in their marriage during the previous year.

The stress process   In general a heart attack, unlike numerous other chronic illnesses, does not usually increase the patient's physical needs for care or for help in carrying out the routine tasks of daily living. The contribution of the patient's wife is consequently focused less upon immediate self-care activities, but rather is oriented to supporting the patient following the illness, to help him to recover his mental equilibrium, and to return to normal everyday life at home and at work. From this perspective, the 'stress of caring' is predominantly a psychological and social strain, with corresponding effects on the psychosocial well-being of the patient's wife. (Psychosocial well-being is assessed in this study using German versions of the anxiety and depression scales employed by Pearlin and Lieberman, 1979.)

Our analytical model has been developed in order to understand more fully some of the mechanisms of this stress process; in this the relationships between the various determinants of psychosocial distress have been considered. The 'stress of caring', which stems either directly or indirectly from their husband's illness, must first be distinguished clearly from general stress in everyday life which is unrelated to the illness but which certainly also affects psychosocial well-being.

The stress, worries and changes caused by the heart attack are represented in Figure 5.3 by box 1. These psychosocial consequences are, as previously indicated, presumed to have a direct effect on the level of the carer's psychosocial distress (box 2). In order to test the second hypothesis, that successful coping with the 'stress of caring' depends upon a variety of conditions a third block of variables is incorporated into the analytical model as 'strains and supports' (box 3). This group of variables includes factors which either mitigate or reinforce the 'stress of caring', the latter in so far as they may impede the process of coping or they may present additional independent stressors. In our model, the positive or negative effect of the variables in box 3 may directly exacerbate the amount of psychosocial distress, or the effect may be mediated indirectly through an influence on the psychosocial consequences of the illness. As the most important determinants of the 'stress of caring' this third block of variables embraces four elements: the severity of the patient's illness; social integration and social support of the patient's wife; personality of the husband; and socio-demographic characteristics (age of the woman, husband's social class and his employment status). Last but not least, a further element is the level of the patient's psychosocial distress, as assessed one year after the heart attack.

The following presentation of results linked to the variables in the analytical model is organized in four sections. First, there is a general overview of the relationships between psychosocial distress and the 'stress of caring', as well as the effects of other sources of stress or determinants of the stress process. The subsequent sections will specifically consider possible determinants of the main elements in the 'stress of caring'. The method of multiple regression has been employed for the analysis; Figures 5.4–5.7 indicate the standardized regression coefficients for the relationships between variables which may be treated as independent factors related to a dependent outcome.

Explaining psychosocial distress Together the variables in the model explain about 30 per cent of the variance in the levels of the spouses' distress. Although, at first sight, this seems a relatively low proportion, it can be argued that psychosocial distress is likely to reflect the total life experiences of the women, whereas the model considers principally only variables relating to the patient's illness.

The coefficients in Figure 5.4 identify the important contribution of the elements of the 'stress of caring' as sources of psychosocial distress. These data provide further confirmation of the stress caused by the patient's illness and of the consequent impairment of the spouse's psychosocial well-being.

Within a marriage, the partners are involved in a dynamic and interdependent process influencing social and psychological events.

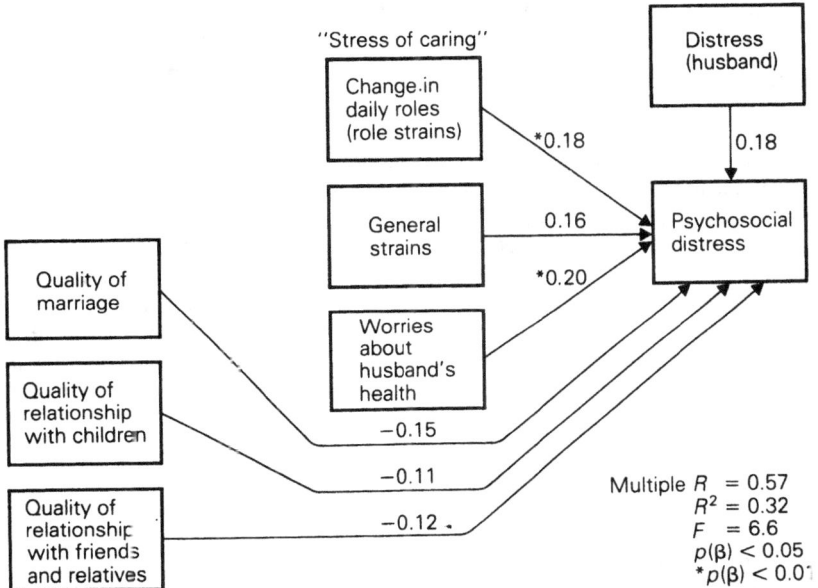

Figure 5.4 Statistically significant direct effects within the analytical model

This general proposition informs contemplation of the entire process of coping with illness within the family. So, for example, it is clear that there was a direct relationship between the levels of psychosocial distress of the patient and his wife. The more that the man felt handicapped by the infarction and its consequences, the more intensely his wife felt unsettled, and the more she reported symptoms of psychological and social disturbance.

The protective and stress-reducing role of satisfactory social relationships is shown in the consistent link between the level of psychosocial distress on the one hand and the level of satisfaction with marriage and with relationships to children, family and friends on the other hand. Marriage which was described by the women as emotionally close and in which the husband came up to his wife's role expectations, clearly brought about a reduction in stress. Likewise women who felt they were, to a satisfactory extent, socially integrated exhibited a lower level of psychological distress.

No direct influence on distress could be demonstrated for the woman's subjective assessment of her husband's state of health. This result can be explained by the high proportion of common variance shared by the variables 'subjective assessment of husband's health' and 'worries about husband's health' of which the latter accounts for more of the variance in the regression equation. The doctor's judgement of the severity of the patient's illness bore absolutely no relationship to the wife's distress. This result owes something to the lack of contact between the general practitioner and the patient's wife, but it also indicates that the experience of the illness and the process of coping within the family are relatively independent of the so-called objective data related to the severity of the illness. Similar results can be demonstrated for the experience of the male heart patients in the main study, whose own definition of their health deviated markedly from the opinions of the hospital doctors (Badura *et al.*, 1987). Their psychological health and management of the illness were relatively strongly related to their own assessment of their health, but showed only a marginal relationship to the medical judgement of severity of the illness.

Among the women supporters, the various social and demographic indicators were not directly linked to the measures of emotional distress. This result is somewhat surprising since in other, comparable studies a general picture has emerged of social class differences in psychosocial well-being (for example, Campbell, 1981). Another, perhaps unexpected, finding can be mentioned at this point. Women with multiple role strains – with, for example, responsibility for a home and paid job, or even with responsibilities for a home, children and employment – were neither more nor less likely to be emotionally distressed (cf. Schott, 1987). This result contradicts the common ideas about multiple role responsibilities and their psychosocial costs. However, several recent studies from the United States, on the everyday stress of women, indicate that psychosocial well-being was greatest among those women who had the most complex role configurations; that is to say, those who were married, had children and were employed (Thoits, 1983; Kandel *et al.*, 1985). At least, our study shows that those women with multiple role obligations did not suffer more distress as a result of their husband's illness. Perhaps the women with multiple roles to perform simply did not have the time or energy to be overly worried by their husband's condition.

Change in daily roles   As already described, the patient's illness is, for a large number of women, bound up with marked changes in marital and family roles. Whether and to what extent these changes constitute stress depends upon three different dimensions. First, it appears to matter whether the patient returns to his usual employment after the illness or he takes early retirement, or he remains unfit for work and takes on the status of a chronically ill or disabled person. Altogether, about 40 per cent of men in this study were unable to

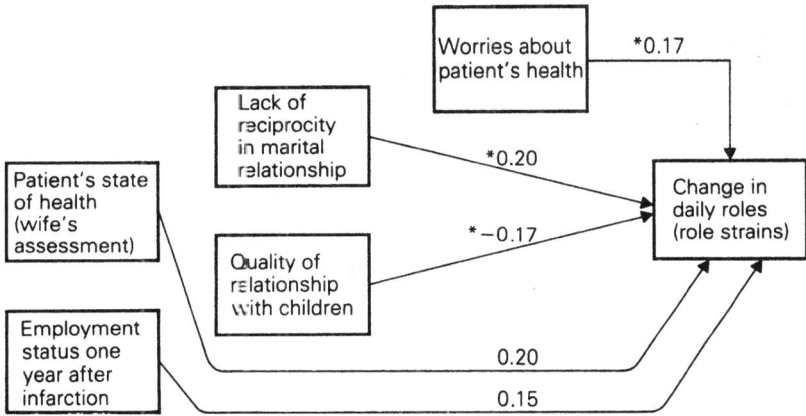

Figure 5.5 Change in daily roles

return to their usual employment, with far-reaching consequences for their daily life, especially, of course, the financial losses they incurred. In addition, for many women it was both unaccustomed and demanding to have their husband at home all day. This was particularly so because the men who did not return to their usual employment were more likely, than the heart patients who did return, to suffer with feelings of depression, and to have difficulties in coming to terms with the illness (cf. Schott, 1987). Second, the extent of change in daily roles is associated with the wife's perception of the patient's health; the more seriously she felt that her spouse's health had been affected, the more change she experienced in the family situation (see Figure 5.5). The same point applies if we consider the extent of the woman's concerns about her husband's health; the more worries she had the more frequently she reported changes in daily roles at home.

These three conditions make a significant contribution to perception of stressful changes in marital and family life. However, the quality of family contact appears to exert a direct and profound influence on this perception of stress. Negative interactions with the spouse and a lack of reciprocity in the marriage aggravate the 'strain'. For example, if a woman feels that her husband expects more from

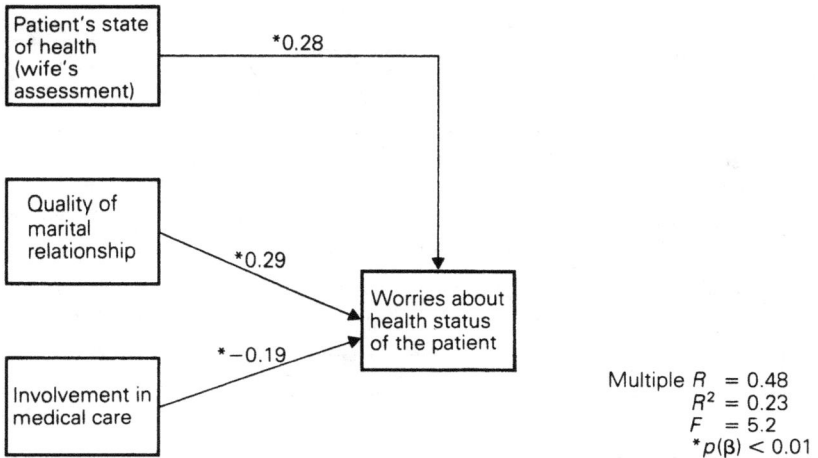

Figure 5.6 Worries about patient's health

her than he is prepared to give and that he is putting himself first to impose his will upon others, then she is considerably less able to cope with problems and demands caused by the illness. The woman's relationship with her children plays an important role in this regard. Women who described themselves as happy with this relationship were less likely to report stressful changes in marital and family routine as a result of the heart attack. It appears then that the quality of family life and relationships is a key to understanding the extent to which the illness has a long-term impact on the daily lives of the marital partners.

Worries about patient's health   The scale of concerns that the wives had about their husband's health one year after the heart attack was, not surprisingly, clearly related to their own assessments of the husband's state of health. Likewise, it is hardly surprising that the extent of the woman's health concerns was directly proportional to the emotional closeness of the marriage. That is to say that, in general, the more love and affection that the woman expressed for her husband, the more she worried about his health.

A further variable appears to be important and significant for separate consideration. A high proportion of the wives (nearly 60 per cent) wished that, in the previous year, they had been more involved in the medical treatment or care given to their husband. This preference and other data on the inclusion of the women in their husband's care indicate an enormous gap, relevant to psychological

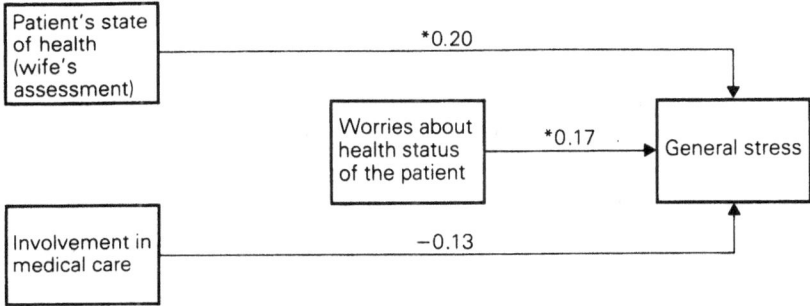

Figure 5.7 General stress

and social concerns, in the medical–curative system. The significance of this result is highlighted by the finding that women who felt they had been extensively involved in their husband's medical care had fewer worries about their husband's health and also showed lower levels of stress. The reassuring effect of involvement in treatment stems, above all, from adequate advice and information. Less than one-third of the spouses felt they had been comprehensively advised on various aspects of life after the heart attack. Women who feel they have been well advised about their husband's illness, about prognosis and risks, are less likely to be led by speculation and are better able to manage the stress caused by illness and the 'stress of caring'.

General stress As was shown in Figure 5.2, the general level of stress among the wives fell continuously over the year following the heart attack; and, parallel with this, the stress caused by the heart attack was also, as a rule, reduced by time – although for most women it did not disappear entirely. Again, the general levels of stress among the wives depended in part upon their views on their husband's state of health; in addition, the extent of their worries about their husband's health and feelings of stress are related quite strongly to each other. These relationships are shown in Figure 5.7 which also reiterates the significance of a lack of involvement in medical care, this time for the general level of stress among wives of the heart patients.

This chapter has concentrated upon significant relationships between psychosocial distress, the 'stress of caring' and possible determinants of the stress process. It is worth noting, however, that some results are important although they are characterized by a lack of statistically significant results in the analytical model. Thus, for example, it was expected that the social and demographic character- istics of the patients' wives would be related to levels of psychosocial distress or the 'stress of caring' – but they were not. Furthermore, personality characteristics of the husband such as type A behaviour (Smith *et al.*, 1983), or his approaches to dealing with the illness failed to show any direct link with the wife's level of stress. Neverthe- less, it may be presumed that the patient's type A behaviour has some indirect influence on coping with stress by spouses, since the wives of type A patients reported lower marital satisfaction, and a greater lack of reciprocity in their marital relationship (cf. Kaufhold, 1987).

Some final remarks   This study had two aims: first to systematically illuminate the significance of psychosocial factors for coping with a chronic illness; and second, to document inadequacies and deficien- cies in the existing organization and practice of medical care. The findings reported here, consistent with others in the study, confirm our basic proposition, that a serious chronic illness not only precipi- tates physical impairment, but also triggers a process of coping with psychological and social stress. This latter depends for a more or less successful outcome on the actions of the doctor but also upon the more general social circumstances of the sufferer and his spouse. So, the extent to which the patient is able to deal with the worries and stress caused by a heart attack is contingent upon both medical treatment and psychosocial care. Such care includes encouragement, exhortation and reassurance – and striking a balance between these facets; but above all it requires sufficient opportunities for discussion with a key doctor, consistent information and adequate advice about medical and social problems or worries of the patient. A second important implication of the research and the main focus of this chapter, is that the wife of the heart patient suffers stress which could be ameliorated if she was also involved, as early as possible, in the process of care and advice. The support of the patient's wife is essential both to help her reduce her own uncertainties, fears and worries, and to help her in her role as the most important social resource of the heart patient. In a marriage the daily contact and the special type of relationship bring about a situation in which the well-being and behaviour of one partner has an immediate impact on that of the other. In the case of a heart attack, as with other chronic illnesses, there is one illness, but in reality there are two patients.

Two general recommendations, derived from the results of the longitudina. study, are placed here, with a view to improving the current situation, at least as experienced in West Germany:

(1) Medical and social science research into chronic illness and associated psychosocial aspects should sharpen its focus on processes within the patient's social network.

(2) In rehabilitation, as well as in general and hospital medical practice, it is essential that more care is taken to ensure there are opportunities for the involvement of family, or at least the spouse, in the treatment and care of the patient. This demands that time is allocated to inform and advise the carers, and to investigate their needs for concrete help that will aid them as they support the patient in coming to terms with life with a chronic illness.

References

Badura, B. (ed.) (1981), *Soziale Unterstützung und chronische Krankheit* (Frankfurt: Suhrkamp).

Badura, B. (1984), 'Life-style and health. Some remarks on different viewpoints', *Social Science and Medicine*, vol. 19, pp. 341–7.

Badura, B., and Waltz, M. (1984), 'Social support and the quality of life following myocardial infarction', *Social Indicators Research*, vol.14, pp. 295–311.

Badura, B., Kaufhold, G., Lehmann, H., Pfaff, H., Schott, T., and Waltz, M. (1987), *Leben mit dem Herzinfarkt* (Berlin, Heidelberg, New York and Tokyo: Springer).

Belle, D. (1982), 'The stress of caring: women as providers of social support', in L. Goldberger and S. Breznitz (eds) *Handbook of Stress* (New York: Free Press).

Berkman, L. S., and Syme, S. L. (1979), 'Social networks, host resistance, and mortality: a nine year follow-up study of Alamedia County residents', *American Journal of Epidemiology*, vol. 109, no. 2, pp. 186–204.

Bradburn, N. M. (1969), *The Structure of Well-Being* (Chicago: Aldine).

Campbell, A. (1981), *The Sense of Well-Being in America* (New York: McGraw-Hill).

Croog, S. H., and Fitzgerald, E. F. (1978), 'Subjective stress and serious illness of a spouse: wives of heart patients', *Journal of Health and Social Behaviour*, vol. 19, pp. 166–78.

Croog, S. H., and Levine, S. (1977), *The Heart Patient Recovers* (New York and London: Human Sciences Press).

Croog, S. H., Levine, S., and Lurie, Z. (1968), 'The heart patient and the recovery process: a review of directions of research on social and psychological factors', *Social Science and Medicine*, vol. 2, pp. 111–64.

DiMatteo, R., and Hays, R. (1981), 'Social support and serious illness', in B. Gottlieb (ed.) *Social Networks and Social Support* (London: Sage).

136   *Living with Chronic Illness*

Doehrman, S. R. (1977), 'Psycho-social aspects of recovery from coronary heart disease: a review', *Social Science and Medicine*, vol. 11, pp. 199–218.

Durkheim, E. (1973), *Der Selbstmord* (Neuwied and Berlin: Luchterhand).

Finlayson, A., and McEwen, J. (1977), *Coronary Heart Disease and Patterns of Living* (London and New York: Croom Helm).

Gottlieb, B. (ed.) (1981), *Social Networks and Social Support* (London: Sage).

Gove, W. (1972), 'The relationship between sex roles, marital status and mental illness', *Social Forces*, vol. 51, pp. 34–44.

Gove, W. (1973), 'Sex, marital status and mortality', *American Journal of Sociology*, vol. 78, pp. 45–67.

Halhuber, C. (1980), *Rehabilitation in Ambulanten Koronargruppen – ein Humanökologischer Ansatz* (Berlin: Springer).

Kandel, D. B., Davies, M., and Raveis, V. H. (1985), 'The stressfulness of daily social roles for women: marital, occupational and household roles', *Journal of Health and Social Behaviour*, vol. 26, pp. 64–78.

Kaufhold, G. (1987), 'Zur Bedeutung des Typ-A-Verhaltensmusters für die Herzinfarktrehabilitation', in B. Badura *et al.*, *Leben mit dem Herzinfarkt* (Berlin, Heidelberg, New York and Tokyo: Springer).

Maclean, U. (1981), *Heart Attack: Survival, Recovery, Prevention* (London: Granada).

Mayou, R., Foster, A., and Williamson, B. (1978), 'The psychological and social effects of myocardial infarction on wives', *British Medical Journal*, vol. 2, pp. 699–701.

Monteiro, L. A. (1979), *Cardiac Patient Rehabilitation – Social Aspects of Recovery* (Berlin, Heidelberg, New York and Tokyo: Springer).

Pearlin, L., and Johnson, J. (1977), 'Marital status, life-strains and depression', *American Sociological Review*, vol. 42, pp. 704–15.

Pearlin, L., and Lieberman, M. A. (1979), 'Social sources of emotional distress', *Research Community Mental Health*, vol. 1, pp. 217–48.

Pearlin, L., Lieberman, M. A., Menaghan, E. G., and Mullan, J. T. (1981), 'The stress process', *Journal of Health and Social Behaviour*, vol. 22, pp. 337–56.

Ruberman, W., Weinblatt, A. B., Goldberg, J. D., and Chandhary, B. (1984), 'Psychosocial influences on mortality after myocardial infarction', *New England Journal of Medicine*, vol. 311, pp. 552–9.

Schott, T. (1987), 'Ehepartnerinnen von Herzinfarktpatienten: Ein Exkurs', in B. Badura *et al.*, *Leben Mit dem Herzinfarkt* (Berlin, Heidelberg, New York and Tokyo: Springer).

Skelton, M., and Dominan, J. (1973), 'Psychological stress in wives of patients with myocardial infarction', *British Medical Journal*, vol. 14, pp. 101–3.

Smith, T. W., Houston, B. K., and Zurawski, R. M. (1983), 'The Framingham Type A Scale and anxiety, irrational beliefs and self-control', *Journal of Human Stress*, vol. 9, pp. 32–7.

Speedling, E. L. (1982), *The family response at home and in hospital.* (New York and London: Tavistock).

Thoits, P. A. (1983), 'Multiple identities and psychological well-being', *American Sociological Review*, vol. 48, April, pp. 174–87.

6 Coming to Terms with Diabetes: Coping Stragegies and Non-compliance

DAVID KELLEHER

Introduction

The symptoms of diabetes have been recognized for several thousand years. Bliss (1983, p. 20) records that:

> A seventeenth century English surgeon called diabetes 'the pissing evile'. The frequent and voluminous urination by severe diabetics (as much as ten to fifteen quarts a day), accompanied by their unquenchable thirst, had caused the disease to be recognised thousands of years before by the Egyptians and Greeks.

A variety of treatments, usually involving a diet, have been tried and diet is still an important part of treatment, but the most important discovery in the treatment of diabetes was the discovery of insulin by two Canadians, Banting and Best in 1921.

Diabetes mellitus is a disease or a syndrome which is caused by partial or complete failure of the pancreas to produce insulin. Insulin is necessary in the metabolism of the body to make use of glucose and without it the bloodstream and the kidneys become overloaded with glucose and a variety of symptoms appear. Long-term 'complications' of diabetes include damage to the micro-vascular system and may lead to kidney damage and loss of vision. People with diabetes also have a higher risk of heart attacks than others and may experience damage to the nervous system which sometimes leads to injury, infection and the onset of gangrene and subsequently to the loss of a limb (West,

1978). About 1 percent of the population of England is treated for diabetes but most authorities estimate that there is another 1 per cent undiagnosed or untreated. The proportion of the population suffering from diabetes is similar or higher in most developed countries, such as the USA and Sweden. In rural, non-industrial countries insulin-dependent diabetes is uncommon and the prevalence of non-insulin-dependent diabetes is low. Studies of people in societies moving towards an urban industrial life-style show the incidence to be increasing (Zimmet, 1982).

Doctors describe patients as suffering from either Type I diabetes or Type II. Type I diabetics usually, but not always, develop the disease in early childhood and, because they are unable to produce any insulin themselves, they have to be treated by having daily or often twice-daily injections of insulin. They are also expected to keep to a diet which balances their intake of food with their demand for energy. Type II diabetics usually develop the disease in middle age and in their case the problem is that they do not produce sufficient insulin to metabolize the glucose produced from the food they have eaten. The treatment of Type II diabetics, or non-insulin-dependent diabetics, is concerned with controlling what is eaten and in many cases by taking tablets which either stimulate the production of insulin in the pancreas or increase the effectiveness of it. About two out of three diabetics are non-insulin-dependent.

Apart from the issues stemming from how the person feels about having diabetes, which will be discussed later in the chapter, there are general problems in successfully managing the treatment. The main symptoms of diabetes are excessive thirst and excessive need to urinate. These symptoms stem from the inability of the body to turn the food which has been eaten into energy; the central concern of treatment is to achieve a balance between the amount of food eaten and the amount of energy used. (The journal of the British Diabetic Association is called *Balance*.) Getting the balance wrong can in the short term bring about the reappearance of symptoms and the problem of becoming overweight, and in the long term increases the risk of developing complications. Changes in a diabetic's pattern of daily activities, changes which may be brought about by shift work or retirement or changes in a person's work or leisure activities or emotional upsets are therefore events which have to be incorporated into the management routine. Keeping to a regular pattern of eating and activity makes achieving the balance easier but also makes for a reduction in the possibility of spontaneous social interaction as will be discussed later.

In the short run diabetes is neither a life-threatening condition nor one that produces severe pain and, given the demands of the treatment regimen, it is not surprising that there is a high level of what doctors call non-compliance (West, 1973; Cerkoney and Hart, 1980; Surwit *et al.*, 1982). The study described in this chapter explores some of the background to 'non-compliance' amongst diabetics and attempts to understand some of the problems involved from their point of view. It is suggested that people with diabetes may come to terms with their illness in several different ways. How they perceive their diabetes affects their perception of themselves just as how they perceive themselves affects how they perceive diabetes; compliance with treatment regimens has costs as well as benefits and is therefore affected by the priority given to being a diabetic, the social and economic resources or support available and the number of other roles to which a person is committed (Thoits, 1983, p. 176).

Although diabetes is not a highly visible impairment, unless 'complications' have developed and brought about the loss of a limb or blindness, it may have disabling effects. These can range from tiredness, which many individuals experience, to impotence amongst men, damaged eyesight and kidney failure. Hopper (1981) discusses whether diabetes is a stigmatizing condition; the data from the study described here suggest that the extent to which diabetics experience social handicap varies, not so much with the degree of seriousness of the condition as seen by doctors, but rather according to how the diabetics themselves perceive it (Kasl, 1983, p. 685).

Like many people who are chronically ill, people with diabetes manage their own treatment regimen and this creates the possibility for them to be autonomous and vary the diet and insulin treatment according to what they are doing and how they feel; but results from this study will suggest that only a few manage their diabetes in this way. More often the people interviewed revealed that they tried to manage their diabetes by giving it a relatively low priority in their lives, making few adjustments to the treatment but accepting some limitations in their life-style as a consequence. The focus of the work described in this chapter explores a relatively neglected area in diabetes research, the patients' perspectives.

Theoretical Perspective

The study of people with diabetes reported here is not a study of a group of people who are peculiar in themselves; while attempting to describe some aspects of the social life that such people experience, this study does not assume that the illness dominates their lives. It is a study of a group of people with an impairment which makes them chronically ill, there is no cure; but in many ways they are very ordinary people, normal people managing a problem.

> I'm the same as the next. You know what I mean, I class myself the same as everyone else, even though I take injections, injections to keep yourself alive, I suppose. But I ain't no different from anyone else. (Mrs A, aged 23)

So the problem has a physical basis but it is also only one of the identities that people with diabetes present to the world of others.

In symbolic interactionist theory social relationships are central to the formation of an individual's identity and self-hood (Mead, 1956) with others. In saying that the other is important in the formation and development of the self, however, it is important to note that the 'I' also has an active part to play in the individual's perception of himself and how he defines situations and typifies the actions of others. In symbolic interactionist theory, then, the individual is far from being a 'cultural dope' reacting to the pressures and conformities of the environment or the labelling of a professional, but is seen as an acting agent in the world. This perspective underlies the present study which attempts to show how people who are coping with or adapting to diabetes and the treatment regimen develop a way of understanding it and of giving it a meaning in their lives. This process of understanding is not so much based on what they know about its aetiology or metabolic effects but rather on how it affects them when they are at work, out with friends, or going shopping and how they think it might affect them in years to come. In attempting to incorporate diabetes into their lives such individuals face issues and problems similar to those we all face when developing additional identities such as becoming a wife or husband, or a parent. Just as some people find it difficult to change their perception of themselves when they get married and go through an unsettled period in their relationships, so some people find it difficult to attribute a meaning to their diabetes, and find it difficult to incorporate the treatment regimen into their everyday lives. Against this backdrop the following conceptual categories have been developed to describe the strategies for living with diabetes among patients in this study: those who manage their diabetes and treatment regimen without altering their life-style are described as 'coping'; those who manage their diabetes and treatment regimen by minimizing the importance of it, but who also make changes in their life-style are described as 'adapting' to their diabetes; while a third group manage their diabetes by continually worrying about it.

The Sample

The people in this sample of thirty diabetics were all aged over 17 and living in London. Twenty of them were randomly selected from a register of 217 patients with diabetes which had been set up by the GPs of three practices with the help of the local hospital. Of the others, five were newly diagnosed diabetics recruited at their first appointment at a hospital clinic and another five were diabetics who had recently been hospitalized. These were selected by a consultant physician as being diabetics with problems. The study was intended to be an exploratory one and it includes both insulin-dependent and non-insulin-dependent diabetics in the sample. Seven of the nine insulin-dependent diabetics were under 40 years of age; the non-insulin-dependent people were, with one exception, all aged over 40. The social class composition of the sample was predominantly working-class with seventeen of them being in occupations such as hospital cleaner, brewery worker, machine operator. Those in non-manual occupations were in jobs such as typist, shop assistant and owner of a small shop. Seven were past retirement age and a further six were economically inactive.

The respondents were interviewed once and in all but three cases interviews were conducted in their own homes. The interviews were semi-structured and tape-recorded. Where appropriate the views of another member of the diabetic's family were sought and observation in waiting rooms and in consultations has also been carried out.

The data collected by these means have most of the limitations and some of the strengths commonly found in qualitative studies with small samples (Locker, 1981). All the interviews were carried out by one interviewer using a checklist of questions, and the study, to that extent, provides reliable data. More important in qualitative work though is the strength and relevance of the interpretation of experience. In this work the analysis was strengthened by the fact that in all but three of the cases the interviews were carried out in the respondent's own home and often involved other family members. In each interview it was stressed that the interview was confidential, that nothing that was said would have any consequences for treatment and that the interviewer was not a doctor.

The process of analysis that has been employed has followed the style of the phenomenological school in symbolic interactionist work (Schutz, 1962). I have attempted to look for similarities between the ways people talked about diabetes and how they incorporated it into their lives. The themes that are highlighted come from a close study of the transcripts, and from notes recalling the interviewees and the settings in which we talked. The concepts that are developed are the second-order constructs of an observer but as the quotes from respondents will illustrate, these organizing constructs are grounded in the expressed feelings of the study group.

The analysis of these data provided two starting points which could be developed and perhaps tested in further work and these provide the structure for the rest of the chapter. First, there are three themes from the data, which are described in the next section, and second, there are the three sets of strategies employed by diabetics in managing their disease and its treatment already mentioned.

Themes from the Data

Three themes emerged from the data and these provide an essential background for a consideration of patients' strategies: the theme of being normal, of the claim to be a normal healthy person; the theme of control, whether there was a sense of being in control of the diabetes or a feeling that it did not dominate daily life; and thirdly the theme of how much of life had to be considered and tailored to fit round the diabetes. I have called this latter theme 'the loss of spontaneity'.

Looking at the ordinariness of life among people with diabetes or any other chronic illness is to look at how they achieve something very important, namely passing as normal members of families and work groups rather than being seen as odd or different. Locker (1983) suggests that chronic illness presents people with three kinds of problem: medical, cognitive and practical and all three kinds of problem have to be managed. The analysis described here is centrally concerned with the cognitive problem of 'Am I a normal, healthy person?' but this problem grows out of and shapes practical problems. One of the striking things which emerged from the analysis, was the number of people who said they regarded themselves as healthy in spite of the fact that they had diabetes. Other writers on chronic illness have also noticed this tendency (Locker, 1981, p. 101). In this study eighteen out of the thirty (60 per cent) rated themselves as healthy whereas others said that they felt they could not be healthy if they had diabetes. The feeling of being healthy was not restricted to people without persisting symptoms nor was it restricted to people on a diet-only regimen; of the nine insulin-dependent diabetics six said they regarded themselves as healthy. Two of the insulin-dependent diabetics who did not see themselves as healthy were newly diagnosed diabetics and it is possible that the recent experience of illness which had led to them being diagnosed was still fresh in their minds.

Several of the people who saw themselves as healthy had symptoms such as very poor eyesight, an ulcerated leg and toes which had become infected as the result of cuts, and in medical terms it is unlikely that they would have been described as being in a good state of health. Those who saw themselves as healthy, whether or not they had persisting symptoms, viewed their diabetes treatment and symptoms, if they had them, as not dominating their lives. They were commenting on what we might call their sense of well-being and this feeling may be derived from a wider range of meanings given to their diabetes than those provided by the medical diagnosis and assessment of their physical statement of health by doctors. Mrs V was a woman with such poor eyesight that she could not go out alone, but thought of herself as healthy because she could do her own cooking and cleaning. On the other hand, Mrs E, an insulin-dependent diabetic who did not see herself as healthy but who was well enough to go to work said:

I was very healthy but due to this diabetes I think of it always, so I am not healthy now.

The experientially grounded concept of well-being is somewhat different from the medical concern with disease, or its absence, and may not always be highly correlated with it. Whether or not this is the case is not the central point here. What will be suggested is that a sense of well-being is relatively common among people with diabetes and this is important in itself in that it affects how someone suffering from diabetes is able to manage it. Patients who felt they were healthy were less likely to worry or agonize over their illness and were more likely to develop more positive strategies for living with the illness. Some of the people said that having diabetes had not changed them at all, but others seemed to be in a continuing struggle with it, as exemplified by one who said:

I ruled it, now it's ruling me.

Others seemed to accept it and the effects on their life. As one man vividly put it:

You can't have the 'flu without sneezing.

Perhaps the most recurring theme in the data was about control, and this refers to how much they were in control of their diabetes, rather than in the medical sense of being well controlled if their blood sugar levels were within the accepted limits. As one woman said,

I think it rules your life. Other people say they don't think it does, they are able to forget about it but I can't.

The theme of being in control, or being controlled by the diabetes is essential to an understanding of its strategic management. Related to the idea of control in the patients' sense were the descriptions of their lives which suggested that many of them had to consider whether eating in the canteen or going for a drink with friends or going on holiday would fit in with their dietary treatment or the timing of their injections. The concept of loss of spontaneity used in the analysis is grounded in these concerns.

A reduction of spontaneity in social interaction seemed to be a common experience. Listening to the respondents' accounts made it apparent that much more of their lives had to be planned, almost ritualized. The timing of injections in relation to meals, the control of what they ate and how much, the planning involved in fitting injections in the enjoyment of a day out, or coping with the office Christmas dinner and everyday eating at work were all mentioned by respondents. Dawn, a teenager, described how she had to dash home from college to have something to eat and her injection before going back for a netball match. Eating had to be related to her injections and treatment regimen, it was not something she felt she could do casually and socially at college. Mr L, a 50-year-old driver, described how he took a bottle of water with him because the drinks from automatic vending machines had sugar in them.

The treatment regimen, the attempt to control the diabetic symptoms and the long-term effects, the 'complications', also reduced their freedom to act in a spontaneous way in social interaction. As a newly diagnosed diabetic Mr R said:

Well normally, as a normal person who can do whatever he wants to do, whatever he wants to eat; but I cannot do that. I couldn't eat what I want.

As a newly diagnosed diabetic he was consciously aware of what he should eat and drink and what was not acceptable except as part of an 'exchange' for another item of his food. After a while diabetics in this study were less aware of the restrictions but the newly diagnosed sufferers were very conscious of their treatment regimen.

Davis (1973, p. 147) suggests that spontaneity is one of the key aspects of everyday interactional situations: 'sociability is furthered by the free and spontaneous initiation of joint activities'; and he goes on to suggest that physically handicapped people have to plan how to get to places, how to handle situations, and this reduces their ability to behave spontaneously. Similarly Locker (1983, p. 71) says of people disabled by arthritis that: 'Thinking it out becomes the order of the day'.

The diabetics in this study, it is suggested, were constrained not just in what they could eat and when, but in that these considerations had the secondary effect of restricting their possibilities of spontaneous social interaction. Further, in deciding whether to join with others in social interaction they may be limiting or at least shaping their interactional roles and the input of others to their restricted image of themselves. This is not to suggest that something called a diabetic personality develops, it is simply that in taking their diabetes into account in their lives the social self is altered. As was suggested earlier, various acquired roles such as wife or manager or parent similarly influence people's definitions of situations and the possibilities of how they can interact socially.

Some patients were less constrained than others. Mr L who took a bottle of water with him when driving his van around was able to say:

I've got a friend who's got a bakehouse, and if I happen to be starving it's nothing for me to go in and pick up a roll.

and in saying that he is showing that he was able to break a routine and go and eat something and have a social chat with a friend despite the limitations of his condition and his treatment regimen.

Transcripts were examined for examples of both spontaneous behaviour, such as having an occasional bar of chocolate, and for examples of them restricting their activities, such as Mrs V who said that she did not go on holiday:

Because, I mean, if you go anywhere, sticking to a strict diet is hard outside, indoors I know just where I am.

By analysing the statements they made about how flexible they were each person was then categorized as being either rated high or low in terms of spontaneity. Out of the thirty in the sample only six were high in terms of spontaneity.

Loss of spontaneity, or reduction of it, is a form of disadvantage, and is experienced as a reduction in the degree of control a person has over daily life. In this sense, loss of spontaneity is a central part of the withdrawal from social relationships that analysts of chronic illness have frequently noted (Strauss and Glaser, 1975, p. 54).

Strategies

Tying in with these themes in the data were the ways that people managed their diabetes, the strategies they had developed. As was described earlier a few were able to feel that they were in control of their diabetes and attempting to be in control has been identified as one of the strategies adopted. These are described as coping with their diabetes. A second group were identified as adapting to their diabetes and the strategy employed by these is described as an overall strategy of normalizing. A third group for whom their diabetes remains both a practical and a cognitive problem are described as worrying or agonizing about their diabetes.

BEING IN CONTROL – 'COPING'

The two central criteria used to differentiate those who were in control of their diabetes from those who were not were (1) the degree to which they followed medical advice and (2) whether they applied it in a variety of situations without restricting their lives in the process. Respondents had been asked what they did if a urine test they had made showed positive signs of sugar; what they did if they were ill with colds; whether they changed their diet or treatment if they were planning to do something energetic; or if they changed their treatment for any other reasons. On the basis of the answers to these questions, and any other volunteered statements relating to their making decisions about altering their treatment, they were classified as being either high or low in terms of being in control of their diabetes. Those who said they ate only a limited range of foods, for example, were said to be low in control. Those who said that they altered the timing or amount of their injections or the timing of meals to accommodate a change in their work or social life were said to be high in control. Only six of the thirty were classified as high in control. The generally low level of knowledge about the mechanics of diabetes was probably a factor in explaining why so few of the patients were actively seeking to manage their diabetes in this way, but they were rated as high in control if they made changes even though the changes made might not have been exactly in accordance with medical advice. Making a change in treatment was defined as change made in the belief that it would be in accord with medical advice even though the effects of making the changes were not always immediately beneficial. One very determined young woman with a family to look after, Mrs B, was gradually reducing the amount of insulin she took because she said she was always going 'hypo', that is, getting the feelings of weakness and confusion resulting from having too low a blood sugar level,

I've told the doctor I'm down to one [unit] and I still go hypo. I think I should cut out the insulin, just the evening. And he said: 'Well let's see how you go. Come back and see me in three months' – which to me, hypos for three months, is not good enough. I've got two babies to look after.

She had had a number of problems with her diabetes and as a teenager she had been reckless in her attitude to eating, but since having two children she felt her diabetes had improved in a way that, according to her, medical authorities seemed to doubt. She was in fact the person in the sample who knew most about diabetes from the medical viewpoint.

Another person who was high in control was a very active man aged 76, Mr S, who carefully kept a chart of the results of his urine tests and then altered his diet if the tests showed positive. He said he had read up about diabetes in 'The Home Doctor'.

A further example of someone who was high in control was an insulin-dependent man in his thirties, Mr Y. He had a physically demanding job and he did not calculate his extra insulin needs very carefully. He either ate a Mars bar between meals if he felt his blood sugar was going low or gave himself extra insulin if he was going out for a drink and a meal with friends. Nevertheless he did make adjustments and in the casual way that fitted his 'macho' image of himself. Thus 'coping' with diabetes in this study meant attempting to control the disease, insisting that it fit in with daily life rather than dominating it.

ADAPTING TO DIABETES – 'NORMALIZING'

An alternative way of managing diabetes was followed by nine people who were not high in control but did regard themselves as healthy. They had given up some social activities such as eating out or going to some of the places they used to frequent but they appeared not to be concerned about these restrictions and accepted them as part of their 'normal' life-style. They accepted as normal the symptoms they experienced and did not make a great effort at controlling their diabetes to eliminate these symptoms. Mr L explained his attitude to continuing symptoms, when talking about the fact that he had to get up several times in the night to go to the lavatory:

I tend to think that if I have any of these symptoms it's probably due to the fact that I've got it and that's it. That is an effect of it, you know what I mean.

He accepted the fact that he felt very thirsty in the evenings and drank a lot of water and then had to get up in the night to go to the lavatory as part of what it is to have diabetes. His involvement with his work and his enjoyment of the food his wife cooked for the family also meant that following a diet was something in the back of his mind rather than dominating his thinking, although he did make the effort to avoid sugary drinks by taking his own drink with him to work. He also did not take his daily tablet because he had been told to take it with his breakfast and he did not usually have breakfast. However, his wife was less than happy with his strategy for handling his diabetes, especially when she was also disturbed at night.

Mr J, another respondent who saw himself as fit and healthy, described his eating habits:

At home here just cabbage, carrots, lettuce, tomatoes.

He said he had cut out rice, only drank Pils lager, did not eat café food because it was 'all greasy' and refused drinks from friends because he did not want to get 'his system upset'. He worked as a street cleaner and said his diabetes caused him few problems unless he rushed about at work, which made him break out into a sweat, which was possibly an effect of his diabetes. He accepted the restrictions and the symptoms but said he did take his tablets and did test his urine three times a week.

Another example of a man who normalized was Mr N who said that his diabetes did not trouble him much and he did not bother much about his diet although he had had a breakdown just after he had been diagnosed diabetic. He then went on to say:

I'm not one of those who ignores everything. It's a thing if you want to keep it under control, you've got to, you know, which I do.

He had given up his place in the pub darts team because he thought he was going out too much. Mr N is an example of someone who tried to hold his diabetes at arm's length. By controlling his life-style he was able to manage his diabetes in a way that kept it out of his mind most of the time. He did not check his blood sugar level but did check his weight carefully, which was perhaps a less threatening part of the regimen. He said that in other people's homes he refused food if it had too much sugar in it on the grounds that he is diabetic.

These nine people who accepted some restrictions on their lives without seeing them as restrictive saw themselves as healthy and managed their diabetes without worrying or agonizing about it. They accepted it as 'normal'; they did not make precise efforts to manage it by using the system of exchanges of foods so that they could continue to eat a varied and interesting range of food. If they did test their blood sugar levels they were more likely to do it as part of routine compliance rather than as a way of gaining information which they themselves would use in planning their eating activities. But neither did they complain about its effects on their lives. They achieved their own balance. Such people were not on the whole regarded by doctors as difficult patients but they are quite an important group to consider when trying to assess how diabetics perceive and manage their diabetes. What they mean when they answer doctors' enquiries by saying they 'feel fine' perhaps needs to be explored further.

Normalization as used in this study shows that some diabetics perceive and manage their diabetes, the process of fitting the treatment regimen in with other daily activities, by reducing the significance of any symptoms experienced and reducing the importance of diet and social activities which might produce problems for them. They were thus able to see themselves as 'healthy'. What started as a strategem, a thought-out way of avoiding difficulties, which is how Davis (1973) uses the term, became an unconscious acceptance of a revised way of living. Diabetes acquired a meaning in their lives by a process of accommodating it within other social roles; the role of diabetic had not become one which had salience across many spheres of their lives, it occupied a relatively low place in the hierarchy of their multiple roles (Thoits, 1983, p. 176).

Whether people view themselves as healthy (whatever that means to them) or not, is a centrally important question which influences how they fit the diabetes into their lives and which may influence their identity and the way they engage with everyday life. Whether or not they see themselves as healthy also influences how they manage their diabetes. Tattersall and Jackson (1982, p. 271) state:

> For most the crucial factors determining the level of control [of blood sugar level] actually achieved are the patient's own motivation and enthusiasm, which in turn depend largely on his emotional response and the way he adapts to diabetes. Therefore the identification and prevention of social–emotional problems are arguably of more importance in preventing complications than new methods of insulin delivery

The analysis in this study suggests that it is not so much the search for and identification of social–emotional problems which is important but understanding the meaning given to diabetes by people experiencing it in their everyday lives. Such meanings, it is suggested, incorporate the individual's perception of the problems related to being a diabetic and the ways actively used to cope with or adapt to the problems. This identification of the patient's perspective is more important than a doctor identifying a particular psychosocial problem.

However, some diabetics in this study had difficulties in giving a stable meaning to their diabetes, and I now turn to this group.

WORRIERS AND AGONIZERS

Half, fifteen, of the sample had some difficulty in giving a stable meaning to their diabetes; they had difficulty in accepting it as a normal part of their life either by giving it a low priority in their life (normalizing) or by being on top of it in terms of feeling confident enough to make adjustments in the treatment according to what activities they were planning (high control). Twelve of the fifteen (80 per cent) regarded themselves as unhealthy. Not surprisingly all but one of the five newly diagnosed diabetics were in this category of seeing themselves as unhealthy.

Typical examples of the worriers included a woman of 75. She said she kept to a pretty restricted diet of salads and boiled fish but would not explain to people that she was diabetic because:

I mean they think it's a terrible thing.

She said she checked on the blood sugar level of her urine but wouldn't alter her diet because:

I wouldn't do it myself, no. No because it's one thing I'm not very clever regarding that.

A man of 58, Mr H, was being treated by diet only and had been diabetic for four years. He tried to keep to a diet and had given up going out to restaurants where he had previously enjoyed eating cakes or pastries. He tried also to get his wife to 'barbecue' (grill) the meat to reduce the fat on it. Overall he felt he was not managing the diet very successfully and he sometimes got up at one or two o'clock in the night to raid the fridge. He thought about his diabetes constantly and was concerned that there was no cure,

in this case you cannot get rid of what is wrong with you and it is always with you.

He was in the process of slowly withdrawing from the running of his shop and handing it over to his son.

These two people were not in great pain or severely disabled by their diabetes but they were worried about it and aware of the effect it was having on their lives and on themselves. Mr H, in particular, thought he had become both irritable and someone who worried over problems without taking action to deal with them. The role of diabetic was high in his hierarchy of roles (Thoits, 1983, p. 177) and had salience across many other roles.

The five people who were classified as 'agonizers' were in a similar position to the 'worriers' in that they were unhappy about their diabetes and it remained a problem for them in their everyday life. They were different from the worriers in the degree of their concern about it. A number of them spoke about being depressed about it. One woman, Mrs E, was several times in tears during the interview. She found it difficult to keep to the diet and felt hungry after meals but in spite of the diet she was still putting on weight. She was an insulin-treated diabetic and found the business of injecting herself a strain, she hated doing it.

> Before I never used to take an injection in my life so I'm very very much scared about needles . . . I manage to do it, but I don't feel alright with it. But I still manage to do it, and worst of all, two times a day, which is so difficult.

The idea that she had an incurable disease worried her a great deal, she compared it to TB which she said was thought of as a terrible disease but she felt diabetes was worse.

Another woman, Mrs D, was also in a depressed state. She lived in council housing with her unmarried daughter and the daughter's three children and was supported by social security payments. Her physical health also seemed poor and she, like all the agonizers, thought of herself as unhealthy. She said she found it difficult to keep to a diet because it was expensive and because the children did not like salads. Her sight was poor and she said she had difficulty in crossing roads because of this, consequently she did not go out very much. She said:

> I don't mix with anyone, just the family.

Her blood sugar level was not well controlled and she had a number of other symptoms besides being overweight and having poor eyesight. Her poor economic circumstances did not help her to feel able to manage her diabetes, which remained a source of worry for her, restricting her activities and encouraging her to see herself as a sick person. Towards the end of the interview she said:

> I do get irritable at times. It's a terrible feeling. I was never miserable, always happy, you know. I can sit here now with the

family and not say one word some days, just sit there with the hump for no reason at all.

One of the interesting points from the analysis is the sex distribution between the four ways that the diabetics saw their diabetes. In the sample as a whole sixteen were women and fourteen were men. In the group who saw themselves as healthy, and managed their diabetes in such a way that it was given a meaning and an ordinariness either by feeling able to control it or by normalizing it, nine were men and five were women. In the group of worriers there were six women and five men: in the group of agonizers there were five women and no men. The pattern suggests that the men in the study were more able to make sense of their diabetes in a non-threatening way than the women; the women were much more likely to worry or agonize about it. This is not surprising given the weight of evidence collected by 'illness behaviour' research which indicates the greater propensity for women to worry about their health and to seek treatment (Scambler and Scambler, 1984, p. 46).

Conclusion

Coping is a word much used by health-care professionals who are keen to find examples of coping strategies which can be taught to people who have not developed them themselves. As it is used in this study, however, coping has referred to the kind of behaviour and meaning which some people have constructed around their experience of having diabetes; they see diabetes as a practical but manageable problem; but, as an experience, it is not something which can easily be taught to others. Those who coped with their diabetes were in a minority, being characterized by having a basic knowledge of how treatment works and the determination to apply that knowledge. They were prepared to alter their treatment regimen rather than reduce their social roles, their engagement with others in the social world. The role of being a diabetic was for them a less salient role in their identity than being a husband, a wife, a worker, or a mother; they did not deny the reality of their diabetes but, by trying out alterations in their medication and exploring the boundaries of their own reactions, they achieved a sense of control. They did not deliberately take risks, but attempted to apply the principles of diabetes care that they had learned from medicine, and were sometimes likely to be labelled as 'difficult' patients because they felt that their own knowledge of diabetes, gained by experience, was more appropriate than the doctor's generalized scientific knowledge (see Freidson, 1975, for a general discussion of this issue).

The theory of multiple identities (Thoits, 1983) suggests that maintaining a range of relationships provides people with a set of positive identities. This set of identities is a source of data for a person to use in shaping the self, providing a basis for a sense of control, a feeling of well-being and 'existential security'. The data from this study suggests that there may be a two-way relationship between adopting a positive coping strategy and having a set of multiple identities which enables them to place or give meaning to their diabetes. Those who were busy with a wide range of responsibilities were less preoccupied with the illness.

For those who coped in this study their diabetes remained a practical problem for them but it was not a disruptive problem at the cognitive level, as they had arrived at a relatively stable meaning for it.

From the evidence of this sample, however, more diabetics manage their diabetes by adapting to it rather than by coping with it. The adapters have minimized diabetes as a practical problem but it remains a problem at the cognitive level and the meaning they give to their diabetes is only relatively stable. Those who have accepted that they have diabetes but have altered their social relations and level of engagement in social life, and who, in some cases have accepted the continuance of some symptoms, are described as being normalizers. In their day-to-day living there is an element of denial that their diabetes causes significant problems as they attempt to achieve a normal but restricted life. They do not take on the diabetic role in public, but backstage in their lives the spectre of it remains (McLean, 1985). They have constructed a place and a meaning for diabetes in their lives by reducing their roles in situations where they feel their claims to being normal are vulnerable.

Those who constantly worry or agonize about their diabetes find that it interferes with their other roles, and their health ceases to be a taken-for-granted resource (Herzlich, 1973) or springboard from which they can manage everyday life. For these people diabetes achieves a dominant place in their identity; it remains a problem at both the practical and cognitive level.

In summary, the experience of chronic illness, for some, is one of existential insecurity, as the British Diabetic Association poster showing people walking a tightrope across Niagara Falls suggests; for others it is much less stressful – the physical disruption of the metabolic system is managed and so is the disruption of the person, the self. It is with describing variations in experience such as these that the present chapter has been concerned.

This study was an exploratory study and the data do not provide answers to questions such as why some people are non-compliant. The evidence does, however, provides ideas for further research and some suggestions for areas which could be given more time for exploration in consultations.

Those responsible for the care of diabetics are already concerned about improving the level of knowledge that diabetics have about their diabetes; the evidence of this study suggests that important though this is it will not be sufficient. It might also be helpful if doctors were able to distinguish those who are high in control from those who deal with questions by normalizing the restrictions they impose on their lives and the symptoms they push to one side. It could also be helpful if doctors gave their attention in consultations not only to the practical problems of managing diabetes but to the cognitive problem of what having it means to an individual. Those described here as worriers or agonizers need support and reassurance with regard to the particular problems they face. In sum, the strategies adopted by patients relate to a broad psychosocial terrain, and this needs careful consideration if the experience of living with diabetes is to be at the centre of medical management.

References

Bliss, M. (1983), *The Discovery of Insulin* (Edinburgh: Paul Harris).

Cerkoney, K., and Hart, L. (1980), 'The relationship between the health belief model and compliance of persons with diabetes mellitus', *Diabetes Care*, vol. 3, no. 5, pp. 594–8.

Conrad, P. (1985), 'The meaning of medications: another look at compliance', *Social Science and Medicine*, vol. 20, no. 1, pp. 19–37.

Davis, F. (1973), 'Deviance disavowal: the management of strained interaction by the visibly handicapped', in W. Filstead (ed.) *An Introduction to Deviance* (Chicago: Rand McNally).

Freidson, E. (1975), 'Dilemmas in the doctor–patient relationship', in C. Cox and A. Mead (eds) *A Sociology of Medical Practice* (London: Collier Macmillan), pp. 285–98.

Herzlich, C. (1973), *Health and Illness: A Social Psychological Analysis* (London and New York: Academic Press).

Hopper, S. (1981), 'Diabetes as a stigmatized condition: the case of low-income clinic patients in the US', *Social Science and Medicine*, vol. 158, pp. 11–19.

Kasl, S. (1983), 'Social and psychological factors affecting the course of disease: an epidemiological perspective', in D. Mechanic (ed.) *Handbook of Health, Health Care and the Health Professions* (New York: Free Press), pp. 683–708.

Locker, D. (1981), *Symptoms and Illness: The Cognitive Organization of Disorder* (London: Tavistock).

Locker, D. (1983), *Disability and Disadvantage: The Consequences of Chronic Illness* (London: Tavistock).

McLean, T. (1985), *Metal Jam, the Story of a Diabetic* (London: Hodder & Stoughton).

Mead, G. H. (1956), 'Mind, self and society', (excerpts) in A. Strauss (ed.) *The Social Psychology of George Herbert Mead* (Chicago: University of Chicago Press).

Rock, P. (1973), *Deviant Behaviour* (London: Hutchinson).

Scambler, G., and Scambler, A. (1984), 'The illness iceberg and aspects of consulting behaviour', in R. Fitzpatrick, J. Hinton, S. Newman, G. Scambler and J. Thompson, *The Experience of Illness* (London: Tavistock), pp. 32–53.

Schutz, A. (1962), 'Concept and theory formation in the social sciences', in M. Natanson (ed.) *Alfred Schutz: Collected Papers I: The Problem of Social Reality* (The Hague: M. Nijhoff).

Strauss, A. L., and Glaser, B. G. (1975), *Chronic Illness and the Quality of Life* (St. Louis: Mosby).

Surwit, R., Scovern, A., and Feinglos, M. (1982), 'The role of behaviour', *Diabetes Care*, vol. 5, no. 3.

Tattersall, R., and Jackson, J. (1982), 'Social and emotional complications of diabetes', in J. Jarrett and H. Keen, *Complications of Diabetes*, 2nd ed. (London: Edward Arnold), pp. 271–85.

Thoits, P. (1983), 'Multiple identities and psychological well-being: a reformulation and test of the social isolation hypothesis', *American Sociological Review*, vol. 48, April, pp. 174–87.

West, K. (1973), 'Diet therapy of diabetes: an analysis of failure', *Annals of Internal Medicine*, vol. 79, pp. 425–34.

West, K. (1978), *Epidemiology of Diabetes and its Vascular Lesions* (New York: Elsevier).

Zimmet, P. (1982), 'Type 2 (non-insulin-dependent) diabetes – an epidemiological overview', *Diabetologia*, vol. 22, pp. 399–411.

7 Accommodating Epilepsy in Families

GRAHAM SCAMBLER and ANTHONY HOPKINS

An epileptic seizure is the product of an abnormal paroxysmal discharge of cerebral neurones and can take a number of forms. Epilepsy itself is sometimes defined as a continuing tendency to epileptic seizures. It is more common than many people realize. At any given time approximately 1/200 of the population will be on anticonvulsant medication for epilepsy which is more or less active. A typical general practitioner in Britain is likely to be responsible for about four adults and three or four children who have experienced epileptic seizures in the last two years, and for another two adults and two children who continue to take medication for seizures in the past.

Despite its prevalence, and a growing awareness among health workers that the diagnosis of epilepsy – conferring the social status 'epileptic' – can prove more of a personal liability than recurring seizures, empirical studies of modes of adjustment to epilepsy or of its effects on family and work roles remain few and far between (Scambler, 1986). Most of those who have written about the psychosocial problems associated with having epilepsy have assumed that these are almost always the result of overt acts of discrimination by 'normals' arising out of the perception of epilepsy as stigmatizing. We have criticized this 'orthodox viewpoint' elsewhere as essentially speculative, and have offered an alternative model which is grounded in our own research data and which, we believe, has greater explanatory potential (Scambler and Hopkins, 1986). As this model underpins much of the discussion below it may be helpful to summarize it briefly at the outset.

The model hinges on a distinction between *enacted* and *felt* stigma. Enacted stigma refers to instances of discrimination against people with epilepsy based on the perception of them as somehow unacceptably different or inferior. Excluded under this definition are instances of what we have called 'legitimate' discrimination – for example, banning them from driving. Felt stigma refers principally to the fear of meeting with enacted stigma, although it also embraces a sense of shame that frequently attends 'being epileptic'.

According to our model, when the diagnosis of epilepsy is made and communicated to them people soon learn to regard their status as 'epileptics' as socially undesirable. Typically, they develop a 'special view of the world' in which felt stigma predominates. Although for much of the time their lives may be entirely normal, uninhibited by their epilepsy, when this 'special view of the world' is 'activated' by 'situational stimuli' – anything from a seizure to a date or a job interview – it predisposes them whenever possible to conceal their condition and the medical label from others; even a witnessed seizure can sometimes be explained away as a faint due to fatigue or to a hot and stuffy environment. Concealment was the first-choice strategy for the great majority of those participating in our study.

This determined policy of non-disclosure has the effect of reducing the opportunities 'normals' have for discriminating against people with epilepsy. In other words, felt stigma promotes a policy of secrecy which, in turn, leads to a reduced rate of enacted stigma. One highly significant consequence of this is that felt stigma tends to be more disruptive of the quality of life of people with epilepsy than enacted stigma. The question of the extent to which felt stigma is justified, however, remains unanswered. It is perhaps the key outstanding question for researchers interested in social aspects of epilepsy.

After giving an account of the goals and methods of the study which generated this model, we shall focus on its relevance for understanding how families cope with the disequilibrium that a diagnosis of epilepsy typically engenders. Special attention will be paid to family responses to the onset and medical diagnosis of epilepsy; to the 'protection' that families often afford to – or foist upon – members with epilepsy; and to various ways in which the intrusion of epilepsy can lead to 'conflict' within families.

Goals and Methods

Our study was essentially exploratory and was designed to yield tentative and provisional answers to three questions. What effects do the onset of seizures and subsequent diagnosis of epilepsy have on the biographies of sufferers? To what extent are these effects deleterious? And, in so far as they are deleterious, how much is this a function of what we later came to call enacted stigma? Given these questions, it was felt that the optimum strategy would be to concentrate on interviews with a small population sample of about a hundred adults with epilepsy. It was decided that participants in the study should be aged 16 or more; have had more than one non-febrile seizure of any type; have had at least one seizure in the two years preceding prevalence day or be on anticonvulsants for more than one non-febrile seizure in the past; and not be in long-term institutional care.

The idea of conducting anything akin to a door-to-door search for a hundred people meeting these criteria was rejected as unrealistic – a decision which effectively excluded people with *undiagnosed* epilepsy from the study. This left two obvious alternative sources: people with diagnosed epilepsy attending selected hospitals or clinics; or people with diagnosed epilepsy on the lists of selected general practitioners. The first would have proved the easier source to exploit but was discounted on the familiar and telling ground that 'any sample of epileptics derived from hospital or clinic sources will reflect the bias in selection of the hospital or clinic' (Bagley, 1971, p. 6). The second was chosen as the least inappropriate source.

Seventeen general practitioners from five practices in and around London agreed to co-operate in the study. One hundred and eight people were identified who satisfied our criteria for inclusion in the sample, giving an overall prevalence of 340 per 100,000 adult population. This figure may be compared with the figure of 540 cases of diagnosed epilepsy per 100,000 total population from an impressive epidemiological study carried out in Rochester, Minnesota, at about the same time (Hauser and Kurland, 1975, p. 26). Three methodological differences are relevant to this comparison. First, Hauser and Kurland studied people of all ages and not just those aged 16 or more. Secondly, they included those in institutional care; if paragraph I.26 of the 'Reid Report' is consulted, these probably number about 30 per 100,000 in England and Wales (Central Health Services Council, 1969, p. 13). And thirdly, they appear to have included in their figure people for whom seizures and medication had ceased; it is likely that this inclusion of 'cured' cases accounts for any residual difference in the figures.

The general practitioners wrote to the 108 patients identified asking them to consent to be interviewed by some colleagues. The letters contained brief descriptions of the research and concluded: 'I will take it that you are willing to see the interviewer unless I hear from you within the next seven days'. Eight people made contact with their doctors and declined to take part. The remaining 100 were approached by us and a further 6 refused to be interviewed. The final sample, then, consisted of 94 adults with epilepsy, giving a response rate of 87 per cent.

We believe these 94 individuals to be representative of adults with epilepsy living in the community; 54 per cent were men and 46 per cent women. The age ranges were almost identical: 16–79 for the men and 16–78 for the women, as were the average ages: 45 for men and 44 for women. Most members of both sexes were married: 65 per cent of the men and 58 per cent of the women. Of the men 29 per cent and of the women 26 per cent were single. One man was separated and two were divorced. Two women were cohabiting, one was separated and four were widowed. Of the total sample 69 per cent had had a seizure in the two years prior to prevalence day (and 36 per cent in the previous month); 31 per cent were on continuing medication for seizures in the past. Those who declined to take part in the study did not seem to differ significantly from those who agreed to help (Scambler, 1983).

Participants were interviewed twice in their homes, once by a neurologist (A. H.) to collect background medical data and once by a sociologist (G. S.). The latter employed non-scheduled standardized interviews (Brown and Rutter, 1966) which ranged widely over the onset of seizures, consulting behaviour, diagnosis and patienthood, the impact and accommodation of epilepsy in friendships, families and employment, and changing perceptions of self and self-worth. Excepting some demographic and other precoded material, data from the taped interviews were transcribed on to sets of 'topic cards'. These corresponded to a series of topics generated during the pilot investigations and explored during the interviews; a set of fifty or more was produced for each person, the precise number depending on his or her age and marital status at onset. The problem of overlap of data relevant to more than one topic, and hence to more than one topic card, was resolved by a system of cross-referencing. The cards brought together and afforded easy access to all statements made during the interviews pertinent to any selected topic. The data on the cards were of course then available for both qualitative and quantitative analysis.

Finally, occasional interviews were conducted with members of respondents' families. This was simply to explore interesting or potentially significant moments in respondents' lives from other angles. In all, conversations were recorded with ten relatives (five spouses, three parents and two sisters). In addition, a number of comments made by the nineteen relatives who, sometimes despite our best efforts, were present for all or part of the main interviews were recorded or summarized on the topic cards.

Onset and Diagnosis

FAMILY RESPONSES TO ONSET

The principal cause of the distress experienced by respondents at onset, affecting four out of five, was the *reaction of others*, notably witnesses of the first seizure. Often, particularly when the victims had neither been aware of having had the seizure nor injured as a result of it, this reaction seemed bizarre and out of place – for example, tearful anguish or the summoning of an ambulance. Not surprisingly in view of the fact that 53 per cent of those who could recall, or knew of, the circumstances of their first seizure said it occurred at home, most witnesses to onset came from the victims' families. Of those whose first seizure occurred at home 60 per cent said it was seen by at least one member of the family.

Questions about how parents, spouses and others 'felt' at the time, or even about what they 'did' cannot be answered adequately from proxy accounts proffered anything up to thirty years later. A multitude of factors doubtless helped fashion these perceptions and actions (for example, seizure type at onset, the personalities of those involved, past experience and present knowledge, the quality of family relationships, and so on). It was possible, however, to discern three typical features of family responses: *concern, bewilderment* and *helplessness*. All are reflected in the following account of onset by a troubled and shaken spouse:

> I just didn't know what the hell was happening: it was as simple as that! I had never seen anybody have a – whatever it was! I didn't know what to do quite frankly. And it was, if I remember rightly, about 2.30 a.m., or something like that, and it was – it was just frightening, that's all I can say. I didn't know what to do. I think that's what frightened me more than anything: I just didn't know what to do, how to cope. I didn't know what I should be doing – whether I should be trying to stop it or, or do something; I just didn't know.

Although in this instance the subject suffered a relatively dramatic *grand mal* seizure, his wife's concern, bewilderment and sense of helplessness characterized almost all family responses to onset. Concern was a natural and predictable product of generally intimate family relationships; as one girl said of her parents: 'Well, they were terribly concerned, naturally, because we're a very close family'. Nearly as many parents and spouses were bewildered as were concerned. Nor is this surprising; as Taylor puts it: 'Ignorance must cover poverty of experience as well as poverty of education – seeing seizures is not an everyday experience' (1973, p. 92). A few people thought they were witnessing a heart attack:

Well, the boys were very frightened; and my husband said he was petrified because he thought I'd had a heart attack, and he didn't think I was going to live. He thought I was going to die, and this was his natural reaction, you know. He was completely shattered.

The majority of parents and spouses were also said to have experienced a profound and disquieting sense of helplessness. This was partly a function of their bewilderment: they had little or no notion of what they could or should do. Their sense of helplessness was not wholly explicable, however, in terms of their confusion. Many *discovered* they could do nothing to help; they could neither intervene or arrest the events surrounding onset nor ease or comfort the victim while they took their inexorable course. They had either to watch and wait or to seek help from some third 'expert' party. In fact, 20 per cent of known family witnesses telephoned for an ambulance.

FAMILY RESPONSES TO DIAGNOSIS

We have suggested elsewhere that the family can be instrumental in the development in people with epilepsy of felt stigma and a characteristic 'special view of the world' (Scambler and Hopkins, 1986). There are precedents for this: the studies of West (1979) in Britain and Schneider and Conrad (1980) in the United States are examples. The latter, having asked how people with epilepsy construct their 'views of others' perceptions', write:

conventional sociological wisdom has emphasized direct disvaluing treatment by others. While this interactive experience is undoubtedly important to study, our data strongly suggest that people with epilepsy also learn such views from significant and supportive others, particularly from parents. Parental training in the stigma of epilepsy is most clear for people who were diagnosed when they were children, but *stigma coaches* were also identified by those who were diagnosed when they were adults (our emphasis). (p. 36)

They continue:

Our data indicate that the more the parents convey a definition of epilepsy as something 'bad', and the less willing they are to talk about it with their children, the more likely the child is to see it as something to be concealed. (p. 36)

They cite the instance of one 34-year-old woman who kept her epilepsy a strict secret since diagnosis at the age of 14. She recalled her parents' reaction:

> Complete disbelief. You know, 'We've never had anything like that in our family'. I can remember that was very plainly said, almost like I was something . . . something was wrong. They did not believe it. In fact, we went to another doctor, and then it was confirmed.

When asked if she had told her husband about her epilepsy before they married, the same woman replied:

> I talked to mom about it. She said: 'Don't tell him because some people don't understand. He may not understand. That's not something you talk about.' I asked her, 'Should I talk to him about passing out?' She said: 'Never say "epilepsy". Its not something we talk about.'

It was equally apparent in our study that parents – much more so than spouses – exercised a considerable influence on respondents' perceptions of the public image of epilepsy. Many parents were certainly told of the medical diagnosis of epilepsy at a time when their children were too young to comprehend it; moreover, some clearly chose to keep the diagnostic label a secret, at least for a while. Doubtless most kept silent to protect their children:

> If it occurred to the rest of the family they wouldn't have told me, because if they attached a stigma to it they would have thought that I would, you know . . . it would have terrified me or something.

Some, however, may have been afraid that the stigma of epilepsy would 'spread' to other members of the family. West, whose study focused on the families of children with epilepsy, writes:

> Parents' conceptions of stigma are not just about the way the child is viewed and treated by others; they and their other children may be felt to be implicated by virtue of their association with a member of the category, epileptic. The affiliational or courtesy aspect of 'felt stigma', however, is difficult to demonstrate because their accounts tend to focus on the implications for the child rather than for the family as a whole. Its importance must therefore be inferred. Parents do not usually say *they* are ashamed to have a child with epilepsy, although they may feel it strongly.
>
> (1979, p. 488)

Family Protection

COPING WITH SEIZURES

It has been suggested that family witnesses to onset tended to experience concern, bewilderment and helplessness. As time passed and seizures came to be recognized as transient and mostly harmless, if bizarre, phenomena, people's concern and bewilderment abated. Their sense of helplessness, however, often persisted (see also Ziegler, 1981). To compensate for this many parents and spouses cultivated roles as *protectors* and *comforters*. If they could do nothing to arrest or curtail seizures, they could at least try to ensure that the victims sustained no injuries as a result of them. One woman said of her parents:

> They just made sure that I hadn't been biting my tongue at all, and just to push a pillow away from my face and make sure there's nothing in the way that can harm me at all, so that I can't crack my head or do anything silly; and just leave me to come out of it myself, not interfere at all.

Parents and spouses could also offer tenderness – often lost on the unconscious or disorientated victim, but affording them relief from their own sense of impotence – and, ultimately, reassurance:

> Mum and dad used to go downstairs and get some, a cold flannel and put it on my head – that's about as much as they could do, I think.

Four out of five in the sample preferred to be in the company of their parents or spouses, or of somebody else in the know, when they had a seizure: they felt 'safe' – from preventable injury, misguided attempts to forcibly subdue seizures, the summoning of ambulances, effusive pity, enacted stigma, and so on – in the hands of those Goffman has called the 'wise' (1968, p. 41). Pearson, quoted by Sutherland in *Disabled We Stand*, has given a graphic account of what can happen if no 'wise' person is present when he has a *grand mal* seizure:

> I was really having them bad . . . They were violent. They were mostly violent because I'd come to and find people holding me down, policemen or whatever, and I became violent because I was being pinned down on the ground by people with their knees in my back. I was always ending up in hospitals and police stations. I just

think the policemen were totally ignorant of epilepsy . . . To them
it was a drunk going berserk or whatever.   (1981, p. 86)

Most respondents may have preferred to be in the company of the
'wise' when they had seizures, but very few wished as a consequence
to be permanently chaperoned *in case* they had seizures. In fact,
family, and especially parental, *overprotection* was the most common
source of anger and resentment against family members.

The ideas that parents tend to be overprotective of children with
epilepsy and that this is potentially harmful is not new. In the 1950s
Ounsted employed the neologism 'hyperpaedophilia' to refer to this
attitude in parents (1955, p. 309). In 1960 Lennox wrote of parents of
children with epilepsy: 'Many parents believe it their duty to keep the
child always in sight and forbid all activities which involve any
danger' (1960, p. 932). In his autobiography former England cricket
captain Tony Greig, who had his first epileptic seizure at the age of
14, writes: 'My family's reaction was primarily one of protection'
(1980, p. 12). He tells how he obstinately resisted their well-meaning
strictures:

> Maybe I was foolhardy, a stubborn martyr. But I was lucky. I came
> to no harm by carrying on just the way I had always done. I never
> had an attack while on a bike, I never passed out while swimming,
> and gradually my family realized that they would take half my life
> away if they insisted on chaining me with safety regulations. So
> they let me do things my way, possibly reluctantly, possibly
> fearfully – but, thankfully, without disastrous consequences.
>   (1980, p. 13)

Many children are less willing or able to counter the parental
tendency to overprotect than Tony Greig was. And Ounsted found,
as have numerous others since, that overprotection can lead to
behavioural and personality problems in early adulthood. Lerman
(1977) provides an account of the 'typical' effects of overprotection
and overindulgence by parents which, although exaggerated, reflects
an established pattern of research findings. Parents generally react to
the diagnosis of epilepsy, he claims, with a mixture of apprehension,
shame, anxiety, frustration and helplessness. This leads to 'an
oppressive atmosphere of secrecy and despair' which has an adverse
effect on the child. The child cannot discuss his or her condition
openly and soon comes to see it as something undesirable. Stigmatization may be experienced at the hands of schoolmates, friends and
neighbours who are in the know. The child often becomes confined to
the home and socially isolated. The intricate skills of social relation-

ships are never learned and he or she remains 'insecure, overdependent, emotionally immature', and is 'inept' when adulthood is reached. Such dire long-term consequences are rarer than Lerman implies, although our study is testimony to the fact that they do occur.

A DARK SECRET

Our data suggest, like Schneider and Conrad's, that parents of chilren with epilepsy frequently function as stigma coaches: through advice and example they prompt 'naive' offspring to define and react to epilepsy as a stigma. Schneider and Conrad (1983) write: 'Children's earliest memories of how parents reacted to the diagnosis seemed to set the stage for how they themselves would interpret epilepsy subsequently' (p. 83). A number of parents in their study adopted what they call a 'closed style':

> Parents who adopted this style were described as 'shocked', 'embarrassed', 'ashamed' and 'fearful' to learn their child's diagnosis. These reactions spoke volumes of negative moral meaning to their children, even though, ironically, in many cases few words about epilepsy were ever actually spoken.   (p. 86)

In our study several parents banned the use of the word 'epilepsy' within the home, let alone outside it. Siblings were often kept in the dark:

> Well, my mum and dad didn't tell my sister much in case she went around telling everybody. It's not something they like to speak about . . . I think they know what's the matter, but no-one speaks about it.

Only half those siblings who shared the parental home with a child with epilepsy knew of the diagnosis.

Interestingly, even fewer, 21 per cent, of the children of a parent with epilepsy knew of the diagnosis. In fact only half of those children who were aged 16 or more and had actually seen their parent have a seizure had been told of the diagnosis. These figures suggest that parents are even more reluctant to discuss their own epilepsy than they are the epilepsy of a child. In a small study of twelve families Lechtenberg and Akner (1984) report that children who were not informed about a parent's epilepsy tended to feel unhappy and let down when they eventually found out. They conclude (p. 84): 'Efforts to conceal the problem breed distrust.'

Very few respondents spoke openly or willingly of their epilepsy outside their families, some having been coached into extreme wariness by parents seeking to protect them from potentially hostile outsiders. Nine out of ten said they rarely disclosed the diagnosis to people who had not thoroughly earned the status of close friend:

> I think I told my closest friends, but I didn't go and broadcast it around, if you like: it wasn't something I was particularly proud of.

Nor were all close friends let into the secret, even if they had first-hand experience of epilepsy:

> I've got a very close friend – as I say, very close, his son has fits – but I've never told him I've had fits.

Normally, people's general reticence about disclosing was the product of felt stigma: they feared that erstwhile friends would reject them or drift away. Some, although no more than one in twenty, claimed to have had experience of this:

> This is what I've found – that whenever I tell anybody that I'm epileptic they don't want to know me at all. I've had friends here: as soon as they know I'm epileptic they don't want to know me at all.

Occasionally, however, an individual baulked at the prospect of eliciting too much sympathy rather than too little:

> I don't tell a lot of them. As I said before, they start feeling sorry for you – you know, pitying you; and you, sort of, don't know where the pity ends and the friendship begins . . . you can't distinguish them. I want them to like me as I am, not feel sorry for me, which is entirely different.

There was a widespread unwillingness also to disclose to boy or girl friends. A choice generally had to be made between what Schneider and Conrad (1980) call 'anticipatory preventive telling' – disclosing in the hope of influencing others' reactions should a seizure occur – and a more or less precarious concealment. Of those who had had more than a single boy or girl friend and were themselves aware of the diagnosis of epilepsy, 13 per cent had always disclosed it, 26 per cent had done so at least once, and 61 per cent had never done so. Almost a third of those who had disclosed at least once said they had suffered broken relationships as a consequence. Only seven single members of the sample had boy or girl friends when interviewed: three had said nothing at all, and four had disclosed the diagnosis of epilepsy;

interestingly, none had disclosed only their seizures. Of the four who had admitted to their epilepsy, three had done so voluntarily when the relationship had matured for several months or more (one being encouraged to do so by the fact that her boy friend, 'a kindred spirit', had diabetes), and one had done so only because he suspected his girl friend had already been told by a female cousin of his, whom she knew well and who was herself dating a boy with epilepsy. None of the four disclosures were made lightly, two of them occurring only five or six years after the start of the relationships.

Most of those who adopted a policy of secrecy in relation to boy or girl friends stressed that they would disclose, as a matter of principle, if they ever became engaged. Intending to do the 'right' thing, however, is not the same as actually doing it. Felt stigma was responsible for the fact that only 33 per cent of the marriages that took place after onset were preceded by a full disclosure incorporating the word 'epilepsy'; and only a further 36 per cent by a partial disclosure involving words like 'attacks' or 'dizzy spells'. There was no disclosure at all in 31 per cent of cases. Disclosure was almost certainly influenced by the witnessing of seizures: 75 per cent of those who disclosed the diagnosis had had a seizure in the presence of their future spouses, compared with 54 per cent of those who disclosed only their seizures and, predictably, none of those who maintained an absolute silence. There was no evidence that concealment jeopardized marriages at a later date.

Disclosures outside the context of family or personal relationships – for example with employers – have been reported in detail elsewhere and need not be documented here (see Scambler and Hopkins, 1980). Sufficient to say that the same pattern was apparent, namely, that people's 'special view of the world', rooted in felt stigma, typically predisposed them to attempt to pass as normal whenever this was feasible. Of those in full-time employment when interviewed, only 5 per cent had volunteered a full disclosure to their employers before starting work, and each of these was experiencing daily seizures at the time. A reasonable generalization to close this section would be that most disclosures of the diagnosis of epilepsy, inside and outside families, are provoked either by a witnessed seizure or by a high probability that a seizure will be witnessed in the near future.

Family Conflict over Epilepsy

When individuals fall victim to chronic conditions which are particularly disabling or stigmatizing their families are often thrown into states of confusion or disequilibrium. As one respondent put it:

My parents had to come to an understanding, and so did I. They had to find their depth, and so did I. We had to walk around rather blindly at first, learning how to treat each other and what to do.

If such families are to survive intact, states of equilibrium have somehow to be restored. As highly focused studies like those of Davis (1963) and, more recently, Voysey (1975) have shown, the homeostatic mechanisms at work can be extremely complex. In this section we illustrate, by means of two extended case studies, how the unwelcome intrusion of epilepsy can lead to tension and conflict between family members, and how in such circumstances family life can be reconstituted. The two families were selected, first, because it was possible to interview independently all the relevant members of both families; and second, because they offered an opportunity to elaborate on two themes already introduced above, concerning the stigma associated with the diagnosis of epilepsy and parental over-protection.

The first case study involves Daniel and Clare Tallit. Daniel Tallit, a hospital laboratory technician, had his first seizure in bed in the early hours of the morning; he was 47 at the time.

I just woke up one morning and my wife said: 'You've just had a fit and I've called the doctor in'.

Clare Tallit, a former nurse, also told Daniel she suspected epilepsy. For his part, Daniel was not convinced that anything had happened *at all*, let alone that he had had a 'fit':

It was a good long while before I believed I'd had that first attack. Really and truly, I thought she was making some fuss out of nothing.

Nor of course was he willing to entertain the to him ludicrous suggestion that he was suffering from epilepsy. When the general practitioner arrived, Clare privately communicated her diagnostic suspicions, but there was no further mention of the word 'epilepsy' to Daniel at this stage. He was, however, referred by the general practitioner to a specialist.

Between the general practitioner's home visit and his consultation with the specialist, Daniel, to Clare's chagrin, vacillated between angry denials that anything at all had occurred during that first, fateful night and a grudging acceptance that 'something *must* have taken place' for Clare and the general practitioner to behave in the firm and decisive ways they did. When in the latter frame of mind, he was inclined to the theory that he must have suffered some kind of 'turn' as a reaction to suddenly discontinuing the 'massive doses' of Librium he had been taking to relieve anxiety caused by a persistent and embarrassing stammer. Clare rejected this theory as nonsense and they quarrelled about it more than once.

Two or three weeks after onset Daniel visited a local specialist who diagnosed 'an epileptiform attack'. Daniel's response was fairly predictable:

> I was quite prepared for them to call it 'epileptiform' because it seemed to me that there's an essential difference there . . . 'Epileptiform' meant to me some sort of fit which wasn't really epileptic, but it had the same effect as the epileptic . . . It isn't necessarily caused by the same thing.

He added:

> I didn't want to be epileptic.

Although Daniel was now prepared to admit to Clare that he must have had a turn of some sort, he remained adamant that he did *not* have epilepsy. Nor had he abandoned his own aetiological theory, in spite of the fact that the specialist had pronounced it groundless; after all, he argued, no alternative theory seemed to be on offer from the medical profession. Clare meanwhile was losing her patience. She neither understood nor sympathized with Daniel's attempts to 'negotiate' a release from the diagnosis of epilepsy:

> She just said it was an epileptic fit, and that I should face it.

Clare told us that she became so frustrated by what she regarded as insufferable obduracy on Daniel's part that their marriage was for a time in jeopardy. Following Ferreira (1963), it might be said that Clare refused to join Daniel in constructing a 'family myth'.

This friction between Daniel and Clare seemed to be directly attributable to their different reference groups or 'perspectives'. Daniel's perception of epilepsy derived from the perspective of the *lay* community, as he had internalized it, while Clare's perception of epilepsy derived almost exclusively from the perspective of the *medical* community, as she had internalized it (she had, of course, been a nurse for a number of years). Less abstractly, Daniel saw epilepsy principally as a stigmatizing label and was chiefly concerned to 'negotiate' its removal, while Clare saw epilepsy principally as a symptom of disease and, as such, strictly non-negotiable (see Scambler and Hopkins, 1986).

By the time of interview, five years and one further seizure after onset, both Daniel and Clare Tallit had mellowed and were willing to admit they had grown more tolerant. Although they still perceived epilepsy differently, a 'truce' – based on love, a modest degree of reciprocal sympathy and a tacit agreement on the non-use of the word 'epilepsy' in each other's company – had permitted a restoration of a state of family equilibrium. Whether or not such a truce would have been possible had Daniel had more than a single seizure since onset is a moot point. As it was, his epilepsy had lost its salience.

The second case study involves the Randall family. When she had her first seizure at the age of 13, a decade before interview, Sarah Randall was living with her parents and two younger sisters, Ann, then aged 11, and Jennifer, then aged 8. It was an extremely close-knit family and Sarah was quickly surrounded by love and attention; her father, a London taxi driver, was especially concerned:

> They were terribly distraught naturally, because we're a terribly close family. My father, being a Piscean, the same as myself, we've got rather the same kind of temperament – I'm a bit better than he is! – he cosseted a bit – well, a bit! – he nearly smothered me.

For all the closeness of this relationship, Sarah soon came to resent her father's overprotectiveness:

> I think, when one's doing something wrong, and you know you've done something wrong, and you know that if you didn't have this particular illness you'd get the biggest hiding, you know, created; when you get away with that kind of thing, you definitely know that something's missing.

As she got older her resentment became more acute:

> My father just used to bring it [her epilepsy] up to make me know that I needed him. You know, as soon as I had my seizures it was like a ball and chain went round me, and he didn't let go. I wasn't allowed to sleep at my friends' houses, things like this, just in case.

The accuracy of this portrait of an overprotective father was confirmed by each of the other three members of the family. Sarah's mother felt her husband, whom she described as 'emotional' and 'highly strung', had behaved 'really badly' from the time of onset onwards:

> He didn't want to leave her. I mustn't leave her. Somebody had to be around her all the time. I did at first, because I think you panic and you don't know what to do, but as time went by I began to realize that it was no good for Sarah doing what we were doing, to pamper her, and so I had to become the hard one, sort of thing.

This led to occasional 'shouting matches' between Mr and Mrs Randall, particularly when Sarah wanted to go out on her own. Jennifer explained what typically happened:

> You see, my mum would say: 'Go out Sarah', and she'd chuck her out . . . But my dad would say: 'What if you have an attack?', or something like this. He doesn't mean to, but he lets his feelings out, which is not very good for Sarah.

Ann told the same story, as the following brief interview extract shows:

Ann: My mum was a bit more practical, and she realized that you've got to look after Sarah more than your own feelings, you know. I can't really explain it, but dad's very kind of, very possessive towards Sarah; he'd rather, sort of, shut her up and protect her, while mum says: 'She's got to learn to live with it' – you know, hope to get married and things like that. I think my dad would prefer her to just sit around, you know, not to go out with boys. The word 'swimming', it's terrible! Not allowed to do that! And drinking and smoking and things like that.

G. S.: Does he actively try to stop her doing things like that?

Ann: Yes. Actually nine-tenths of the rows in this house are because of that. If she goes out, you know, dad says: 'Don't do this. Don't do that'. My mother sort of screams at him to shut up and, you know, sort of says: 'She's 23 years old'.

G. S.: How does Sarah react?

Ann: She doesn't like being molly-coddled. She gets very, very worked up about it, very emotional.

For his part, Mr Randall was well aware of his family's, and especially his wife's, disapproval of his attitude towards Sarah:

> I get accused of pampering her . . . but, I mean, if you put yourself in my place, and you know the kid stands just a couple of feet from

the side of the platform, or she wants to go heights and you've read in a book that she's not supposed to go heights – all I'm trying to do is make her aware of the thing that she's epileptic. She's got to live with it, but she's also got to safeguard herself from hurting herself . . . But she [his wife] won't have it. She says I pamper her, I worry too much over her, or stop her from doing this, or I spoiled her, or I made her as she is today, which is not really true.

He seemed unrepentant. He recalled a party to celebrate the New Year which Sarah had wanted to attend. Jennifer had already given us an account, entirely consistent with those of her mother, Ann and Sarah herself:

She was going to this party, and straightaway my dad jumped in and said: 'Going to a party all by yourself? Walking through the streets? What if you happen to have an attack?' It was all coming out, and he shouldn't have said it! Now my mum was thinking exactly the same thing, but she kept it inside and said: 'You go'.

Mr Randall justified his intervention in the following, revealing terms:

She wanted to go into a neighbourhood which I thought was a very rough, frightening neighbourhood where a lot of rape has happened . . . Being a cab driver, I know all these things. I seen it: I was 25 years on nights and I know what can be done. And I said to her, the trains didn't go exactly where she wanted, she had a long walk, and I was very worried about her. But she upset herself because she said I was trying to put her off . . . This is my fear, in case she had an epileptic fit, that somebody might pick her up, put her in the cab and, sort of, rape her; and I think this would be a great big damage to her.

Despite having, on average, only one seizure every nine months or so, Sarah normally stayed at home seven evenings a week, shunning all forms of social intercourse. In fact she went out so rarely, doubtless mainly because of the long-term influence of her father, that when she did venture out she behaved with a manifest lack of maturity. As her mother expressed it:

She doesn't know how to behave in company; it's a terrible thing to say, but she doesn't.

This lack of maturity, according to both Ann and Jennifer, was most apparent in the company of men. Ann told me that:

If we're out with a group of fellows she giggles a lot; she acts sort of immature, I suppose that's the best way to put it.

When she's out she often becomes very, sort of, boisterous, which puts others off, because she's so kind of restricted and she's so uptight in case she has an attack or something.

Jennifer explained how and why she and Ann were generally apprehensive when accompanying Sarah:

I'd like to say to her: 'Sarah, come out with me', but I can't for the simple reason, because she doesn't go out a lot – the last time she came out with us she was very embarrassing. I don't know whether you've noticed but she's very boisterous, she's sort of overpowering . . . and she'll just say the first thing that comes into her mind . . . it's very embarrassing at the time . . . and I find myself making excuses for her. I feel very guilty afterwards for doing it.

Summarizing, then, Sarah had by the time of interview lost the will to go out and mix with others, especially men, and spent most of her time closeted at home with her parents. Ann was probably right when she portrayed her as a particularly sad victim of felt stigma:

I think she thinks she'll get very serious with a fellow, it will be the real thing, you know, and she'll tell him and he'll be off. That's what she's scared of. That's why she won't go out most of the time, in case that happens.

She lived, Ann said, in a substitute world of dreams, constructing daily fantasies in which men were invariably the protagonists. Not surprisingly, on those rare occasions when she did find herself in male company she lacked the social skills to cope.

Everybody in the family held Mr Randall to be primarily responsible for Sarah's unhappy, cramped life-style. Mrs Randall told us:

I honestly think she would have outgrown it by now had she been pushed out on her own a bit more. She's in; she's always in! You know, as a child she's always been among grown-ups: she's never been a child, if you understand!

A state of family equilibrium could only be maintained by means of a conspiracy involving Mrs Randall, Ann and Jennifer to coax and cajole Sarah to socialize and to circumvent and, if necessary, 'shout down' Mr Randall's well-intentioned but misguided protests. If Mr

Randall had mellowed a little (and only a little) over the years, then, as his wife put it:

> I think that's pure perseverance on our part – swearing tactics, you know!

Conclusion

In discussing the effects of epilepsy on individuals and their families we have concentrated on a number of ways in which the stigma associated with the medical label and the seizures themselves can disrupt family equanimity, and we have illustrated some of the coping strategies commonly employed. It is paradoxical that physicians charged with treating people with epilepsy are both aware of the problems that epilepsy can cause in families and generally unwilling or reluctant to include discussion of such problems on the agenda for consultations. One of the principal complaints against physicians – and against hospital specialists in particular – is that they are preoccupied with the 'management of epilepsy' and disinterested in wider aspects of care (Scambler, 1986). West has suggested that most lack what he terms a 'stigma ideology' for epilepsy: they have neither researched nor thought out any systematic counsel for people faced with psychosocial problems because of their epilepsy. He adds: 'the physician is in danger of legitimating the stigma of epilepsy, not by talking about it, but by *not* talking about it' (1979, p. 647).

Ziegler has argued that assistance for the parents of children with epilepsy in coping with its psychosocial correlates must become part of 'the overall treatment plan'. He writes of physicians and parents as potential 'clinical partners' (1981, p. 344). Schneider and Conrad similarly insist that physicians and adult patients should be 'coparticipants in care'. They ask:

> While physicians are experts in the treatment of disease and disorder, can they claim to 'treat' the social experience of illness? What would such treatment be? How, for instance, could a doctor 'treat' the relationships of dependence that developed with family members, or the way others respond to witnessing a seizure, or the person's perception of the stigma surrounding epilepsy?
>
> (1983, p. 228)

It must be acknowledged, they continue, that 'illness is something too complex for any single person, no matter how highly trained, to manage' (p. 229). Care should be shared. It may be asking a lot of physicians to expect them to evolve 'stigma ideologies' of the kind envisioned by West, but open discussion arising out of an open agenda can be therapeutic in itself; and over time, if they listened to their patients, physicians might become increasingly well informed and effective counsellors.

References

Bagley, C. (1971), *The Social Psychology of the Child with Epilepsy* (London: Routledge & Kegan Paul).

Brown, G., and Rutter, M. (1966), 'The measurement of family activities: a methodological study'. *Human Relations*, vol. 19, pp. 241–63.

Central Health Services Council (1969), Advisory Committee on the Health and Welfare of Handicapped Persons. 'People with epilepsy' (London: HMSO).

Davis, F. (1963), *Passage through Crisis* (Indianapolis: Bobbs-Merrill).

Ferreira, A. (1963), 'Family myth and homeostasis', *Archives of General Psychiatry*, vol. 9, pp. 457–63.

Goffman, E. (1968), *Stigma: Notes on the Management of Spoiled Identity* (London: Penguin)

Greig, A. (1980), *My Story* (London: Stanley Paul).

Hauser, W., and Kurland, L. (1975), 'The epidemiology of epilepsy in Rochester, Minnesota, 1935 through 1967', *Epilepsia*, vol. 16, pp. 1–66.

Lechtenberg R., and Akner, L. (1984), 'Psychologic adaptation of children to epilepsy in a parent', *Epilepsia*, vol. 25, pp. 40–5.

Lennox, W. (1960), *Epilepsy and Related Disorders*. Vols. 1 and 2 (London: Churchill Livingstone).

Lerman, P. (1977), 'The concept of preventive rehabilitation in childhood epilepsy: a plea against overprotection and overindulgence', in J. Penry (ed.), *Epilepsy: The Eighth International Symposium* (New York: Raven Press).

Ounsted, C. (1955), 'The hyperkinetic syndrome in epileptic children', *Lancet*, vol. 2, pp. 303–11.

Scambler, G. (1983), '"Being epileptic": sociology of a stigmatizing condition', unpublished PhD thesis, University of London.

Scambler, G. (1986), 'Sociological aspects of epilepsy', in A. Hopkins (ed.), *Epilepsy* (London: Chapman & Hall).

Scambler, G., and Hopkins, A. (1980), 'Social class, epileptic activity and disadvantage at work', *Journal of Epidemiology and Community Health*, vol. 34, pp. 129–33.

Scambler, G., and Hopkins, A. (1986), 'Being epileptic: coming to terms with stigma', *Sociology of Health and Illness*, vol. 8, pp. 26–43.

Schneider, J., and Conrad, P. (1980), 'In the closet with illness: epilepsy, stigma potential and information control', *Social Problems*, vol. 28, pp. 32–44.

Schneider, J., and Conrad, P. (1983), *Having Epilepsy: The Experience and Control of Illness* (Philadelphia: Temple University Press).

Sutherland, A. (1981), *Disabled We Stand* (London: Souvenir Press).

Taylor, D. (1973), 'Aspects of seizure disorders: II. On prejudice', *Developmental Medicine and Child Neurology*, vol. 15, pp. 91–4.

Voysey, M. (1975), *A Constant Burden: The Reconstitution of Family Life* (London: Routledge & Kegan Paul).

West, P. (1979), 'An investigation into the social construction and consequences of the label "epilepsy"', unpublished PhD thesis, University of Bristol.

Ziegler, R. (1981), 'Impairments of control and competence in epileptic children and their families', *Epilepsia*, vol. 22, pp. 339–46.

8 *The Experience of Stigma: Living with Rectal Cancer*

LEA MACDONALD

Introduction

Cancer is among those diseases that particularly evoke feelings of fear, dread and revulsion. It is not only the victims of cancer and their families, and the public in general for whom cancer is frightening and stigmatizing. It is difficult for the medical and nursing professions as well, because it involves not only the treatment and management of the disease but, very often, the care of the dying patient. Despite much professional activity and some improvements in diagnostic and · therapeutic procedures, outcomes of cancer, in terms of cures leading to increased survival of adult cancer patients, have not noticeably improved in the last fifty years.

Growing concern for the well-being of cancer patients in the community and efforts to direct and improve services to them were among the reasons for examining in detail the quality of life of cancer patients. Patients with cancer of a single site were selected in order to control for clinical variations in treatment. Rectal cancer was especially suitable for study. It is a fairly common disease accounting for 10 per cent of cancer diagnoses, and affects all strata of the population. The male: female ratio of incidence is 1.8 to 1 at ages 65 and over, the years of greatest risk. Five-year survival, corrected for other causes of death, is about 32 per cent and has remained relatively unchanged over the last five decades (Office of Population Censuses and Surveys, 1981; 1984).

Two-thirds of rectal cancer patients are left with a permanent colostomy following amputation of the anus and rectum. A colostomy is an incontinent, artificial anus formed by an opening from the abdomen into the colon. The colostomy, with no sphincter to control it, can release faeces and flatus unpredictably, generally into a plastic bag attached to the abdomen with adhesives, a belt, or both. So the person with a colostomy may be defecating while cooking, eating, working, sleeping, making love, or engaging in any other activity.

These patients obviously face complex problems of physical, emotional and social adaptation. The shame, taboos and fears associated with mutilation of the body, with faecal incontinence, with seeing and handling faeces, and with cancer made it clear that we should investigate the stigma perceived by patients with rectal cancer. Stigma is the result of interaction between individual and community values through which the individual feels devalued, and subject to negative stereotyping. This study identified damaging social influences as perceived by the patient. Other people were not asked about their attitudes and behaviour towards rectal cancer patients and colostomy; questions concentrated on the subjective assessment of perceived stigma.

Rectal cancer is a disease of the affluent Western world, most likely induced by exposure to common environmental features of modern life, probably dietary (Wynder, 1983). It fits very neatly into Freidson's (1970) well-known social typology of 'legitimate' and 'illegitimate' categories of medical conditions and impairments. For example, there appear to be no differential class or occupational risks of contracting the disease and, unlike lung cancer, no unequivocally demonstrated protective actions that individuals may take to prevent it. Thus, no one contracts rectal cancer because of what might be construed as an irresponsible life-style. Moreover, there appears to be no relation between personality type and risk of contracting the cancer; nor has it been linked to stress factors or to psychosomatic reactions to adverse life-events (Brown *et al.*, 1974; Haney, 1977). The only individual attributes associated with rectal cancer are age and sex. There is no evidence that the person who contracts rectal cancer is in any way psychologically predisposed. Early presentation of symptoms has little or no relation to survival from the disease. That is, duration of symptoms is not related to the invasiveness of the cancer nor to its malignancy (MacArthur and Smith, 1984). So rectal cancer patients who delay in seeking medical advice for symptoms do not necessarily jeopardize their chances of survival.

Thus, rectal cancer can be considered among the category of diseases in which the sufferer is a true victim, in no way responsible for the condition. According to Freidson (1970) rectal cancer is 'unconditionally legitimate' and the disease does not involve a notion of responsibility on the part of the victim (Sontag, 1977). In particular, the stigma of this potentially embarrassing and potentially mutilating condition comes from the disease, its treatment and iatrogenic sequelae, as the following brief description of the symptoms, diagnosis and treatment shows.

The clinical aspects of rectal cancer suggest that diagnosis of the disease must be an overwhelming shock to most patients, whether or not they are formally made aware of the diagnosis. Symptoms are rarely severe or dramatic. Rather, they tend to be mild, chronic and insidious. The most frequent symptoms are changes in bowel habits and blood mixed with stool. The relatively non-specific nature of these symptoms often makes diagnosis difficult and delays in seeking medical attention understandable (MacArthur and Smith, 1984). Verification of the general practitioner's initial diagnosis involves a number of humiliating, painful and potentially frightening procedures such as endoscopic examination (Wilson-Barnett, 1978). The traumatic nature of the patient's encounter with diagnostic procedures and the extreme post-operative dependence on others for the management of body functions may have a damaging effect, particularly if the patient is insensitively treated or left in ignorance of what is being done (Johnson *et al.*, 1973).

Treatment for rectal cancer involves the majority of cases in radical mutilating surgery, life with a colostomy, and low expectation of survival. Although new techniques to reduce the number of colostomies are constantly being sought (Heald, 1980), most rectal cancer patients must inevitably face the double burden of cancer and colostomy. However, within a year of surgery, the majority of patients, including those with colostomies, have recovered from surgery and, if they survive for five years, are considered by their surgeons to be cured (Goligher, 1975).

The fact that so many of these people are elderly or close to retirement age may mean that their private problems are disguised and normalized by old age. At a general level, there is a great overlap between problems that may be encountered by the elderly and problems of living with rectal cancer which poses real difficulties in defining and measuring the special needs of these patients (Arluke *et al.*, 1979). For example, elderly women living alone with few relatives close by may constitute a group at special risk of remaining frequent users of medical care (Wan and Soifer, 1974; Kovar, 1977), as much or more as a consequence of being elderly and alone than as a consequence of having had cancer and perhaps a permanent colostomy.

Despite the serious problems associated with the disease, there has been no large-scale community-based study of rectal cancer patients carried out in the UK. Nor has there been a study which tries to depict the extent to which these patients may be living a full family and community life. Although the social consequences of rectal cancer are conspicuous, there has been no specialized social study of these patients. Indeed, there have been few sociological contributions to the public debates about cancer and the problems of cancer patients.

The disease of rectal cancer provides an important case for investigating the relationship between the biomedical and social production of illness and health. This is because rectal cancer patients do not differ in any discernible way from the general population, except that they have been victims of cancer. The choice between an anal-sphincter-saving operation (excision of the cancer and anasto-mosis of the bowel) and an anal-sphincter-sacrificing operation with formation of a permanent colostomy appears to depend largely on the distance of the cancer from the anal verge and on the preferences, skill and clinical judgement of the surgeon – not on the characteristics or social status of the patient. In effect, therefore, the patient is, with few exceptions, randomly assigned to mutilating or non-mutilating surgical procedures.

Intensive studies of colostomy patients show that they must work through profound intra-psychic problems associated with reactions to loss of part of their body (Orbach and Tallent, 1965). In some respects, this is similar to the grief and mourning associated with the loss of a family member (Speck, 1978). But there is a social dimension to this process. People who have lost a spouse are expected to take up their lives after a period of mourning, but in a new social position – that of the widowed (Lynch, 1977). Without carrying the analogy too far, it can be said that rectal cancer patients are expected to take up their lives after a period of convalescence, but in an ambiguous and impaired social position – that of the chronic patient with the invisible but ever-present threat of cancer (Zahn, 1973). Rectal cancer patients with colostomies have additional visible and invisible burdens: the diagnosis of cancer, the problems of physical deviance and the intra-psychic problem of incorporating a new body image into their concept of themselves. Their new social position is that of the chronic patient with a permanent stigma which, although hidden, is always in danger of becoming manifest (Ablon, 1981). In looking at the problems of rectal cancer patients, it was important therefore to include relative freedom from perceived stigma in the examination of their quality of life along with the already fairly well identified factors of physical, emotional and social health.

Methods

Although a large cross-sectional study is limited in depth and is unable to present a dynamic picture of changes over time, it has definite advantages when the purpose is to provide a representative sample of a defined category of respondent. It was decided to conduct a cross-sectional survey because interviewing patients only once would minimize inconvenience to families and to patients who might be very ill. Moreover, a single interview would avoid distortions due to changes in care by professionals because they were aware that the study was being carried out. The data were linked to the date of diagnosis recorded in the South Thames Cancer Registry and could provide some understanding of the experiences of patients at intervals of between one and twenty years since diagnosis and treatment of the disease. This was a population-based rather than a hospital-based study. The strength of the selected method is that it provided a representative sample of rectal cancer patients, independent of the potential biases of particular hospitals and treatment regimes. This approach, however, had the disadvantage of requiring negotiation of multiple ethical approvals, Local Medical Committee approvals, consultant surgeon permissions and general practitioner support.

Six health districts in South-West and South-East London with a total population of about 1,500,000 were selected for study because they were within one hour's drive of St. George's Hospital Medical School. After obtaining approval from all the appropriate ethical committees, support for the study was sought from each Local Medical Committee and each Division of Surgery. All general practitioners were circulated with a description of the study. The South Thames Cancer Registry then supplied the hospital case number, date of diagnosis, hospital atttended and name of the consultant surgeon of all patients diagnosed as having rectal cancer and treated by radical surgery between 1958 and 1978, who had an address in one of the selected health districts and who were not known to have died. A letter, requesting permission for the release of the patient's name and address and to approach the patient for interview, was sent to the 143 surgeons on the record of the 644 eligible cases, to their successors, or to the head of the appropriate Division of Surgery.

One district Division of Surgery decided *en bloc* not to participate (a loss of 89 cases), surgeons at one hospital did not wish their patients to be interviewed (a loss of 21 cases) and one surgeon did not reply to repeated communications (a loss of 10 cases). Six other cases were excluded on the specific request of the surgeon. A letter, explaining the study and requesting consent to be interviewed, was sent to the 518 cases for whom consultants' permission had been obtained. Of these, 25 died before they could be interviewed, 24 were terminally ill, 21 had moved outside the study area, 7 could not be traced, and 21 did not wish to be interviewed.

Each patient was interviewed at home by one of a team of twenty-eight specially trained health visitors who did not previously know the patients. They used a semi-structured questionnaire which had been developed and piloted among rectal cancer patients attending surgical out-patients clinics.

In addition to the question of perceived stigma, the study was designed to yield information on the following groups of topics: quality of life – physical, emotional and social health – as perceived by the patient and assessed by both the general practitioner and the health visitor. We also used the Leeds scale for the self-assessment of anxiety and depression (Snaith *et al.*, 1976). Level of perceived stigma was included in the definition of quality of life. Clinical variables comprised details of symptoms, other chronic illnesses, and medication (MacDonald and Anderson, 1985). Disability was assessed using an instrument developed by Garrad and Bennett (1971). Buffer variables, which might protect patients against poor quality of life, included use of medical and community services, satisfaction with services, and personal, family and socioeconomic circumstances.

A stigma self-rating measure was devised, consisting of statements about avoidance of others, avoidance by others, feelings of self-consciousness, of unattractiveness, and of being different from other people. Typical statements are: 'I feel less attractive than I used to'; 'I feel self-conscious and embarrassed about myself'; 'I feel odd and different from other people'. Items were scored from 0 (complete disagreement) to 3 (complete agreement) with each statement. In the absence of independent judgements about patients' feelings of stigma, we could not determine a cut-off point based on total scores. The arbitrary solution was to use the extremes: 0 or 1 (negligible stigma) on every item against the rest, that is, 2 or 3 (some stigma) on any item. Responses were also tabulated by dividing scores above and below the median. Severe stigma was defined as the upper 15 per cent of the frequency distribution of scores. The scale was supported by additional questions about perceptions of changes since surgery – in self-esteem, in physical appearance when fully dressed, and in married life (MacDonald and Anderson, 1984).

Results

A PROFILE OF THE POPULATION

A total of 420 interviews were successfully completed, half happened to be with men and half with women; 265 (63 per cent) had a permanent colostomy. The others had been left with a functioning

Table 8.1   *Social and Economic Characteristics, Presence of Colostomy, and Number of Years since Surgery*

	<65		Age 65–75		75+		Total
	M	F	M	F	M	F	M & F
	(n=64)	(n=52)	(n=80)	(n=80)	(n=66)	(n=78)	(n=420)
	%	%	%	%	%	%	%
Marital status							
Single	6	8	6	5	2	14	7
Married/							
cohabiting	81	67	82	46	72	18	60
Widowed	5	15	11	41	26	68	29
Separated/							
divorced	8	10	1	8	0	0	4
Living alone	8	19	10	39	23	56	27
Left school,							
age 14 or less	63	52	69	66	73	71	66
Employed							
Part-time	6	21	14	6	5	0	8
Full-time	70	17	5	1	2	0	14
Gross weekly							
household income							
<£60	10	36	52	71	75	91	58
>£100	56	40	20	13	10	4	22
Social Class							
Manual	51	49	52	48	65	59	54
Non-manual	49	51	48	52	35	41	46
Housing class							
Owner-occupier	65	56	58	53	55	46	55
Private tenant	13	21	19	16	17	23	18
Council tenant	22	23	23	31	28	31	27
Colostomy present	69	65	70	55	59	62	63
Years since surgery							
1–5	58	65	59	46	44	47	53
6–10	23	23	23	30	27	18	24
11+	19	12	18	24	29	35	23

rectum after excision of the cancer and anastomosis, that is, the removal of part of the intestine or bowel (referred to subsequently as 'anastomosed patients'). About half the patients were within one and five years of diagnosis and treatment, about a quarter within six and ten years and a quarter had survived for more than ten years. The demographic and socioeconomic characteristics of the population studied and their years since surgery are shown in Table 8.1

A third (34 per cent) of the patients were aged under 65 years, 38 per cent were between ages 65 and 74, and 28 per cent were over 75 years. Three-fifths of the patients were married, although only 18 per cent of women aged 75 and over were married. More than a quarter lived alone; again the oldest women were disadvantaged in this respect, with more than half living alone. Two-thirds of patients had left school at age 14 or younger. Among patients under retirement age, a quarter of men and three-fifths of women were not in employment. The majority of patients had a household income of under £60 a week (1982 prices), the proportion rising to 90 per cent of very elderly women. More than half the patients owned their home, about a quarter were council tenants, and a fifth were renting privately.

Patients in this survey were likely to be long-term residents of their community, .o have at least one relative living in the neighbourhood or in London, and to be in contact with the relative at least once a week. However, 14 per cent of patients were isolated indoors, in that they left the house less than once a week, the proportion rising to 31 per cent in older women. Colostomy patients were more than twice as likely as those with anastomoses to be isolated indoors. A quarter of patients left the house less often than before bowel surgery, and while 45 per cent of them attributed this to the bowel condition, the rest blamed old age or disability. The frequency of contact with friends and relatives was not associated with the presence of a colostomy; in the majority of cases (84 per cent), the pattern of social relations had remained unchanged since bowel surgery. Although the great majority of patients maintained contact with the outside world by means of television (93 per cent) and newspapers (83 per cent), more than a third had, since surgery, lost interest in their customary non-family activities and more than half participated less in activities outside the home. Colostomy was associated both with reduced interest and participation in customary outside activities, as Table 8.2 shows.

THE IMPACT OF CANCER

Respondents reported a variety of symptoms, some general, some specific, to rectal cancer. More than a quarter of respondents did not sleep well, a fifth had a poor appetite and 40 per cent had low energy

Table 8.2   *Social Activities by Age, Sex and Colostomy*

| | Age <65 | | Age 65–74 | | 75+ | | Colostomy | | Total |
	M (n=64) %	F (n=52) %	M (n=80) %	F (n=80) %	M (n=66) %	F (n=78) %	Yes (n=265) %	No (n=155) %	(n=420) %
Leaves house < once a week	8	14	4	13	14	31	18	8	14
Sees relatives < once a month	17	10	23	26	22	16	17	24	20
Sees friends < once a month	19	26	24	26	39	31	27	29	28
Loss of interest in social activities	36	27	36	34	38	56	43	31	38
Less participation in social activities	45	38	65	53	64	74	63	49	57

Age v. leaves house, less participation $p<0.001$; v. sees friends, less interest, $p<0.05$; v. sees relatives not significant.
Sex v. leaves house, less participation $p<0.001$; v. less interest, $p<0.05$; v. sees friends, sees friends not significant.
Colostomy v. leaves house, less participation, $p<0.01$; v. less interest, $p<0.05$; v. sees relatives, sees friends not significant.

levels. A third were in pain in the fortnight preceding the interview. Four-fifths of respondents had another chronic ailment or impairment apart from rectal cancer, the most common being arthritis, and three-quarters regularly used one or more medicines. Multiple illnesses were more common in those over 75 years (35 per cent) than in younger patients (20 per cent). The tendency to 'normalize' chronic illness is well illustrated by these patients. When asked to assess their physical health, 71 per cent of respondents said that in comparison with others of their age, their own physical health was good or excellent. There were no significant differences when age, sex, or the presence of a colostomy were taken into account.

In addition to generalized symptoms and other ailments, patients suffered from a number of specific complications of bowel surgery such as excessive uncontrollable flatus, malodorous stools, urinary complaints and diarrhoea. All of these symptoms may produce feelings of shame and embarrassment especially in public.

SEXUAL PROBLEMS

A common side-effect of bowel surgery is loss of sexual capacity. Less than half the patients were physically capable of sexual activity. Compared with anastomosed patients, those with a colostomy were more likely to lack sexual capacity (61 v. 42 per cent) and to ascribe this to their bowel condition (50 v. 17 per cent). As one man said: 'Since my operation I just can't seem to do it.' The proportions of those stating that they were incapable of sexual intercourse increased significantly with age (widows and single women over 65 were not asked about sexual activity). Table 8.3 provides a summary of the findings. Among those without sexual capacity, 54 per cent of men and 20 per cent of women considered this a complication of surgery. The others blamed old age and other ailments. 'What do you expect at my time of life?' commented a 77-year-old man.

When asked about the degree to which they were interested in sex, 57 per cent of men and 76 per cent of women stated that sex was not at all important to them. As with sexual capacity, interest in sex declined with age. Colostomy patients did not differ significantly in their interest in sex from those with an anastomosis. Forty per cent of men and 20 per cent of women felt that their bowel condition was responsible for reducing their interest in sex and this perception was more common in younger men and women. Those with a colostomy were more likely to ascribe reduced sexual interest to their bowel condition (36 per cent) than those with an anastomosis (20 per cent). Although impotence in men is often a result of nerve damage during extensive bowel surgery, women are also affected and some of the problem is likely to be as much a consequence of shame and

Table 8.3 *Sexual Capacity and Interest in Sex by Age, Sex and Colostomy*

	<65 M (n=64) %	<65 F (n=45) %	Age 65–74 M (n=80) %	Age 65–74 F (n=44) %	75+ M (n=66) %	75+ F (n=14) %	Colostomy Yes (n=206) %	Colostomy No (n=107) %	Total (n=313) %
No capacity	49	19	58	43	75	81	61	42	54
No interest	26	47	59	79	87	87	69	62	67

Age v. no capacity, no interest $p<0.001$.
Sex v. no capacity, no interest $p<0.001$.
Colostomy v. no capacity $p<0.01$; v. no interest not significant.

embarrassment as of physiological damage. These feelings can have a profound effect on the patient's self-esteem and alter family relationships. As one woman remarked: 'I feel so embarrassed about my body, I can't think that anyone would want to with me.' A man said: 'I've just lost interest – fancy making love when your colostomy is working.' Another said: 'We just don't want to these days. We've slept in separate beds since my operation.'

DEPRESSION AND ANXIETY

Against this backdrop it was not surprising to find that, based on the Leeds scales, 25 per cent of respondents were classified as depressed and 26 per cent as anxious, as shown in Table 8.4. Depression and anxiety, both overall and severe, were observed most commonly in women under age 65. A colostomy was not associated with the presence of anxiety or depression overall. However, significantly more colostomy patients were severely depressed. Anxiety, as a clinical category, but not depression, declined significantly with the number of years since surgery, apparently as the threat of death from cancer receded with each additional year of survival.

DISABLEMENT AND SUPPORT

A minority of respondents (16 per cent) were disabled in that they could not carry out routine household tasks. For the most part, disabled respondents mobilized their friends and relatives to perform personal and household tasks. In connection with the most frequent disabilities, 70 per cent of those unable to walk outdoors unaided depended on a relative for assistance and a further 9 per cent on a friend. Of those who did not travel without assistance, nearly two-thirds could count on the help of a relative and a further 12 per cent called on a friend. Similar high proportions of those who could not carry out routine household tasks depended on their relatives and friends. In the case of domestic tasks, relatives from outside the household contributed a considerable amount of support.

Partly as a result of two major disabilities, which both involved restrictions on venturing from home, the elderly, in particular the oldest women, were at greatest risk of becoming isolated. Those who lacked friends and relatives to help them (20 per cent) were very likely to be dependent on the social services and other formal supports. And, in fact, the bulk of social service support was given to the elderly disabled among the survey population.

Even among respondents who appeared to be in need and yet were not in receipt of services, there was little expressed demand. Nearly all who did not receive services said they neither needed nor wanted them. Nevertheless, the health visitor interviewers identified 15 per

Table 8.4 *Emotional State by Age, Sex and Colostomy*

| | <65 | | Age 65–74 | | 75+ | | Colostomy | | Total |
	M (n=64) %	F (n=52) %	M (n=80) %	F (n=80) %	M (n=66) %	F (n=78) %	Yes (n=265) %	No (n=155) %	(n=420) %
Depressed	22	39	18	26	17	31	26	24	25
Severe	3	13	1	3	1	7	6	1	4
Anxious	31	40	17	30	18	20	28	23	26
Severe	1	13	0	5	1	2	4	2	3

Age v. depression, severe depression, anxiety, severe anxiety $p<0.05$.
Sex v. depression, severe depression, anxiety, severe anxiety $p<0.05$.
Colostomy v. depression, anxiety, severe anxiety not significant.
Colostomy v. severe depression $p<0.05$.

cent of cases – most of them colostomy patients – as having immediate urgent unmet needs for medical, nursing, or social services. (They were able to arrange services for them.) This disparity revealed, in part, the extent to which these patients were unwilling or unable to make use of available services. It suggests that more intensive professional monitoring of patients at home would increase demands on the services to some extent, but would also improve patient care.

COMMUNICATION AND SATISFACTION WITH SERVICES

The results with regard to satisfaction with services also suggest that patients were unwilling or unable to complain. Most respondents were satisfied in general terms with the services they received. Those who were not, tended to acknowledge their dissatisfaction to the interviewers but felt that there was no way of resolving their complaints. This is because most dissatisfaction was with the quality and quantity of professional–patient communication.

Some dissatisfaction revolved around not being taken seriously by the GP. One women said:

> He's very abrupt. He never listens to me. He always thinks it's my nerves. There's nothing I can do.

Other patients complained about the consultant's apparent unwillingness to acknowledge that the patient knows something about his or her own condition. One man commented:

> He doesn't care what I say. He thinks I'm mucking him around. I don't know what to do. It never enters his head – he's such a know-all.

Evidently, these sorts of dissatisfactions were extremely difficult for patients to formulate and articulate, and even more difficult to complain about. The survey findings indicated that a fifth of those respondents who wanted discussions with their doctors in hospital, or in the community, were not satisfied with the level of communication.

THE HOSPITAL EXPERIENCE

More specifically, upwards of a quarter of patients, particularly those with a colostomy, expressed dissatisfaction with what they were told about the operation, and a fifth complained that they were not told enough about the bowel condition while in hospital. Lack of preparation for the possible consequences of surgery and the colostomy meant that the first reaction to the stoma of nearly half the colostomy patients was shock, fright, disbelief, or despair. By contrast some accepted the colostomy as a necessary part of treatment and these patients tended to have been well prepared in advance for the possibility.

Memories remained vivid. The experience of horror at the thought of a mutilated body and an unnatural anus is illustrated by the comments of two patients. One woman, eight years after surgery, said:

I wanted to die – I told him [the surgeon] not to let me live like this – they made that ugly thing on my perfect body – I got some glass and tried to cut it off.

A man, ten years after surgery, said:

I didn't look at it for weeks – but when I saw it, I thought it was horrible and unnatural.

Others were more stoic, but still upset. A woman, five years after surgery, commented:

I wanted to learn how to manage it [the colostomy] because I wanted to go home – but I shall never get used to it.

However, some patients were less affected. A man, two years after surgery, recalled:

Well, I just accepted it – I knew it had to be done.

Some patients complained about insufficient information. A woman said:

I should have been told what a big operation it was, what a risk it was. They said I would need to wear a bag, but I didn't know what a colostomy was.

Another said:

They never told me I wouldn't be able to control it [bowel motions]. Nobody explained it to me.

By contrast, others didn't want to know. A man recalled:

I didn't want to know anything. I knew I had cancer and I left it all to the doctors.

Some patients felt they were pressured into surgery. A woman remarked:

> I didn't want to have it. I said I couldn't live with it. My husband said I was to have it, and that was that.

COMMUNICATION AFTER DISCHARGE

Communication is also difficult when there is little continuity of follow-up care. More than half the respondents were attended by a different doctor at each surgical follow-up, although more than a quarter of these patients definitely would have preferred to be attended by the same doctor.

In the community, nearly half the patients had had no discussions about the bowel condition with their general practitioner since leaving hospital, at least one year and a median of four years before they were interviewed. Anastomosed patients, especially, said that their doctor had not discussed the bowel condition with them. Moreover, the great majority of patients had not communicated with other community professionals about their condition.

No respondent, except for a few who complained of delay in diagnosis, had anything but the deepest appreciation of the high quality of clinical care and treatment they received. Nevertheless, dissatisfaction was closely related to the perception of poor physical, emotional and social health, to feelings of stigma, and to the presence of specific medical problems and disability. That is, despite verbalized gratitude, those with less favourable outcomes were more dissatisfied. The evidence of this study suggests that patients' well-being could be enhanced considerably by more and better communication with health-care professionals in hospital and in the community.

PERCEIVED STIGMA AND ITS CORRELATES

The several measures of perceived stigma devised for this study revealed that some rectal cancer patients did not feel stigmatized by their condition, as is shown in Table 8.5. However, younger patients, particularly younger men, were more at risk of feeling stigmatized than older patients, according to the stigma self-rating measure and the indicator of quality of married life. The effects on family relationships were marked among these patients. One man commented:

> It has put a barrier between us. We have no sex life. The atmosphere has changed. We always think about health.

Table 8.5 *Stigma self-rating and supplementary questions by age, sex and colostomy*

	<65		Age 65–74		75+		Colostomy Yes	No	Total
	M (n=64) %	F (n=52) %	M (n=80) %	F (n=80) %	M (n=66) %	F (n=78) %	(n=265) %	(n=155) %	(n=420) %
Stigma self-rating									
Some stigma	57	53	46	51	31	58	54	41	49
Severe stigma	22	30	12	12	6	17	26	13	16
Feelings about self worse	40	39	24	33	40	43	43	27	37
Appearance worse when fully dressed	11	21	10	19	11	23	20	9	16
Married life worse*	48	27	27	27	19	9	29	14	23

* Single people and those divorced or widowed before surgery were not asked this question.

Age v. some stigma p<0.01; v. severe stigma p<0.01; v. feelings about self and appearance not significant; v. married life p<0.001.

Sex v. some stigma and appearance p<0.01; v. severe stigma p<0.01; v. married life p<0.001; v. feelings about self not significant.

Colostomy v. some stigma and appearance p<0.05; v. severe stigma and appearance p<0.01; v. feelings about self and married life p<0.001.

Another said:

The colostomy disgusts my wife. She won't sleep with me.

A woman remarked:

We have separate rooms now, but I'm much more dependent on my husband.

Women of all ages were vulnerable to the self-consciousness and embarrassment of a noticeably changed appearance. One woman said: 'I feel with a fitted dress everyone can see it [the colostomy].' Another commented: 'I know people can see the bulge [of the colostomy]; I have to wear loose and shapeless dresses.' Another remarked: 'It [the colostomy] shows on one side unless I cover it up with a loose jumper.'

The indicator of lowered self-esteem did not vary with age and sex, but showed, like all the stigma indicators, that colostomy patients felt more stigmatized than those with anastomoses. Many men and women felt that they had been assaulted and made to feel unclean. The symbolic meaning of the surgery and fear of pollution (Douglas, 1966) is very evident. A woman said:

I don't like going out among people. I lack confidence – I'm embarrassed all the time.

Another woman said:

I feel dirty – I never feel clean. I think having a colostomy is like when you read in the paper of girls being raped. I feel like that.

Another remarked:

I feel apprehensive when I go out of the house. I never used to – I feel terrible.

One man commented:

It's not the same. I always feel embarrassed in company.

Another said:

I used to be very lively and now I'm all inside myself.

Another recalled:

> It's ruined my life. I worry about letting myself get dirty or smelly.

As a result of these feelings, many colostomy patients tried to conceal the fact that they had a stoma, even from health professionals. Fewer than half said that the stoma had been seen by their GP or by a district nurse. Many even concealed it from their husbands or wives. A third had never shown the colostomy to their spouse and more than four-fifths had never shown it to anyone else outside the hospital.

Although a tenth of those with colostomies followed no special routine for a day out, a tenth were so concerned with concealment that they never left home for a full day. The others took extra supplies of underclothing, cotton wool and colostomy bags, fasted or used drugs in preparation. A quarter of colostomy patients said that the stoma still worried or offended them and half that it had drastically altered their way of life.

The fear of exposure restricted many patients' lives. Many of the emotional and social problems reported by colostomy patients were perceived by themselves as arising from shame and embarrassment caused by noise and odours from the stoma, fears of offending other people, and self-disgust at the need to handle bags of faeces and to clean faeces from the front of the body.

Some respondents were acutely anxious in public. One man said:

> I get embarrassed in other people's houses. I'll use the toilet – I have to take supplies and bags with me. It takes long, and I don't like to ask people where I can dispose of the bag.

A woman remarked:

> If I go for a meal, I have to tell them I can't eat certain foods, it makes me uncomfortable.

Another said:

> It has created an embarrassment especially when I pass wind in company. It's not easy to accept a dinner invitation or go on holiday.

However, if a colostomy were the sole reason for feelings of stigma, those without a colostomy would not feel stigmatized. Yet a considerable proportion of anastomosed patients also felt stigmatized. The

Table 8.6   *Correlation Coefficients: Stigma with Other Variables by Colostomy*

| | Colostomy | | |
	Yes ($n = 265$)	No ($n = 155$)	Total ($n = 420$)
Quality of life variables			
Poor physical health	0.40[c]	0.42[c]	0.40[c]
Poor emotional health	0.65[c]	0.73[c]	0.67[c]
Poor social health	0.28[c]	0.20[c]	0.25[c]
Clinical variables			
More specific medical problems	0.36[c]	0.29[c]	0.34[c]
More disablement	0.25[c]	0.12[d]	0.22[c]
Buffer variables			
More service use	0.04[d]	0.24[b]	0.10[a]
Less satisfaction with services	0.22[c]	0.18[b]	0.21[c]
Less personal/social resources	0.08[d]	0.01[d]	0.06[d]

[a]$p<0.05$ [b]$p<0.01$ [c]$p<0.001$ [d]not significant

following section shows the association between feelings of stigma and other variables for colostomy and anastomosed patients separately.

STIGMA AND OTHER VARIABLES

Table 8.6 shows the relation between feelings of stigma and the summary variables obtained by principal component analysis for colostomy patients and anastomosed patients separately. The highest correlations occurred between feelings of stigma and poor emotional health for both groups of patients. Specifically those who felt stigmatized were much more likely to have perceived their emotional health as poor (39 v. 12 per cent) and to have scored as clinically depressed (38 v. 12 per cent) or anxious (42 v. 10 per cent). They were more likely to have had a self-reported 'nervous breakdown' since surgery (12 v. 3 per cent).

Feelings of stigma and poor physical health were also correlated. Perception of poor physical health was more closely associated with feelings of stigma in anastomosed than colostomy patients (47 v. 37 per cent). In both groups, the proportion of patients who did not feel stigmatized but who none the less perceived poor physical health was substantially lower (17 per cent). Feelings of stigma and poor social health were more highly correlated in patients with a colostomy than in those with an anastomosis. Feeling stigmatized was not associated with levels of social interaction between patients and friends and relatives, but, particularly among colostomy patients, was associated with restriction of other social activities. Those who felt stigmatized were more likely to leave the house less frequently than once a week (24 v. 10 per cent), to be less interested in customary social activities (53 v. 30 per cent), and to participate in them less (73 v. 51 per cent). In the anastomosed group, the same tendencies were observed, but the differences did not reach statistical significance.

Feeling stigmatized was correlated with the presence of specific medical problems. In both groups of patients, those who felt stigmatized were more likely to sleep poorly (34 v. 23 per cent), to have a poor appetite (27 v. 11 per cent), and to have low energy (47 v. 33 per cent). Feelings of stigma among colostomy patients was associated with pain (44 v. 28 per cent), sexual incapacity (67 v. 55 per cent), other complications of surgery (58 v. 46 per cent), the use of analgesics (45 v. 27 per cent), and the use of tranquillizers (14 v. 4 per cent).

Feelings of stigma were also significantly correlated with the inability to carry out routine domestic tasks among colostomy patients (27 v. 15 per cent), but the correlation between stigma and frequent use of services was higher in anastomosed than in colostomy patients.

Having a job, higher income, a higher social and housing class, and other socioeconomic factors did not appear to buffer any category of rectal cancer patient against feeling stigmatized by their condition. The better-off were, of course, immune from the dependency attached to poverty, unemployment, council housing, the negotiations required to receive cash benefits, and the like. But, evidently, the felt stigma of cancer and a mutilated body was powerful enough to overcome the protection of privileged social position.

There is clear evidence from this study that feelings of stigma are closely associated with behaviour, but in a selective way. In terms of personal relationships, both those who did and those who did not feel stigmatized maintained close and frequent contact with family members and friends. Also, feelings of stigma were not associated with having a job: the same proportion in both groups were working. However, in the realm of recreational activities outside the home, and interest and participation in informal community life, those who felt stigmatized were much more likely to have cut themselves off, particularly if they had a colostomy. This sort of isolation may indeed represent secondary deviance (Lemert, 1951).

It is not possible to provide definitive answers to the problem of stigma management because this study did not investigate other persons' attitudes and behaviour towards rectal cancer and colostomy. However, those who felt stigmatized were significantly more likely to complain that their GP did not discuss things sufficiently with them (39 v. 23 per cent) and that they saw a different doctor each time they attended hospital (38 v. 19 per cent). These findings suggest that professional attitudes and the organization of care play some part in the stigmatization of these patients.

Discussion

In concentrating on the social consequences of chronic and degenerative disease and the often cumulative complications of radical surgery, this study has tried to avoid the purist sociological insistence on illness as solely a social problem. Undoubtedly, sociology's strong focus on illness as deviance and on stigma as a consequence has been valuable, because it has helped to show how the broad definition of health proposed by the World Health Organization (1958) can be spelled out in terms of the suffering produced by the social patterning of illness. Nevertheless, labelling theory as the explanation of ill health and stigmatization is as partial in its own way as the medical model which it seeks to replace. It was not the intention of this study to replace the medicalization of social problems by a sociology of medical problems which would argue that they are not medical at all (Illich, 1975).

Although it would be expected that years since surgery would have an important effect on quality of life, a surprising finding of this study was that controlling for survival time did not add appreciably to an understanding of the needs and problems of respondents. It appears that patterns of adaptation to cancer and colostomy become fixed soon after surgery and do not vary greatly after that. This suggests that whatever pre- and post-operative preparation, advice and services are offered to rectal cancer patients may affect them throughout the remainder of their lives. Although a number of specific physical problems related to colostomy appeared to diminish with longer survival time, the results showed that most patients with problems continued to have them. Therefore care and advice should not be confined to the early years after diagnosis and treatment, but should be continued even for long-term survivors who may need help.

A central problem for social policy and service planning is how to strike a balance between promotion of voluntary aid and its replacement by statutory services. It is evident from this study that much goodwill and readiness to help was found among friends and relatives of those in need, but there is always a danger that official provisions could be rationed so as to exploit this voluntary aid. Certainly, it cannot be argued that voluntary aid is always necessarily better than official services, for family and friends may give help in such an idiosyncratic and even haphazard way that it could often be provided more routinely and more expertly by statutory agencies.

The results of this study suggest that it is a lack of available relatives as much as a lack of active goodwill, which justifies the argument that the state must complement and supplement the efforts of volunteer help. Whatever the interaction between compassion and availability, and whether or not respondents lived alone, a fifth had little or no contact with their relatives elsewhere or had no living relatives, and would sooner or later become heavily dependent on state services. This extreme category is a strong argument for state services playing a part in supporting the elderly in need in the community.

However, the utilization of formal services itself involves ambivalent attitudes, of rights on the one hand, and fears of dependency on the other. Unless the particular category of service recipients is represented by an effective pressure group, or is incorporated into a universalistic political culture which affirms service as a right such ambivalence will continue. However, in the case of rectal cancer patients, no such solidarity has evolved and, given their short life expectancy, there seems little prospect of their adopting such protective organization or winning such universalistic recognition along with other chronically ill and elderly patients. Indeed the Colostomy Welfare Group in Britain is simply a secretariat which sends out volunteers to visit individual colostomy patients. No meetings or group activities are held.

Yet, many rectal cancer patients live reasonably normal lives and are not overwhelmed by their condition. The colostomy patients among them learn to accommodate to their stomas relatively well and most carry on their usual activities despite their problems. Some patients have physical, emotional and social problems that are as much a consequence of ageing and accumulating chronic ailments as of having cancer and perhaps a colostomy. A large fraction of patients, however, suffer from a poor quality of life because of their experience of the stigma of cancer and colostomy.

Results of this study strongly suggest that the most important improvement in care should be more sensitive and thoughtful attention to the frequency and quality of communication with patients. It is difficult to interpret the findings about lack of communication with patients, except in the light of professional reluctance to talk about cancer. The problem of what, and how much, to tell cancer patients about their diagnosis continues to cause controversy. In the present study, interviewers did not use the word 'cancer', nor did it appear on the interview schedule or in any letters to patients. Although it is not possible to determine if respondents who did not spontaneously mention cancer were actually aware of their diagnosis, half of those with a colostomy and a third of those without, spontaneously mentioned this diagnosis. Moreover, more than 10 per cent expressed gratitude that they had been told about cancer and more than 10 per cent complained that they had not been told. Some patients complained that discussions had been held with members of the family instead of with themselves directly.

The evidence about the harmful effects of stigma is clear. Therefore, particular efforts are needed to help patients with mutilating or disfiguring disabilities and those suffering from cancer to resist the additional burdens of stigma and its social and psychological effects. Although this has been an evaluation of cancer care, controlling for cancer of a particular site, it is likely that patients suffering from other cancers and other chronic disabling and degenerative conditions have similar unmet needs for improved communication and professional awareness of the damaging effects of stigma.

References

Ablon, J. (1981) 'Stigmatized health conditions', *Social Science and Medicine*, 15B, 5–9.

Arluke, A., Kennedy, L., and Kessler, R. C. (1979), 'Re-examining the sick-role concept: an empirical assessment', *Journal of Health and Social Behaviour*, vol. 20, pp. 30–6.

Brown, J., Varsamis, J., Loews, J., and Shane, M. (1974), 'Psychiatry and oncology: a review', *Journal of the Canadian Psychiatric Association*, vol. 19, pp. 219–30.

Douglas, M. (1966), *Purity and Danger: An Analysis of the Concepts of Pollution and Taboo* (London: Routledge & Kegan Paul).

Freidson, E. (1970), *Profession of Medicine: A Study of the Sociology of Applied Knowledge* (New York: Dodd, Mead).

Garrad, J., and Bennett, A. E. (1971), 'A validated interview schedule for use in population surveys of chronic disease and disability', *British Journal of Preventive and Social Medicine*, vol. 25, pp. 97–104.

Goligher, J. C. (1975), *Surgery of the Anus, Rectum and Colon* (3rd edn) (London: Baillière Tindall).

Haney, C. A. (1977), 'Illness behaviour and psychosocial correlates of cancer', *Social Science and Medicine*, vol. 11, pp. 223–8.

Heald, R. J. (1980), 'Towards fewer colostomies – the impact of circular stapling devices on the surgery of rectal cancer in a district hospital', *British Journal of Surgery*, vol. 60, pp. 198–200.

Illich, I. (1975), *Medical Nemesis: The Expropriation of Health* (London: Calder & Boyars).

Johnson, J. E., Morrisey, J. F., and Leventhal, H. (1973), 'Psychological preparation for an endoscope examination', *Gastro-intestinal Endoscopy*, vol. 19, pp. 180–2.

Kovar, M. G. (1977), 'Health of the elderly and the use of health services', *Public Health Reports*, vol. 92, pp. 9–19.

Lemert, E. M. (1951), *Social Pathology* (New York: McGraw-Hill).

Lynch, J. J. (1977), *The Broken Heart: The Medical Consequences of Loneliness* (New York: Basic Books).

MacArthur, C., and Smith, A. (1984), 'Factors associated with speed of diagnosis, referral and treatment in colo-rectal cancer', *Journal of Epidemiology and Community Health*, vol. 38, pp. 122–6.

MacDonald, L. D., and Anderson, H. R. (1984), 'Stigma in patients with rectal cancer: a community study', *Journal of Epidemiology and Community Health*, vol. 38, pp. 284–90.

MacDonald, L. D., and Anderson, H. R. (1985), 'The health of rectal cancer patients in the community', *European Journal of Surgical Oncology*, vol. 110, pp. 235–41.

McKeown, T. (1976), *The Role of Medicine: Dream, Mirage, or Nemesis?* (London: Nuffield Provincial Hospitals Trust).

McPeek, B., Gilbert, J., and Mosteller, F. (1977), 'The end result quality of life', in J. Bunker, B. Barnes and F. Mosteller (eds) *Costs, Risks and Benefits of Surgery* (New York: Oxford University Press).

Office of Population Censuses and Surveys (1981), *Cancer Statistics: Incidence, Survival and Mortality in England and Wales*, SMP5 (43) (London: HMSO).

Office of Population Censuses and Surveys (1984), *Deaths by Cause*, OPCS Monitor, Ref. DH2, 84/2. (London: Government Statistical Service).

Orbach, C. E., and Tallent, N. T. (1965), 'Modification of perceived body and body concept following the construction of a colostomy', *Archives of General Psychiatry*, vol. 12, pp. 126–35.

Pinker, R. (1973), *Social Theory and Social Policy* (London: Heinemann Educational).

Snaith, R. P., Bridge, G. W. K., and Hamilton, M. (1976), 'The Leeds Scales for the self-assessment of anxiety and depression', *British Journal of Psychiatry*, vol. 128, pp. 156–65.

Sontag, S. (1977), *Illness as Metaphor* (New York: Farrar, Strauss & Giroux).

Speck, P. (1978), *Loss and Grief in Medicine* (London: Baillière Tindall).

Wan, T. T. H., and Soifer, H. (1974), 'Determinants of physician utilization: a causal analysis', *Journal of Health and Social Behaviour*, vol. 15, pp. 100–8.

Wilson-Barnett, J. (1978), 'Patients' emotional responses to barium x-rays', *Journal of Advanced Nursing*, vol. 3, pp. 37–46.

World Health Organisation (1958), *The First Ten Years of the World Health Organisation* (Geneva: WHO).

Wynder, E. L. (1983), 'Dietary fat and fibre and colon cancer', *Seminars in Oncology*, vol. 10, pp. 264–72.

Zahn, M. A. (1973), 'Incapacity, impotence and invisible impairment: their effects upon interpersonal relations', *Journal of Health and Social Behaviour*, vol. 14, pp. 115–23.

9 Living with Renal Failure on Home Haemodialysis

JOHN MORGAN

Introduction: Renal Failure and its Treatments

Renal failure is a serious condition, causing death if it is not treated promptly. Normally functioning kidneys remove excess fluid and waste products from the blood and convert them to urine for excretion. When this function is impaired, the waste products accumulate in the blood in poisonous concentrations, causing unpleasant symptoms including tiredness, headaches, dizziness and nausea. Loss of renal function may occur quickly or over many years. The ideal treatment is transplantation of a functioning kidney from a donor or cadaver: it completely replaces the function of the failed kidney, and has none of the serious restrictions of other treatments. If there are no post-operative complications, the individual should be restored to normal life within a few weeks. The success rate is relatively good nowadays: in European countries about 60–70 per cent of the transplanted kidneys last at least three years, and about 90 per cent of patients with a transplant survive for at least three years (Kramer *et al.*, 1985, pp. 30–1).

Not all people with renal failure can be treated with transplantation. There is a shortage of kidneys, as well as surgical facilities, and it might be several years before a person can receive a transplant. If the transplanted kidney fails, another form of treatment will be needed, even if only temporarily. For some people with renal failure, transplantation may be contra-indicated for medical reasons, while for others, the risks of transplantation are judged to be unacceptable and they opt for alternative treatments which they see as safer, even if less than ideal. In 1983, 56 per cent of people treated for renal failure in the United Kingdom were being treated by methods other than

Table 9.1   *Current Treatment of People with Renal Failure in the UK*

Current treatment	% of those being treated 31 December 1983* (Total number=8559)
Transplanted kidney	44
Peritoneal dialysis	15
Hospital haemodialysis	17
Home haemodialysis	23

* % of those treated by renal replacement therapy.
Source: Kramer *et al.*, 1985, p. 13.

transplantation (Table 9.1); almost all people with transplants would have been treated by other methods at some time. None of these other methods is completely satisfactory, since renal function is only partly replaced, and all methods require a significant modification of life-style permanently, or until transplantation. Where some renal function is retained, conservative treatment using drugs, severe dietary restrictions, and limited fluid intake may be adequate. Complete renal failure requires treatment by dialysis, either peritoneal dialysis using the lining of the abdomen to filter out waste products from the blood; or by haemodialysis, in which the individual's blood is passed through an artificial kidney (a 'kidney machine'). Until recently, peritoneal dialysis has usually been a hospital-based treatment, but the development of continuous ambulatory peritoneal dialysis (CAPD) means that many more people with renal failure can be treated at home by this method (Gokal, 1986, provides an up-to-date account of this technique and its implications).

HAEMODIALYSIS

Haemodialysis has been a major long-term treatment for people with renal failure for some time. Currently, about 40 per cent of UK patients receiving treatment for renal failure are treated this way (see Table 9.1); this proportion is much lower than in the early 1970s, when transplantations and (especially) peritoneal dialysis were less well developed (Brunner *et al.*, 1972).

The treatment is carried out two or three times a week for a total of 12–30 hours, depending on the system used. The artificial kidney and a control and monitoring unit together make up the 'kidney machine'. A variety of artificial kidneys are in use: some, now in widespread use, are disposable after each treatment, while others are re-usable after careful cleaning and reconstruction. The patient's blood system is connected to the artificial kidney by two tubes. These are long enough to permit some degree of movement around the equipment (roughly a radius of 5 or 6 feet), although patients are normally on a bed or in a reclining armchair during dialysis. Access to the patient's blood system is usually effected by one of two methods. One way is to connect the blood lines to a semi-permanent 'shunt', which is basically two short tubes connected surgically into a vein and an artery in one of the patient's limbs. A successful shunt may last for several months or more. The alternative method, which is now more common, is to connect the blood lines to two hollow needles, which are then inserted into a vein which has been artificially distended by a minor surgical operation for this purpose (a 'fistula'). The insertion of the needles ('needling') is done with the aid of a local anaesthetic, and since the fistula is normally in one of the patient's forearms, 'needling' is more conveniently carried out by a nurse or helper, although some patients do 'needle' themselves.

Haemodialysis was first developed nearly thirty years ago, and in Britain it became available through the NHS in 1965. Although facilities were limited for a number of years afterwards, the position improved somewhat in the 1980s. By 1965, methods and equipment had been developed which also enabled suitable patients to carry out their treatment in their own home. For these people, the hospital renal unit was attended only for initial training, periodic check-ups, and for back-up treatment when things went wrong or in illness. The consequences for patients and their families of this form of treatment – home haemodialysis (HHD) – form the subject of this chapter.

In contrast to other European countries, the UK has always had a majority of haemodialysis patients on HHD. Whatever the benefits for patients and their families of home treatment over hospital, the balance in Britain for many years reflected the limited NHS resources available for treatment of renal failure: quite simply, HHD enabled more people to be treated (Robinson, 1978). For the NHS, home treatment was cheaper than a hospital, because it used patients' homes rather than hospital buildings, and patients and their helpers (usually a spouse) carried out the treatment rather than nursing staff. But, as we shall see, the demands made of patients and helpers by HHD are considerable; not all people with renal failure can meet them and some can only be given haemodialysis in hospital. The cost comparisons which favour HHD do so because only NHS costs are usually considered. Many of the costs falling to patients and their families – lost earnings, disruption of life-style and social relationships, for example – are difficult to compute and are not accounted for (see, for example, studies reviewed by Drummond, 1981).

In the early years of the HHD programme, each patient who could not be transferred to HHD meant a hospital place taken up (if one was available) which could in the long term have been used to train and support several home dialysis patients. Understandably, too, all concerned with this fairly novel treatment – patients, families, medical and nursing staff – were keen to see it succeed, with patients returning to their usual occupations and ways of life. A number of authors have used occupational rehabilitation (usually taken to mean employment rehabilitation) as the main measure of success (for example, Brynger *et al.*, 1980, pp. 51–4). The argument that home dialysis was an effective way of restoring people to the workforce, and enabling them to continue to support dependents, was one which was deployed to support allocation of greater resources to the programme (for example, Buxton and West, 1975). Moreover, these consider-ations played a large part in the way patients were selected for dialysis. The ideal patient was a young or middle-aged working man with a steady job, a supportive family, and otherwise in good health. Older people, for example, were unlikely to be accepted (and therefore died) until fairly recently: in the UK in 1975 only 8 per cent of new patients accepted for any type of renal replacement therapy were aged over 55, increasing to 19 per cent in 1979 and 35 per cent in 1983 (Kramer *et al.*, 1985, p. 17).

The way selection criteria were chosen, and ethical and other issues related to the method of selecting patients, are not our concern here. But it is important to note that the return to normality (especially occupational normality) became a major and often explicit goal from the early days of the programme. This had implications for the care and training of patients, and for the relationship between staff and patients (Alexander, 1976), as well as for the selection of patients for treatment.

A Study of HHD Patients

In 1973, following a discussion with a holiday neighbour who happened to be a renal physician, I made several visits to two renal units in the Midland. In both places, there was concern amongst unit staff that although a number of problems and risk factors affecting rehabilitation of HHD patients were known, there had not been a broader study of the lives of patients (and their families) on HHD. At that time, very little research had been done on the impact of HHD on the lives of patients and their families. Most studies were confined to patients and spouses, rather than the wider family. Several studies were by psychologists or psychiatrists (for example, Menzies and Stewart, 1968; Hassall, 1972). Typically, these examined the psychological impact on patients and spouses of the new uncertainties and restrictions in their lives as a result of HHD (depression, anxiety, marital disharmony, for example) and considered what professional support could be given to help. A much smaller number of studies had focused on the practical problems encountered in establishing patients at home (for example, Gordon and Cattell, 1970; Gower and Stubbs, 1971). But there was a growing realization amongst medical and nursing staff that conditions at home were important influences on the success of the treatment and of rehabilitation. Some renal unit staff were also becoming uneasy at the importance given to occupational rehabilitation as the principal measure of success (Gordon and Cattell, 1972).

In the summer of 1973, I conducted a short, descriptive study of the impact of HHD on the daily lives of patients and their families. The study was intended to provide a broader account than others had done, and hopefully (not being a care professional myself) provide a perspective closer to the concerns of patients and helpers.

AIMS AND METHOD

The aim of the study was to explore what were the costs and consequences of HHD for the lives of the patients and their families. What resources – financial, material, social – had they been able to draw on, and how had they used them, to deal with these consequences? The selection of these topics resulted from preliminary discussions with staff and a small number of patients at two renal units. It is worth emphasizing that the study focused on the impact of the *treatment* of renal failure, rather than the condition itself. Renal failure is fatal if untreated, and in that sense it is difficult to disentangle the effects of the disease from those of this particular treatment, which (imperfectly) replaces the function of the kidneys.

The study examined the experiences of forty-four patients from one renal unit in the Midlands (although extra insight was provided by visits to other renal units in the Midlands and London). Criteria for inclusion of patients in the study were that (1) they were currently being treated by HHD and (2) they had been first established at home for at least six months. Patients were interviewed using a semi-structured interview schedule, and interviews lasted between 45 minutes and 4 hours (mean 1.6 hours).

Nine patients were interviewed while dialysing. In eighteen interviews, the patient's helper (usually spouse) was present for all or most of the interview; in eight, for only part of the interview. Only one spouse-helper was seen separately. Three patients had parent-helpers, and in each case they were present through most of the interview. For nineteen patients, the helper was not seen at all or only briefly introduced. These differences were largely a result of the timing of interviews: when patients were interviewed during the day, helpers were more likely to be at work. The effect of this was that only one husband-helper was interviewed and some of the data therefore more strongly reflect the experiences and views of wife-helpers. Sensitive questions, about personal relations, for example, would have required separate interviews of the helpers. These questions were avoided, since only one interview per patient/partnership was possible in the time available. It is likely that the view obtained in joint interviews was more of a consensus: certainly, it was rare for strongly held conflicting views to be expressed. On the other hand, it enabled factual data to be cross-checked, and this happened (apparently with advantage) on a number of occasions. In some interviews, recall of detail was obviously limited for some questions; accuracy of memory is in any case a basic hazard of retrospective surveys. For those who had been on HHD for a number of years (eight had started HHD more than five years earlier), the task was clearly more difficult.

Conducting interviews in patients' homes, and the independence of the researcher were important factors in eliciting full and frank answers to questions. All respondents were clear I had come from Birmingham University and not from their renal unit, though they were also clear that I had visited the unit several times and had discussed the study with unit staff. The fact that respondents were critical about aspects of unit practice and sometimes even of individual staff suggests an acceptance of my independence and my assurances of confidentiality. Respondents were able to introduce their own topics and were encouraged to speak freely. None in the sample refused to be interviewed, and although three people were a little reticent, most respondents were very pleased to be interviewed and were glad to talk freely about their experiences.

THE RESPONDENTS

Tables 9.2–4 show some of the characteristics of the patient-respondents. Not surprisingly, these characteristics reflect the selection criteria operating in this renal unit (and many others) at the time. A sample of patients drawn more recently would contain more women, more elderly and young people, and more from ethnic minorities, for example. The majority of respondents in the study were middle-aged married men and a majority had dependent children. None had complicating illnesses when taken on to HHD, though a few had

Table 9.2   *Patients' Sex, Civil State and Dependent Children*

Sex	Married		Single	Total
	Dependent children	*No dependent children*		
Men	20	6	2	28
Women	9	4	3	16

Table 9.3   *Patients' Age*

Age	20–9	30–9	40–9	50–9
Patients	8	20	8	8

Table 9.4   *Time since HHD First Established (years)*

Years	½–1	1–2	2–3	32–4	4–5	5–6	6–6½
Patients	10	6	6	7	7	6	2

developed non-acute illnesses later (in addition to the expected conditions associated with renal failure). Time since they were first established on HHD was quite varied, ranging from six months to six and a half years. Clearly, longer-established patients were more likely to have experienced changes in their own condition. Seven patients had experienced a failed transplant.

THE PATIENT CAREER

In renal failure, HHD is one of several alternative treatments, and a patient may have been treated by other methods before becoming established on HHD. Even when established on HHD, the ability of patients and families to cope with home treatment and its consequences will probably change over time. The treatment itself will change as technical improvements are made, hopefully with benefits for patients. The method of treatment may change: a kidney transplant may become available, for example. The patient's own condition may change, and require extra treatment for other illnesses. In short, for people with renal failure and their families, the usual uncertainties of life are substantially added to.

This means that our understanding of the impact of renal failure and its treatment must encompass a long-term view. Medical sociologists use the idea of a 'patient career' to help understand this continuing experience. By using the term 'career', we are acknowledging the importance of considering future prospects as well as past experience in understanding the lives of people with chronic illness. By analogy with the occupational career, we are examining an individual's experience of living with chronic illness, as it affects his independence, status, and relationships with other people. For example, in the employment career it is possible to be promoted or made redundant, so the HHD patient may be 'promoted' to the greater independence (and risk) offered by treatment with a transplant; premature death, too, is a real possibility in these patients' careers. (See also Gerhardt, 1981, who develops the concept of career in relation to renal failure.) In Britain, the patient careers of many people with renal failure include periods of time with HHD treatment: it was these periods of their experience which provided the focus for the study.

Life on HHD

THE TRANSITION TO HHD

It is misleading to think of the transition from normal healthy life to the condition of living with a chronic illness as a simple, single-stage transition. In renal failure, this is particularly the case, since there are alternative treatments which may well change for a given individual over time, just as that individual's condition and ability to cope with the illness and treatment will also change. It may be helpful to begin by considering the simplest sequence of steps in the career of a patient who progresses from gradual renal failure through to well-established HHD without complication. There were a number of people like this in the study, and Mrs B is one example. After suffering partial kidney damage in her early twenties, she was maintained on conservative treatment for nearly twelve years. During this time, she married and had two children. Her kidneys finally failed and she was maintained on hospital haemodialysis for five months (as an out-patient for most of the period) and began HHD when she was 34 years old. She had been on HHD for six years when interviewed, without major problems. She regarded transplantation as too great a risk to take until her children were independent.

Five phases of this basic career can be distinguished:

(1) the onset of renal failure;
(2) hospital treatment for end-stage failure (that is, when there is little or no kidney function left);

(3) training for HHD (at hospital);
(4) the first weeks on HHD;
(5) HHD well established.

The onset of renal failure may happen very quickly or take several years. Clearly, a longer period allows for more gradual psychological and practical adaptation to the uncertainty and restrictions of the illness and its treatment, but it also has the price of a longer period of unpleasant symptoms, especially tiredness, headaches, and the rigours of conservative dietary treatment. *End-stage renal failure* is the second phase. It is a very short phase: the patient will die unless treated. If the patient is to be treated, he is taken into hospital (in 1973 treatment was not available for all people in end-stage failure and some died). Patients become seriously ill as end-stage failure is approached, and in the first and second phases they may well have to seriously limit or give up much normal activity: work, social and family responsibilities. Early treatment is beneficial in limiting this consequence (see also Auer, 1983), but depends on the availability of facilities. The certain knowledge that the condition is fatal, and the uncertainty of whether treatment will be available are causes of great anxiety for patients and spouses (or just patients, as the case may be) at this time. Spouses may have to bear the greater burden of this anxiety since the patient may be too ill to be much concerned (Hassall, 1972).

Once the patient is accepted on to the HHD programme, much of this anxiety gives way to gratitude and relief. After only one or two dialyses, the patient makes rapid recovery and enters the third phase, which is a *period of training and adjustment*. HHD requires a number of practical, psychological and social adjustments to be made by patients and their families. Many of the adjustments have to be made as soon as dialysis begins. For example, the dietary restrictions commence even before dialysis begins; psychological adjustments to the fact that life depends on the machine begin as soon as a patient knows that he is to be taken on the dialysis programme; homes have to be adapted and equipped and the technique of dialysis completely learnt before a patient can be established at home; and if the patient was a wage-earner, the financial adjustments begin on the day he loses his earnings or goes on to sickness benefit. All these things will affect the whole of the patient's household, not just the patient and helper. After a short time, if the patient is well enough to go home, he (and later the helper) can travel to the renal unit for dialysis sessions, though the travelling has time and cost consequences.

The fourth phase begins when training is complete and the first dialysis at home takes place. Typically, it seems to take up to six months from this point for patients to become well established. During this first six months they might encounter several emergencies or crises while dialysing – machine faults, mistakes made in the routines, technical and medical emergencies. All patients in the Midlands study told me that they had experienced such mishaps during this *initial period at home*; but 'it all seemed far worse at the time'. Once a regular routine for preparation, dialysis and clearing up had been established, together with the experience of one or two emergencies, almost all said that home dialysis became 'part of life', 'just routine' (see also Hudson, 1971, for an interesting discussion of this phase). It should be said, though, that very few patients were experiencing serious problems of employment, medical complications, or difficulties with family relationships; it is possible that they might have made a less benign judgement in more difficult circumstances.

At this point, the *transition to established HHD is completed* and the fifth phase is reached. The transition from first to fifth phase can take as little as six to nine months in straightforward cases. Others take much longer, especially if they have a transplant before being later established on HHD following failure of the transplanted kidney. Mr A's career is an example. He was an engineer, whose first symptoms appeared when he was 46 years old. He began getting frequent bouts of cramp and feeling tired; on holiday that year, he also noticed that he became breathless very quickly. In the following two years, his symptoms worsened and he lost more and more time off work. He was finally admitted to a renal unit and put on conservative treatment for two months (a special salt-free diet and very low fluid intake). At the end of this period, he commenced hospital haemodialysis on an out-patient basis and also began training with a view to establishing HHD. He took some time to adjust physiologically to dialysis, and had several in-patient spells at the renal unit. For the whole of this three-month period on dialysis, he was off work. Just as he was becoming competent with self-treatment he was given a kidney transplant. After a further two weeks he was discharged home feeling fit and well, though, because of drug therapy to prevent rejection of his transplanted kidney, he put on weight. Mr A returned to work.

Three years later (aged 52) his transplanted kidney began to fail, and after about six weeks he had to recommence hospital dialysis and training for HHD. Once again, though, he was given a transplant before starting home treatment (eleven weeks after beginning hospital dialysis); he returned to work. The second transplant also failed, after nearly three years: Mr A was now 55 years old. He began hospital dialysis again, and six weeks later was established on home treatment. At this point his employer offered him early retirement, which he accepted.

Mr A was 60 when interviewed. In the five years following the failure of his last transplant, he developed some of the long-term side-effects of dialysis: calcium deposits under the skin, and continuous severe itching. He hoped to have an operation on his parathyroid gland which might ameliorate these effects.

Mr A's experience is not *very* unusual. In the Midlands study there were seven people on HHD who had had one failed transplant, and five who had had complicated careers like Mr A.

As Mr A's case illustrates, the career continues even when the fifth phase of established HHD is reached: any or all of the patient's condition, treatment method, or means of coping, can change over succeeding years. Compared with the transitional phases, changes may be less frequent, though their impact may be no less sudden. In the Midlands study, I chose people who had reached the fifth phase and much of the discussions with them, and the data collected, related to this later period of their patient careers.

SOME CONSEQUENCES AND COSTS

HHD has a variety of consequences with which patients and their families have to cope; these vary between phases of the patient career. What follows is not intended as a comprehensive review: the focus is mainly on patient careers from the fifth phase onwards, when HHD was well established. One way of examining the impact of renal failure and HHD is in terms of the limitations placed on the lives of patients and their families: how is the potential to maintain and improve quality of life limited? Four ways in which this occurs are:

(1) diversion of resources from maintenance and improvement of quality of life to coping with the illness and its treatment:
(2) loss of some of these resources;
(3) uncertainty about future demands and resources available; and
(4) limitations on freedom of action and choice.

The resources considered here are personal energy and effort, money, and time.

People on dialysis suffer reduced physical fitness and loss of stamina. Haemodialysis produces chronic anaemia, which is a major cause of their fatigue, though periodic blood transfusions help mitigate this. The build-up of waste products in their blood between dialyses can also make them feel unwell. Indeed, some felt and looked permanently unwell, and some had developed other medical problems since beginning HHD (some unrelated to renal failure). If a patient has to cope with illnesses in addition to renal failure and HHD, such problems can become demoralizing and depressing. However, the majority of patients said they felt reasonably well (except immediately after dialysing), but they tired easily and were limited in their range of physical activities.

'Feeling well' or 'poorly' are, in any case, subjective experiences. In the (quite proper) pursuit of occupational rehabilitation and a return to some sort of normality, it is easy for care professionals to forget that patients may *feel* ill, and that their health is in a permanently precarious condition. Given also that patients are based at home and are self-treating, this oversight is not unexpected. As the unit's senior registrar observed: 'All the working patients are more than sick enough to warrant a doctor's note under normal circumstances' – a significant comment in the light of earlier observations about patient selection and pressure for rehabilitation. Nevertheless, some were surprisingly fit and lay people could probably not distinguish them from any other healthy adult.

In the Midlands study, all but one patient dialysed overnight (most were on a regime of 3 times per week for 10 hours each session), and loss of sleep exacerbated the problem of fatigue. Only a minority (32 per cent) said they usually slept well while dialysing; five (11 per cent) said that they would never try to sleep while dialysing in case something went wrong. For example, one person explained how, when he was dialysing in hospital, one of the blood lines came apart while he was asleep, and he had lost a quantity of blood before a nurse noticed and woke him up. Although machines have alarms to arouse patients in the event of such emergencies, this had not allayed his fears. Cramp could also disturb sleep and this seemed to affect a number of patients. Helpers generally slept much better than patients, although six (14 per cent) said they did not try to sleep when the patient was dialysing, even if the patient managed to get some sleep. Dialysis sessions have become much shorter since the early 1970s: 3 times per week for 4 hours each session is much more usual (Brynger *et al.*, 1980, p. 63) and enables dialysis to be completed during the evening. Removing the need to dialyse overnight will have been a substantial benefit.

Awareness of limited physical activity very much depended on what level of activity patients had been used to. For example, men who were in heavy manual work or played football regularly; women who played tennis frequently in the summer, or went dancing regularly: all were much more keenly aware of the effect of their condition on their physical activity than, say, an office worker whose major interest in life was stamp collecting, or the housewife who had always had daily help with the housework. Just over one-third of respondents had had to stop one or more major activities or interests, usually because they involved some sort of physical effort, and sometimes because they no longer had enough time. It is interesting that out of thirteen housewife patients, however, only five had arranged extra help with housework from outside of the household (two local authority home helps, two privately arranged helps, and one sibling). Most had extra help from relatives, but only on an occasional basis. The cost was mentioned by six as a constraint.

Such limitations are bad enough when they deprive patients of a major leisure activity, but they may be more problematic if they limit employment potential, and therefore income. This can happen in two ways. First, a patient may have been engaged in heavy manual work, for which he no longer has the strength or the stamina; or, secondly, whatever form of employment he is engaged in, he may be so weak and tired after the dialysis session (especially if he lost sleep) that he is unable to go directly to work, and may have to miss as much as a full morning's work, three times a week. Either case could (and did) lead to loss of employment or considerable reduction in earnings.

Nine patients who had been in full- or part-time employment had stopped work temporarily or permanently: three were working fathers and were seeking re-employment and the remaining six were women who had given up work for the foreseeable future. Two of these were young single women living with their parents, and four were working wives (two part-time) whose earnings had been important supplements to the family income. Of the nine patients out of work, or who had given up work, only one man said it was because he was too fatigued, although he expected to adjust to this and begin work later in the year (he had been home for only seven months). One woman said fatigue was part of the reason, although she had other medical problems. The remaining women said that dialysis chores took up so much time, they did not have 'enough time' to work now. However, all those who had had to change from full-time to part-time (four men and one woman) had done so entirely because of dialysis fatigue, which was aggravated in three cases by loss of sleep while dialysing. Two of these men were given lighter jobs (full-time) by their employers, and another had to find a new employer (he was with his third employer in two years since becoming established on HHD).

Superficially, the employment situation of the married men appeared to be fairly satisfactory – only three out of twenty-six were not working, and they hoped to be working in the near future. However, over one-third of the married men had experienced considerable or total loss of earnings. Even though the other two-thirds were earning the same or only slightly less than they had been before kidney failure, almost all of them believed that their earning *potential* had been affected. Most felt that because of their condition they could not now expect the same rate of promotion, and that they were also effectively tied to the same firm, since the chance of finding a new employer was believed to be poor for dialysis patients. Other patients were known to them who had lost their old jobs and had had great difficulty finding new positions.

The great majority of employers were reported to have been sympathetic to the plight of the patients, and in several cases where it was necessary, had either modified the job or found lighter or less demanding work for patients. A few patients were less fortunate: three had had their employment terminated. A fourth patient was made redundant just before he began dialysing at home (though not for that reason), and managed to find a new job only after a number of unsuccessful applications (which was regarded as unlucky in the early 1970s). Another man had been the production manager of a small company, and could not continue to hold the position because he found the strain too great (he tried to go back to the job, but collapsed in the first week). Nevertheless, the firm had been very sympathetic and continued to pay his salary for nearly a year, as well as offering part-time work if and when he wanted it.

Of all those still working, 62 per cent had remained with their old employers, and 24 per cent had successfully found new employment either full- or part-time. The search for new employment often took several months (in one case, two and a half years) and numerous unsuccessful applications. It was alleged that this was often because the applicant was a 'kidney patient' and the prospective employer 'did not want to take the risk', as one patient put it. There was no firm evidence that any one occupational group suffered this particular prejudice more than any other, but on the question of employment generally, heavy manual workers seemed much more likely to need job modification or change, and given an unsympathetic employer, could be faced with having to find new employment. On the question of earnings, the degree of loss depended to some extent on how sympathetic the employer was, but again, salaried staff on the whole suffered less than manual workers paid by the hour; not surprisingly those whose earnings had depended to a large extent on overtime or more highly paid night-shift work were also hit harder. (Gerhardt, 1985, found similar evidence of differential experience in her study of seventy men in the late 1970s.) These were the experiences of the late 1960s and early 1970s: it seems unlikely that many in the study would have fared as well in the 1980s.

In eight cases, reduction in the husband-patient's earnings had to some extent been compensated by his wife-helper going to work.

Seven helpers had begun work (five of them full-time) since their husbands had experienced kidney failure, to make up for their husbands' reduced earnings. One wife-helper had changed from part-time to full-time employment for the same reason (her husband had lost his job and was still unemployed after eighteen months). It is interesting to note that in only one case did a husband-helper lose earnings, and that through a change from night-shift to day-shift working, rather than shorter working hours. In a different arrangement 4 wife-helpers had given up jobs to spend more time on housework and dialysis chores, in order to help husband-patients maintain their working hours (see also Gerhardt, 1985).

Patients' helpers have important, though varying, functions in the management of dialysis. In the case of the married patients, the helper was always the patient's spouse; in the case of single patients, it was one or both parents. During the training programme at the unit studied, patients were encouraged to be completely independent of the hospital (except in emergencies), and as independent as possible of the helper, who should only help the patient to 'go on' the machine at the beginning of a dialysing session, to 'come off' at the end of the session, and to be available in an emergency. Part of the rationale of this emphasis on patient self-reliance was that where patients depend too heavily on spouse-helpers, the partnership can fail (see, for example, Hall, 1972, p. 138). In spite of this, I found that the majority of helpers (66 per cent) gave a considerable degree of help, and therefore time, at most or all stages in the dialysis routine. This suggests that couples worked out what was best for them, rather than what health professionals thought was appropriate. Several couples used phrases like 'team effort' and 'a partnership' in describing their arrangements, and in some cases, at least, it was clear that extra help with dialysis was seen as a way of giving the patient more time for other things: going to work, and time with the family were mentioned by several patients. Gerhardt, among others, has noted the importance of this type of support in enabling patients to remain in work. (Gerhardt, 1985).

Only a small minority of patients (10 per cent) received the minimal level of help from their helpers, for which patients were trained. In two cases, explanations were offered almost apologetically: 'He's got enough to do with his work', or 'she doesn't like blood and medical things'.

Preparation for dialysis, dialysis, and clearing up afterwards are the major regular time costs in the lives of patients and helpers. In the Midlands study, the time spent on dialysis 'chores' (everything except dialysis) varied considerably between patients. Nearly one-third of the patients said that preparation took 2½ hours or more; this included 'standing by' while the machine went through the sterilizing cycle, and probably accounts for much of the variety in the reported preparation time, since the cycle of some types of machine takes longer than others. Clearing up for the majority of patients (70 per cent) took no more than one hour, and in many cases, this part of the routine was completed before breakfast. Cleaning and rebuilding the artificial kidney took between 30 minutes and 1 hour for 80 percent of respondents.

Typically, then, dialysis chores were taking about 4 hours for each session – 12 hours weekly. Dialysis itself was a further 10 hours per session, so patients in the study were giving up 42 hours a week to dialysis sessions alone. When extra time is added for (usually infrequent) sessions which did not run smoothly, and for periodic visits to the renal unit for check-ups, there was a substantial loss of time. Patients were strongly encouraged to dialyse overnight, so that time loss for ordinary activities (work, leisure, time with family) was minimized, but even this arrangement effectively lost three evenings weekly. If sleep was seriously interrupted, overnight dialysis became much less advantageous.

Some Changes since 1973

In some respects, the experience of the patients and helpers in the Midlands study would be different today. For example, treatment facilities have expanded since 1973: more transplants are done, and it is now easier to start dialysis earlier in end-stage failure and avoid the debilitation and disruption to lives that afflicted the more seriously ill patients in the study. Since the early 1970s, there have also been significant changes in treatment methods which have reduced the time costs. In 1973, HHD made heavy demands on the time of patients and helpers which affected employment and social life. Disposable artificial kidneys would have saved them at least half an hour each session, and dialysis times could be 6 hours per session less. Total session times of about 12 hours would now be roughly halved; these are clearly substantial benefits.

There are other changes which would disadvantage them. For example, the employment prospects of the group would probably be worse, given the currently high rates of unemployment, especially in the Midlands. Employers would be less able to be generous in allowing time off or job modification. Finding a new job would be considerably more difficult. The patients' own condition could well have worsened since 1973, even if they have survived: unpleasant long-term side-effects of haemodialysis have steadily become apparent.

Uncertainty and Limited Choice

These examples of change over a thirteen-year period draw attention to the uncertainty of the patient career. All of us live uncertain lives, of course, but living with renal failure and its treatment multiplies those uncertainties. Respondents in the Midlands study – helpers and patients – were aware of this, and the topic invariably cropped up in a number of places during interviews. Three issues in particular seemed to highlight the heightened sense of uncertainty: employment prospects, social and holiday arrangements, and views about kidney transplantation.

The impact of illness and treatment on employment prospects and holidays and social arrangements illustrates well the problems of uncertainty and, linked to that, limitations on freedom of action and choice. Earlier, we saw that some patients felt tied to current employers because of uncertainty about the chances of finding another job at all, let alone a sympathetic employer as well. As Mr A's case illustrated, there was always the uncertainty of whether their relatively good health, and therefore their job, would continue.

One occasion when the total dependence of patients on dialysis was particularly felt was when families thought about holidays. Patients cannot safely continue for more than four days without dialysing, and this fact in itself rules out a traditional two-week family summer holiday free from dialysis. In addition there may also be complications over accommodation – the patient has to be certain of finding establishments which can cater for his diet (unless the family is on a self-catering holiday, of course). In 1973, the problem of regular dialysis on holiday had been partly solved by some renal units providing seaside (or countryside) dialysis facility; eleven units were known to have such facilities in 1973. The Midland renal unit had a Portakabin in the grounds of a hospital on the South Coast, containing the dialysis equipment, and beds for the patient and helper. Understandably, the heaviest users of this type of facility were those with dependent children. Since then, facilities of this type have expanded (Stout, 1985), and 'portable' kidney machines have been developed which allow greater flexibility.

For a considerable number of patients, however, a 'holiday' was not really a 'holiday' unless it was free of dialysis, and all patients without dependent children said that in 1974 they expected to take long weekends or four-day holidays, free from dialysis. Of those with children, over one-third said that although they hoped to have a Portakabin holiday in 1974, they would also try to take some additional period free from dialysis. But whatever arrangements they made, choice was limited to no more than four days without dialysis, or a longer period in special accommodation.

Uncertainty plays a part here, too. Like any other plans that these families made, last-minute disappointments had to be expected. An unsuccessful dialysis session immediately before going on holiday, or the night before a planned evening with friends, can mean that the plans have to be delayed for at least 24 hours so the patient can repeat the dialysis session successfully. Even when the holiday was under way, a problem during dialysis, or unexpected illness, could seriously disrupt or even terminate the holiday.

A successful transplant could remove all the limitations of freedom of action and choice, and all of the uncertainties of HHD. But there would still remain the uncertainty of whether the transplant would eventually fail, and whether the patient would survive the failure. Some patients had known individuals who had died after being transplanted, and for them, the sense of risk seemed heightened. If HHD was going well, a few patients decided the risk was too great and elected not to keep their names on the transplant list. One woman's view was typical of several patients (men and women). She had two young teenage children and said she would not consider a transplant until they had left home. Her husband's work took him away from home a great deal, and she was concerned that if there were complications, she might be in and out of hospital a lot. Death, too, was an appreciable, if small, risk which seemed to her unnecessary to take.

Some problems for the future   In the twenty years that the NHS has provided renal replacement therapy, a number of changes have occurred which have implications for our understanding of the impact of renal failure and its treatment on patients and their families; this should also guide the way care and support is provided for them. First, there have been a number of advances in medical knowledge and technology which have been beneficial for patients in the safety, flexibility and convenience of treatment: several of these have been mentioned already. Second, there has been some expansion of resources, although there are still shortages. These changes have both contributed to a third change in the composition and needs of the client group which has altered significantly since the early 1970s. Renal units can now be less selective in who they take on to renal replacement therapy. The consequence of this is a case load which will include patients for whom the impact of renal failure and its treatment is likely to be less easily coped with, since personal and family resources may already be absorbed in the task of coping with other illnesses or problems. Such people will require greater and more varied support from renal unit staff (see, for example, Bol-Vries, 1983; Auer, 1985). Their treatment also raises important questions about whether and how an acceptable quality of life can be maintained for such people. In a cost-limited health service there are also difficult ethical questions to be faced when attempting to allocate funds to the treatment of one group of patients rather than another.

A fourth change, which has received only limited attention in the literature, is the increasing numbers of people who have been on HHD for a very long time. In 1973, patients and partners who had been established on HHD for five or six years were generally satisfied with their circumstances. For them, HHD was 'the normal way of life now'; they had 'got used to it' or they 'didn't notice it, except when things went wrong'; it was 'no bother now, quite routine'. How many feel like this after, say, ten years or more? How much had this (apparently acceptable) 'new normality' been tainted by the development of unpleasant side-effects such as Mr A experienced? How has the recession of the 1980s affected them? It is possible that what was once seen as the routine of new normality has become relentless drudgery with the passage of time, and perhaps with the added disadvantage of unemployment and uncomfortable or painful side effects. A larger proportion of HHD patients will now have had one or more (failed) kidney transplants. What is the effect of this in the longer term?

A fifth change is the rise in unemployment. Occupational rehabilitation has remained an important goal for renal units and patients, although its definition appears to have broadened to include part-time work and even unpaid occupations. But part of the importance attached to the occupational rehabilitation goal was a belief that it actually helped patients and families to cope better, for example, by giving a sense of purpose and self-esteem, perhaps as a distraction from the treatment, and as a much needed source of income. Two questions arise: first, have patients on HHD fared worse than healthy individuals of comparable relevant characteristics (age, sex, qualifications, and so on)? Second, if unemployment amongst established HHD patients has increased, what effect has this had on their well-being? For example, Gerhardt (1985) discusses evidence suggesting that non-working patients have poorer survival rates than working patients. Reduced income must further limit life-style and choice for patients and their dependents. Employment, especially for men with dependents, is an important source of self-esteem and purpose. If employment helped to make life on HHD bearable, loss of employment must be felt particularly badly by patients.

Other changes could also be identified which have consequences for the quality of life and care of patients. But it is important to ask how far research evidence can enlighten us about the impact of such changes, and indicate appropriate responses. The heterogeneity of patients with renal failure makes them a difficult population to study if we are seeking generalizable and predictive findings rather than qualitative insights. The study reported by Hardiker *et al.* (1984) is a good example of an in-depth, small-scale, investigation which is rich in qualitative detail, and provides a basis for theory building rather than generalization (as the researchers intended). Earlier literature of the 1960s and early 1970s must be re-evaluated given the considerable changes since then. Much of this and more recent literature is written by authors who are practising care professionals, who have neither the time nor resources to conduct the larger-scale studies now needed. The time dimension is important, but is particularly difficult to study. This chapter has emphasized the importance of viewing the patients' experience as a career, which evolves over a number of years. Cross-sectional studies, even retrospective studies, cannot do justice to this dimension. In the future, we should attempt longitudinal or follow-up studies which can explore patient careers over a longer period.

References

Alexander, L. (1976), 'The double-bind theory and haemodialysis', *Archives of General Psychiatry*, vol. 33, pp. 1353–6.

Auer, J. (1983), 'Social and psychological implications of acute presentation in end-stage renal failure', in EDTNA, op. cit., pp. 67–8.

Auer, J. (1985), 'Quality of life of diabetics on renal replacement therapy: special problems need special solutions', in Stevens and Monkhouse, op. cit., pp. 96–9.

Bol-Vries, E. (1983), 'Psycho-social aspects of treating mentally handicapped patients with renal replacement therapy', in EDTNA, op. cit., pp. 48–51.

Brunner, F. P., Garland, H. J., Harlen, H., Scharer, K., and Parsons, F. M. (1972), 'Combined report on regular dialysis and transplantation in Europe, 1971', in *Proceedings of the 7th Conference of the European Dialysis and Transplant Association* (London: Pitman), p. 3.

Brynger, H., Brunner, F. P., Chantler, C., Donckerwolche, R. A., Jacobs,C., Kramer, P., Selwood, N. H., and Wing, A. J. (1980), in B. H. B. Robinson and J. B. Hawkins (eds) *Proceedings of the European Dialysis and Transplant Association*, vol. 17 (London: Pitman).

Buxton, M. J., and West, R. R. (1975), 'Cost-benefit analysis of long term haemodialysis for chronic renal failure', *British Medical Journal*, vol. 3, p. 376.

Drummond, M. F. (1981), *Studies in Economic Appraisal in Health Care*, (Oxford: Oxford University Press).

European Dialysis and Transplant Nurses Association (1983), *A Selection of*

Psycho-Social Papers Presented by Social Workers at EDTNA Conferences between 1973 and 1982, (Birmingham: British Association of Social Workers, for the European Dialysis and Transplant Nurses Association).

Farmer, C. H., Bewick, M., Parsons, V., and Snowden, S. A. (1979), 'Survival on home haemodialysis: its relationship with physical symptomatology, psychosocial background and psychiatric morbidity', *Psychological Medicine*, vol. 9, pp. 515–23.

Gerhardt, U. (1981), *Patient Careers in End Stage Renal Failure*. (Social Science Research Council end of grant report no. HR5013) (London: Social Science Research Council).

Gerhardt, U. (1985), 'Family rehabilitation in end-stage renal failure', in Stevens and Monkhouse, op. cit., pp. 87–95.

Gokal, R. (ed.), (1986), *Continuous Ambulatory Peritoneal Dialysis* (Edinburgh, Churchill Livingstone).

Gordon, P. (1972), 'No end of a treatment?', *New Scientist*, 9 November, pp. 326–9.

Gordon, P., and Cattell, W. R. (1970), 'Home conditions – the limiting factor in domiciliary dialysis', *Proceedings of the 7th Conference of the European Dialysis and Transplant Association* (London: Pitman).

Gordon, P., and Cattell, W. R. (1972), 'Blind spots in home dialysis', in *Proceedings of the 9th Conference of the European Dialysis and Transplant Association* (London: Pitman), pp. 35–41.

Gower, P. E., and Stubbs, R. K. T. (1971), 'Some administrative problems in adaptation of homes for home dialysis', *British Medical Journal*, vol. 3, p. 637.

Hall, G. H. (1972), 'Home dialysis for chronic renal failure', *Royal Society of Health Journal*, vol. 92, no. 3.

Hardiker, P., Pedley, J., Olley, D., Littlewood, J. L., and Walls, J. (1984), *Coping with Chronic Renal Failure* (Leicester: University of Leicester School of Social Work).

Hardiker, P., Pedley, J., Littlewood, J. L., and Olley, D. (1986), 'Coping with chronic renal failure', *British Journal of Social Work*, vol. 16, no. 2, pp. 203–22.

Hassall, C. (1972), 'Psychological problems in long-term care', in *Treatment of Renal Disease* (*Nursing Times* supplement) (London: Macmillan).

Hudson, K. (1971), 'Some social and emotional implications of dependence on machinery', *British Journal of Social Work*, vol. 1, no. 2.

Kramer, P., Broyer, M., Brunner, F. P., Brynger, H., Challah, S., Oules, R., Rizzoni, G., Selwood, N. H., Wing, A. J., and Bales, E. A. (1985), 'Combined report on regular dialysis and transplantation in Europe, XIV, 1983', in A. Davison and P. J. Guillou (eds) *Proceedings of the European Dialysis and Transplant Association*, vol. 21 (London: Pitman), pp. 5–63.

Menzies, I. C., and Stewart, W. K. (1968), 'Psychiatric observations on patients receiving regular dialysis treatment', *British Medical Journal*, vol. 1, p. 544.

Robinson, B. H. B. (1978), 'Selection of patients for dialysis and transplantation', in J. L. Anderton, F. M. Parsons and D. E. Jones, *Living with Renal Failure* (Lancaster: MTP Press).

Stevens, E., and Monkhouse, P. (eds) (1985), *Proceedings of the European Dialysis and Transplant Nurses Association*, vol. 13 (London: Pitman).
Stout, J. (1985), 'The EDTNA holiday project 1984', in E. Stevens and P. Monkhouse (eds) *Proceedings of the European Dialysis and Transplant Nurses Association*, vol. 13 (London: Pitman).

10 *The Experience of Psoriasis under Treatment*

RAY JOBLING

Psoriasis – a Chronic Skin Disorder

Psoriasis is a skin disorder which in varying degrees, affects some 1–2 per cent of the population, in other words in excess of a million people in Great Britain alone. It can take several forms but characteristically it shows itself as dull pink or red patches on the skin, which may be small or localized, and which commonly appear on the elbows, knees, or scalp. The lesions may be extensive and it is far from unusual for affected individuals to find huge areas of their bodies affected by the disorder. The patches of psoriasis become covered by distinctive silvery scales of skin which peel away constantly in a shower of fine dandruff-like dust, or in much larger pieces or snow-like flakes. Sufferers can experience itchiness or irritation, and the patches may crack open painfully. The temptation to touch or pick at the loose scales can lead to bleeding. There are complications of the condition including for a minority of sufferers a related form of arthritis. In rare cases of generalized exfoliative psoriasis, basic body functions may be interfered with (for example, temperature regulation) to an extent that seriously threatens the individual concerned.

The basic biological defects underlying psoriasis are imperfectly understood, although there is an inherited predisposition to it. 'Cure' is therefore not a possibility, and even control can be difficult. Clearance, albeit only partial, is possible, but is only temporary. Those experiencing an onset of psoriasis are likely to have to learn to live with a rather unpleasant chronic complaint (Jobling, 1977). For those only marginally affected this is a matter of no more than minor inconvenience. They may not be fully aware of it and therefore never seek professional medical diagnosis, treatment, or advice. However, those who experience more widespread psoriasis, or who find that it obtrudes into their everyday lives by interfering with physical, psychological, or social functioning inevitably consult their doctors. They also not only 'try' a rich variety of over-the-counter remedies, but consult practitioners of complementary medicine (homeopathy and acupuncture, for example).

Management of the physical and social impact of the condition is particularly crucial in view of the exceptional significance accorded to skin disease by the general public. Skin disorders generally offer one of the most striking examples of 'stigmatizing illness', and serious psoriasis has a number of special features which serve to mark it out as an exceptional case even within that broad designation. There is evidence for example that the biblical condition commonly translated as 'leprosy', was not in fact the disease now known as Hansen's disease, but rather psoriasis. Skin disease has connotations of *shame and guilt* in many cultures, and has long attracted social condemnation (Hulse, 1975).

Those who develop psoriasis are potentially challenged by semipermanent disfigurement, which is damaging to social attractiveness and self-esteem in the many circumstances where their lesions may be revealed to the world. Moreover, the constant shedding of an unusual, unaesthetic body product, namely waste skin, which is difficult to manage, makes self-presentation and a normal everyday life all the more difficult. Actual or anticipated threats of social rebuff abound. Additional to this comes the suspicion of culpability through poor personal hygiene; and the widespread perception of skin conditions as exceptionally infectious or contagious.

Psoriasis sufferers who are more than minimally affected seek medical help, not only in an effort to control the disease, at least in the basic sense of removing its symptoms, but also to demonstrate that they are indeed 'ill', and that they are accepting an obligation to do something about it. They seek treatment, therefore, for social as well as physical reasons (cf. Jobling and Coles, 1985). The course of the disease is none the less typically chronic, and it is commonplace for psoriasis patients to pursue a 'career' of treatment lasting many decades. For such individuals their experience of psoriasis is fundamentally shaped by their treatment regimens. These are typically demanding of time, of energy, of economic resources, and not least emotionally. Psoriasis, or more properly, 'psoriasis-as-treated', can be hard *work*. (Jobling, 1977, cf. the discussion by Strauss *et al.*, 1982.) The work-load falls not only upon the affected individual but also upon the family. Psoriasis is in this sense a condition of families as much as of individuals. Coping with the physical aspects of treatment, for example, application of ointments or laundering soiled linen, is one obvious element. The provision of psychological support is another. Families can also develop a coherent, understandable 'story-line' which explains the nature, origins and implications of the condition, so that contradictory information and meanings are not conveyed to outsiders. There is a recognition that the whole family, and not just an affected individual, is potentially at risk of stigmatizing misperceptions. Aspects of family life may well be organized around the control of information about one member's psoriasis. For example, family holidays may be chosen which exclude public bathing.

Family members may therefore become crucial to impression management and the presentation of the self, in individual efforts to counter stigma. They represent, moreover, a significant resource (and force) in the work performed at a collective level by psoriasis associations.

Psoriasis – Research and Analysis

There is a substantial medical literature on psoriasis, characterized by major controversies about its aetiology and the most appropriate and effective therapeutic regimens or modalities. Recently, interest has grown in the psychosocial aspects of the disease, and dermatologists in particular have become more conscious of the need to attend to the quality of life experienced by their patients. Typically, however, this stops short at little more than a straightforward recognition of the need to make ointments more aesthetically acceptable.

My own initial interest in the disorder stemmed from personal experience of it, and its treatment, over more than thirty years. Following a well-established tradition in the sociology of health and illness (cf. Roth, 1963), the primary impetus towards analysing aspects of that experience came during a period of in-patient hospital treatment. Subsequently the subjective experiences of psoriasis sufferers who were members of a 'self-help group', the Psoriasis Association, were the basis of an exploratory postal survey with 300 respondents (Jobling, 1976). This was developed in an interview study of thirty-five psoriasis patients attending out-patient skin clinics in a north London hospital and twenty patients in another in the English Midlands. Here the emphasis was upon the experience and impact of treatment rather than upon the 'biological' disease as such. The basic object of the enquiry was to compare the doctors' knowledge, understanding and evaluation of the treatment regimens with that of patients using them at home. A comparative element in the research became possible when patients, doctors, and nursing and other staff in psoriasis treatment centres in four other countries, were added in a major widening of the study. The principal research methods employed have been observation, unstructured interview, and participation in group discussion involving psoriasis patients, relatives, and professionals from a number of relevant occupations. Over a period of years, moreover, it has proved possible to draw upon participant observation in meetings of psoriasis associations not only in Great Britain, but a number of countries (the USA, the Scandinavian countries, Western Europe and Israel, in particular).

Two authors who themselves suffer from psoriasis and have received treatment for it over many years have written autobiographically and in fiction about both the disease and therapies. In the USA John Updike has published two fascinating *New Yorker* articles significantly entitled 'Journal of a leper' and 'At war with my skin' (Updike, 1955; 1976), which draw upon his own experience; and he has given the disorder to a leading character in his novel, *The Centaur* (Updike, 1963). The British writer Dennis Potter has discussed his own struggles with psoriasis and related arthritis in published interviews, in his television drama *The Singing Detective*, and similarly afflicted a character in the novel *Hide and Seek* (Potter, 1973). It is instructive and illuminating to draw upon the detail of these powerful and perceptive accounts grounded as they are in personal experience.

This research programme, spanning more than a decade, has brought into focus a number of different problems. One has been of recurring importance – the professional organization of illness by medical practitioners, in this case most especially specialist dermatologists; and the imposition of a routine 'work-load' upon psoriasis patients. The content, character and demands of patient work placed upon psoriasis sufferers derives very largely from the therapeutic theories and preferences of the doctors they consult and who manage (indeed direct) their 'case'.

This has been one of the 'classic' concerns of the sociology of medicine. Eliot Freidson, for example, in a celebrated discussion, wrote in relation to chronic illness (Freidson, 1975) that patients

> develop new organization of their lives, an organization flowing from the professionally-defined demands of their treatment . . . develop a round of life tempered by their own view of their illness and organized by the demands of regular professional observation and treatment of their difficulty. It is important to bear in mind that such a round of life is *not* organized by the disease and the biological incapacity it may produce, but by the professional conceptions of the disease and of what is needed to treat it: the disease becomes a professionally organized illness.   (pp. 311–12)

On entering the professional domain the patients have a given organization of experience, and even manifestations of the illness, imposed upon them. In common with those suffering from many other chronic illnesses, psoriasis patients become involved, long term, with doctors whose demands may seem simple in the consulting room, yet which impose an arduous regimen in the world of everyday life. As Freidson indicates, the social organization of treatment creates the conditions by which the experience of being ill, relationships with others when ill, and the life of the sick person become organized (Freidson, loc. cit.). The psoriasis sufferer must cope not simply with 'the biological entity' but psoriasis under particular forms of treatment. While undoubtedly part of the 'solution', therapeutic regimens are equally undeniably part of the 'problem'.

This simple but fundamental insight is ignored, or at best taken for granted by many dermatologists in relation to psoriasis and its treatment. They can be unaware of or inattentive to the implications of their therapeutic decisions and recommendations. These consequences may be substantial, not only in terms of the demanding work they are in effect expecting of their patients, but also through the impact made upon the interpretation of the meaning of the illness, and the effects that this has on the social reputation of the individuals concerned. Lay (non-medical) people and those among whom they must move in everyday life often have difficulty understanding or making sense of the disorder which afflicts them. 'What does it all mean?' is a perfectly reasonable question. If formally put to medical professionals, answers may not be forthcoming; or if they are, they may be confusing, difficult to understand, or couched in terms far from guaranteed to convey clear information to a lay person. It is scarcely surprising therefore that lay people fall back on a vernacular, 'folk' knowledge, supplemented by a common-sense reading of apparently significant messages or signs conveyed without any deliberate intent, by doctors, nurses and the like. Nurses in particular may sometimes be relied upon to decode the doings and sayings of doctors to a degree that might surprise them, with the least qualified auxiliaries being more important in this regard than fully qualified staff. The choice of treatment and its form is potentially a major source of information and a basis for interpretation by patients, relatives and the wider public (cf. Roth, 1963). The process of making sense of treatment may be at times a matter of intuition as much as intellect, and it is not too far-fetched to see it in quasi-anthropological terms as the decoding of systems of symbols. The rituals of psoriasis treatments deserve attention from those who would seek to understand the basis of the disease's pronounced stigmatizing effect.

Psoriasis – the Medical Treatments and their Implications

The psychosocial functions of the skin are similar to its physiological functions. On the one hand it represents the barrier between the person and the world and, on the other, a major point of contact and exchange with it. The skin is visibly the 'person' and the relationships of others to him or her are based in part on the visual impression it makes. More than this, as a visible organ which expresses emotion that is difficult to control, it has long been assumed that a disordered relationship of the person to the world, particularly a morally dubious or shameful relationship for which the person must bear blame, will show itself on the skin. Conversely a disordered skin hints strongly at a disordered or disorderly person who brings it upon himself. This guilt may be physical in the sense that culpable dirtiness may be alleged or it may be moral in basis, in which case 'dirtiness' or rather 'uncleanness' is thought to be rooted in misbehaviour or 'evil intent' (cf. Douglas, 1973). In either case those with skin disorder should, it is believed, quite properly feel ashamed.

There is no doubt that however unjustifiable in rational, factual terms, those with psoriasis do feel ashamed, guilty and in some cases deeply disturbed. The interview studies referred to earlier provided evidence of this. Asked the worst thing about having psoriasis, sufferers repeatedly respond in clear terms.

> Revulsion against one's body and a feeling of never being really clean.   (Man, 69 years, psoriasis for 20 years)

> One always feels unclean. In my young days I would never expose myself to view.   (Woman, 53 years, psoriasis for 30 years)

The constant shedding of skin scales is one aspect of this sense of uncleanliness.

> One feels unclean – with the constant shower of scales.
> (Woman, 44 years, psoriasis for 24 years)

> I have always felt a sense of shame. I feel it most when I look at my body. I try to hide it even from my friends, especially from friends in fact. But the scales make it difficult. It is such a dirty disease.
> (Woman, 70 years, psoriasis for 12 years)

The mingling of physical and moral concepts can be pronounced, illustrating the powerful stigmatizing potential of the condition.

The American novelist John Updike, himself a long-term sufferer, has expressed in dramatic imagery the impact of the disorder on self-esteem and the vulnerable feelings it generates (Updike, 1976):

> spots, plaques and avalanches of excess skin . . . expand and migrate across the body like lichen on a tombstone. I am silvery, scaly.
>
> Puddles of flakes form wherever I rest my flesh . . .
>
> The name of the disease, spiritually-speaking, is humiliation . . .
>
> They glance at me and glance away, pained.
>
> My hands and face mark me. In a month I can wear gloves. But even then my face will shout 'enormity': the livid spots beside my nose, the crumbs in my eyelashes, the scurvy patch slipping along my left cheek, the silver cupped in my ears.

Updike describes his life with psoriasis as 'a nightmare'. The British writer Dennis Potter (1976) expresses his feelings thus:

> I sometimes almost think that I've chosen my illness. Some people carry with them a very obscure sense of – if I say 'shame' you're bound to misunderstand, 'guilt' would be a better word, a metaphysical sense of my relationship to the world and therefore to God. My response to the world is one of 'anxiety', that's a better word than either 'shame' or 'guilt'.

'Sin' is a word preferred by another sufferer, who feels that it can be inherited through generations. The predisposition to psoriasis is of course genetically transmitted, a fact well known to psoriasis patients.

> My father was covered from head to foot. When he undressed the scales fell like snow and covered the carpets in white dust. The trouble goes back generations on my father's side; an ancestor being a wealthy squire, spent his adult life with any woman who cared to sleep with him, whether it be maid or servant, or even a hag. Hence it being a case of placing the sins of the father onto the children.   (Man, 72 years, psoriasis for 51 years)
>
> It is not easy to live with psoriasis because it is in some ways a reflection of ourselves, and we feel that we must be eternally on show as being miserable, wicked creatures, with visible signs of our inner wickedness.
>   (Anonymous contributor to a 'Living with Psoriasis' series)

The physical disorder is deeply felt to be moral guilt; and it is extremely difficult to control the incriminating evidence of pollution (cf. Reif 1975 on controlling polluting body products). The lesions are either openly on show, or there is a risk of chance disclosure. Preserving identity can involve sophisticated strategies of avoiding situations and settings involving such risk, or constantly covering up; but management of the skin flakes presents a complication.

In group discussion psoriasis sufferers often share experiences. The following comments were made during a tape-recorded discussion involving eight British psoriasis patients.

A: When I was a teenager fashions were difficult. There weren't as many long sleeve dresses. I suffered terrible embarrassment. I would buy two dresses a year. Because having braved one sortie to the shops I would not go again until I really needed them. It was too much of an ordeal. I like to buy my clothes in shops where I can pick it up and take it home, try it on, see how it looks . . . or I buy on a club.

B: I agree. I always think they are going to get something else out and come in the cubicle . . . I always think, God they're going to see it.

C: Changing rooms worry me. I won't use shops with big, shared changing rooms. You can't wear dresses you would like anyway. I wanted to buy a halter neck for a change, but of course I couldn't.

B: I don't buy dark clothes because the scales are light. Suede is a problem. Scales show up and you can't brush them off – unless you've remembered to carry a little brush in your handbag.

D: It's more embarrassing to go anywhere with a dark carpet. It shows up, and you leave a trail behind you.

A: Going away on holiday that's a time. You leave a trail in the bedroom. I always like a light carpet.

D: I take extra sheets with me. If they make the beds I don't want them to see it. You learn to cope like that. You don't want them to find a bed full of scales, or covered in grease.

The reference to the additional problem posed by 'grease' is important. It shows how the ointment treatments prescribed for psoriasis provoke their own additional burden. The discussion continues.

D: Finally we bought a caravan to get away from all that. My husband wanted it. He said I wasn't getting any break. In hotels I was always brushing, sweeping, cleaning up. I spent three quarters of the holiday clearing up after myself. And I was having to have nappies over the pillows to keep the grease off the hotel's linen. We use the caravan now.

The role played by spouses in joining forces to cope with problems is important. Their support is vital. It does evoke a further sense of guilt, however, about the burden being imposed on relatives. There is, too, the anxiety or disappointment caused by the unattractiveness of the condition, which affects even those benefiting from a secure relationship.

> I wanted to go to bed sweet smelling and not greasy. I didn't want to be a scaly, unattractive, smelly mess.
> (Woman, 53, psoriasis for 30+ years)

The ointment-based treatment regimens for psoriasis which have prevailed for decades generate an arduous demand, every day for weeks on end and hours of work, sometimes with little obvious reward. Moreover the regimens in their very nature can serve to reinforce the sense of disgrace involved in the disorder. Some patients do actually say that they feel they are being punished.

> I said to myself, 'Oh my God, what have I got myself into?'. The tar and pyjamas were dirty looking and stained. And they got worse – greasy and sticky. They are never washed. And then you have to strip in front of the doctor every day . . . It all felt like I was being punished really. (Hospital in-patient)

Life with psoriasis under treatment can become an embarrassing chore.

> The whole house, much to my embarrassment, filled with a pervading stink of tar, and my hair hung in matted, greasy, evil-smelling hanks! To make matters worse at least four applications of shampoo had to be used to remove the tarry grease to an extent where I could mix socially, and the psoriasis got no better! What's more, I seemed to spend half my leisure time in the bathroom.
> (Anonymous contributor to a 'Living with Psoriasis' series)

Many dermatologists are acutely aware of the dangers of committing a physical 'insult' to the skin in over-aggressive therapy. Yet they may be less than alert to the psychosocial insult they inflict upon their patients.

Even when clearance is near the patient rarely experiences the so-called 'remission' so often declared in dermatological research reports.

> In ten years I've been into hospital 12 times I think it is. The coal tar or dithranol [ointment] treatment cleared me up in 3–4 weeks. But even then I got no relief really. The ointment stained, 'burned', all my skin so that even though the psoriasis had gone I couldn't wear sleeveless dresses or skirts. By the time the stains had faded the psoriasis had come back.
>
> (Woman, 20 years, psoriasis for 12 years)

The psoriasis patient compelled to undergo long-term treatment both at home and perhaps with successive spells of hospitalization, involving experience of one of these regimens, suffers from the 'Sysyphus syndrome'. In Greek mythology Sysyphus was condemned by the gods for his misdemeanours to roll a huge boulder to the summit of a steep mountain. He laboured long and hard. Just as he achieved his objective the rock escaped his grasp and rolled to the bottom. Sysyphus was forced to begin again and again. He had neither relief nor satisfaction from ever accomplishing his task. So overwhelming may be the burden of the work involved in these ritualized tasks that the patients (and the co-workers in their households) almost collapse into the asylum and convalescence of the hospital ward which offers rest and recuperation just as much as formal 'treatment'. They need not only respite from the disease and the daily work of coping with it in ordinary social intercourse, but also from the rigours of the home-based ointment regimen. As they progress through the period of their stay not only are the efforts to improve their skin, but also to restore them to 'working fitness', that is, full capability to resume their self-care duties. Accordingly as time goes on during the hospitalization more and more is expected of them as active participants in the treatment process. Those judged to be fully fit in the general sense are required to start work on day one and be engaged in their own treatment. Nor is the work only physical. In a few highly specialized psoriasis treatment centres at least, patients must contribute formally to psychosocial tasks through involvement in group (therapeutic) sessions, and less formally through everyday interpersonal exchanges with other patients and staff.

The most widely applied topical treatments for psoriasis, the 'Goeckerman' tar/UV and 'Ingram' dithranol/UV regimens are often described as 'rituals'. They involve strict conformity over weeks, months, or even years, to a programme of repetitious, daily (even twice-daily) bathing, rubbing and scrubbing. This is followed by anointment with oils, creams, pastes, or ointments, some of which may involve a subjectively noxious smell. This may be done alone, or it may implicate others especially spouses or parents, in a co-operative 'observance' of the rituals. Regular exposure to the sun's rays (or at least an equivalent produced by a machine) is another component. All of this may take up to several hours a day. It all adds up to an extraordinary, demanding process bringing all too often, as we have seen, little by way of physical relief. Those involved in it, and those who constitute an audience for it, must ask themselves as they do of the disease itself, 'What does it all mean?'. Such a question may be voiced consciously and explicitly, or inwardly in a more latent way.

Certainly one must question the meaning of such involved, arduous duties to such little obvious positive end. Given the character and content of the regimens the outcome for many is a reinforcement of feelings of dirtiness and disgrace. Yet simultaneously and paradoxically this self-imposed feeling and experience of disgust followed by self-induced relief – the smearing in foul substances and the washing away of them – may be serving to handle the profound sense of 'guilt' which many psoriasis sufferers do have. To follow the anonymous author of an article in the *British Medical Journal* (1976), 'Washing away at acne', the washing is a 'ritual of purification'. So too perhaps is the sunbathing, just as the ointment is a ritual punishment. The 'healing' process has a symbolic character and may be as active at a psychosocial as it is at a physical level.

These ointment regimens for psoriasis have a psychosocial impact in at least three other ways. First, they may contribute to the shoring up of the person by the reinforcement of his apparently crumbling and dangerously vulnerable body boundary. I have touched upon this earlier. Second, even though the ritual/regimen is working far less than perfectly in its intended physical way, heavy involvement in it is indisputable evidence for oneself and significant others (family, colleagues and friends) that one has subjected oneself to patienthood. A heavy commitment to patient work under professional medical supervision provides socially acceptable essential proof of a 'genuine' physical illness. This is important because there is ambiguity about whether a ('mere') skin disorder 'counts' as illness in the ordinary sense, for the purposes of making allowances for the individual. It also demonstrates that one is working hard at doing something about it (albeit with only modest success), thereby showing willingness and commitment to do something by way of accepting the essential burden of adjustment. The disorder and its offensiveness must be visibly seen to be being attacked if not brought under complete control by the 'offender' himself. Erving Goffman (1963) among others has pointed to the importance of this in the process of managing stigma. It is an obligation imposed upon the obtrusively different as a minimum condition for continued, even partial, social acceptance. They work hard to show that they accept their offence and they are doing their best to expiate and atone for it, and to control it. Third, it is plausible that these ritualized routines serve to manage what psychologists have called cognitive dissonance. The anthropologist Victor Turner (1965) provides this insight for us.

All rituals have a fundamental common characteristic. They increase tolerance for cognitive dissonance. Those who participate in ritual become capable of combining an unrealistic expectation with an undesirable reality.

There are other therapeutic possibilities for those with chronic psoriasis all of which have social and psychological implications.

PUVA

During the last decade considerable interest has centred upon an innovation involving the oral administration of a drug (psoralen) and exposure to long-wave ultra-violet radiation (UVA). This process, known as photochemotherapy or PUVA (psoralen + UVA), relies upon the photosensitizing effect upon the skin of the drug. It produces not only distinctively pronounced tanning, but also a remedial effect upon psoriasis. Arguably it has promised much to patients, in that it frees them from the demand of daily ointment regimens, clears the condition relatively effectively and speedily, and is technically quite simple to administer. Unfortunately, if perhaps predictably, it does not work for all; it produces in some unwanted immediate side-effects or a worsening of their condition, and involves long-term statistical risks of mutagenicity and carcinogenicity. Although initially it was introduced on a trial 'experimental' basis, the speed and scale of its introduction as a therapy was dramatic. Thousands of psoriasis patients underwent PUVA, initially with enthusiasm. Freed from the chore of the Goeckerman or Ingram ointment regimens, and all they entailed, PUVA seemed a godsend. It worked and did so apparently painlessly. People literally moved their homes to be close to a clinic offering it.

John Updike, who underwent the treatment invested PUVA with near magical properties (Updike, 1976). Before PUVA the images attached by him to psoriasis and those afflicted by it (under 'topical' treatment) are instructive. They involve such terms as torture, loathsome, hate, humiliation, enormity, hideous, filthy, foul, untouchable, nightmarish, excrement and dreadful. After PUVA the emphasis shifts markedly and other terms come to the fore: miracle, passable, fair, beautiful, free, whole (Updike, 1976).

PUVA itself is referred to as 'the cleansing fire'. It is invested with magical, miraculous qualities. Yet ambiguity and uncertainties remain. There are side-effects. Updike now feels queasy and 'itches with subtle rage'. He worries about the disease being driven beneath the surface: 'fleeing to deeper tissue, and will wait there to be reborn in more devilish and loathsome form'. While he revels in current freedom from his psoriasis and dreams of continuing clearance, he fears that failure is bound to come. To be a 'PUVA failure' and taken off the treatment is to become 'a leper among lepers, doubly untouchable' (Updike, 1976).

This problem of losing what appeared to be a bright prospect of relief via a relatively simple process, after years of hard therapeutic work without much lasting benefit, has been commented on by Dutch psychologists who studied PUVA patients. They were found to have had unrealistic hopes, with an ever-present threat of being let down. A period of uncertainty which provoked high anxiety was followed by disappointment as the treatment failed. The outcome was depression and aggression (De Korte *et al.*, 1977). Failing on PUVA means to retrogress both physically and socially. It represents a significant demotion in one's therapeutic career (cf. Jobling, 1977). An American PUVA patient commented in an interview on what happened when the treatment began to make him sick, and exacerbated his condition.

I made an appointment to see the doctor. He really shocked me. I didn't expect him to nominate me for candidacy back here [a treatment programme relying upon coal tar ointment, baths and UVB]. I don't know what I expected but it wasn't that.

Updike's denial of access to PUVA when his doctor decides to remove him from the treatment had a serious impact. He regrets, too, that he can obtain it from nowhere else (Updike, 1976):

I cannot work, I cannot smile. I know now the box [the cabinet containing the UVA lights], that is the torture. It is there, out there a magical prism . . . Boston has a single hexagon of divine nectar, a decompression chamber admitting me to Paradise; and it is locked.

Later, having been returned to the PUVA programme and benefiting from it, he enjoys no sense of security for he fears that the disease will return. Perhaps worst of all, and most perceptively, he realizes that removal of his symptoms and freedom from the organizing disciplines of treatment represent a dramatically significant change which is not all for the better. The disorder has for so long been part of himself and his relationship to others. Now that it has gone he is a new person with a new relationship to the world and people in it (Updike, 1976):

> I feel between myself and my epidermis a gap, a thin space where a wedge of spiritual disassociation could be set.

He feels a personality change. It results in greater alienation rather than less. Others feel it too, and respond to him accordingly.

Some therapeutic staff have intuitively grasped that these problems exist, though others are insensitive to it. The technology of PUVA is 'cold' and on its own 'inhumane' by comparison with the interpersonal contact demanded by 'topical' ointment regimens. One American PUVA patient commented on it in discussion:

> There is no concern at all in the PUVA programme . . . sometimes I would try to talk to them [the staff] a little but I would never get any responses. They are just moving people in and out. That's a little cold – especially with something like psoriasis which is so stress related. You'd think they would want people to feel at ease.

Staff at another PUVA centre, however, are aware of patients' psychological needs:

> Here, if you touch the patients it's an extra, unlike in the hospital where you have to bathe them [as part of a Goeckerman regime]. So we try to make a point of it . . . I mean I'm touching someone and I'm a person. That helps them not to feel so bad about having a crumby skin disease. They expect you to want to avoid touching them. I can tell they like it [when you do] . . . I even touch the psoriasis . . . that's just my own philosophy, not necessarily the policy here . . . I guess that's the influence of my own nursing training.

This nurse went on to comment upon the pride that improving patients take in their bodies, to the extent that they begin to 'parade' their nudity beyond what is strictly required by the circumstances of treatment.

> I let them have their privacy if they want it, but once they feel good about their body they don't care.

Interestingly when PUVA was initially being officially researched in a major multi-centre trial in the USA, strict protocols were established to ensure that each centre delivered the treatment in identical terms. No one, however, apparently attended to the psychological and social components of the delivery of PUVA, and one centre did differ markedly from another. The results from the different centres varied considerably, and it is obviously possible that the psychosocial component played its part in this (cf. Jobling, 1978). PUVA has now become an established therapeutic option in many countries, although the initial optimism concerning its role in the management has become tempered by knowledge of its modest results and continuing anxieties concerning side-effects. There has been little further enquiry into the psychosocial aspects of it.

CLIMATOTHERAPY

Climatotherapy and thalassotherapy (treatment by sea bathing), while not numerically major treatment modalities for psoriasis in the USA or Britain, are more important on the continent of Europe. For Central Europeans they are a natural extension of spa treatments, which have continued to be important in Germany, for example. In the Nordic countries the state health authorities have funded therapeutic visits by psoriasis patients to the Israeli Dead Sea centre, the Canary Islands, and elsewhere, for some time. In recent years psoriasis patients have begun to bathe in one of Iceland's pools of naturally hot water, believing in the healing qualities of the water and its chemical constituents.

British patients do in growing numbers invest upwards of £1,000 for a course of treatment in Israel. Typically a Dead Sea treatment involves a 28-day stay. The 'scientific' basis of the modality is the screening out of much UVB 'burning' radiation and the consequential longer periods of exposure to UV therapy made possible. It is also possible that the mud which many patients apply to themselves, and the salts in the water in which they bathe have a therapeutic effect. Psychologically, too, relaxation, the great separation from the 'normal' world, the isolation and the quiet probably have an impact. Freedom to expose oneself completely to public view in the protected environment of the centre is also important, and equally, so is the collective sharing of feelings and experience with fellow sufferers in group settings. It is also likely that the very 'pilgrimage' to the 'healing' shores of the sea in the 'Holy Land' has significance for some. For many, such pilgrimages have become an annual event.

GROUP THERAPY

The only major modality for psoriasis to give calculated prominence to psychosocial factors and processes is psychotherapy, especially group therapy (Coles, 1965; 1967). It may involve closed group psychotherapy of an intense, demanding type. Or, it may take the form of relatively open group discussion, employed alone or in combination with other forms of treatment. The former, stronger version typically involves psychotherapists as such, and its setting and context is clinical psychology or psychiatry. Involvement with psychiatry is not without its reputational consequences for the psoriasis patient, for it may communicate (however 'falsely') to both patients and others, psychological weakness or sickness. To put the skin patient into the same connotational category as the psychiatric patient may bring some limited therapeutic benefit, but entails too great a risk of stigma 'fallout'. Even the very unusual, atypical, deviant nature of the therapy and therapists (albeit in the 'softer' form) may serve to reinforce the 'special' character of the disorder and the patient. Is it not better perhaps to be 'normally' ill and 'normally' treated, however unsatisfactorily? There are risks too that aggressively applied psychotherapy (individual or group) can be invasive, intruding further into the person than justified by the disorder itself. The treatment (just as with other modalities) can become more problematic than bargained for, and in some cases more so than the skin disorder prompting recourse to it.

However, the modality is attracting increased interest, and patients in particular are asserting its attractions. In Scandinavia, for example, psoriasis associations have promoted it and in the case of Finland they have participated in pilot schemes. It differs significantly from other modalities in setting improvement in the skin as such as only one objective, and making it perhaps only a minor one. More importance is given to subjective feelings, coping behaviour and life pattern. Regular, 'ritualized', involvement in small group discussion and activity, including public 'confession', expiation and forgiveness is of great interest. The theoretical or ideological basis of group therapy is provision for the creative use of morbid experience not in pursuit of 'cure' in the physical sense, nor even symptomatic control, but rather the general development and enhancement of the *whole person* involved. Health is defined not in terms of the absence of symptoms of disease, but more positively in terms of personal confidence and autonomy.

Contemporary group therapy for psoriasis parallels the biblical case of Job's illness, so brilliantly considered by Jack Kahn (1975). Stricken by skin disorder Job followed the cruel cultic rituals strictly, compulsively, obsessively, sacrificing and humiliating himself in a drive towards perfect wholeness, completeness and blamelessness (cf. Stekel, 1949). These fail him and he turns to comforters who 'ritually' share his dejection, sit by him, keep silence with him and act out his grief. They identify with him and provide group support and interaction which will finally draw from within him the resources with which he himself will construct his *own* 'cure'. The therapy consists of group experience, 'Job and his comforters', through which he abandons the striving towards physical perfection and achieves instead a more general state of health. In the process he enjoys a better quality of life.

A natural and logical extension of small group structures and processes is the development of wider association, which of course serves other purposes too. This extends the possibilities of the modality via collective organization, negotiation and work at the level of the community, society and even on an international stage (Coles and Jobling, 1985; cf. Duller and van Veen-Vietor, 1986). Psoriasis associations should be seen as an integral part of the therapeutic process in its widest sense. There are some signs that this fact is receiving increasing recognition among dermatologists, especially in terms of the contribution which may be made to psychosocial support processes, political advocacy, and co-operative endeavours with the interested professionals (Coles and Ryan, 1975; Jobling, 1978; Swanbeck and Jobling, 1984; Coles and Jobling, 1985).

Participation in small group discussion is undoubtedly helpful to the minority of psoriasis patients involved in it and to their relatives. It assists in long-term adaptation to the circumstances of a life with the disorder, as well as being vital in short-term crises. For many, however, recognition comes that individual adaptation is not enough, and that collective action to remove the sources of problems is imperative. Psoriasis associations therefore provide not only assistance at an individual level but, like many other self-help organizations move in the direction of mutual aid through social/political advocacy (Coles and Jobling, 1985). For a 'hard core' few part of the experience of the disorder is an active, public, representative career. This has been aptly termed 'adopting career patient status' (Jobling, 1977; cf. Gussow and Tracy, 1968).

Discussion

In the present state of knowledge psoriasis cannot be prevented or 'cured' in the sense of eliminated completely, so the objective set by doctors is realistically, containment. However, the drive for close-to-complete clearance of the symptoms on a relatively long-term basis dominates the lives of many (perhaps most) patients. It is, too, one of the fictions of dermatological practice that this is achievable. Thus patients' 'worlds' can be organized demandingly around the disciplines of treatment in a way which comes to dominate their everyday lives. Increasingly, however, dermatologists recognize that reaching a sensible balance between the disease and its treatment, weighing costs and benefits rationally, should be the objective. Such a process requires sophisticated two-way negotiation between therapists and patients, involving also family members who are a key element in the situation. More, it demands an understanding from all concerned that psoriasis is not only a physical 'biological' disorder, it is (in common with other skin disorders) a social and cultural phenomenon of considerable complexity. It must be seen as such, and dealt with as such, if a better quality of life is to be achieved for those directly affected by it. Information, knowledge and perspectives relevant to the psychological and social dimensions are essential (Jobling and Coles, 1985; Jobling, 1987a). Sociological and psychological concepts and analysis are also important to future developments in therapy. It is remarkable that despite the obvious 'social' implications of extensive, visible skin disease (like psoriasis) there has been so little formal sociological enquiry and analysis. Dermatologists have only rarely sought it from professional social scientists, and only slightly less rarely strayed into the field themselves, beyond a few simple enquiries and statements. Typically 'psychological' contributions to debate in dermatology (outside the specialized context of 'psychosomatic' disorders) attract scornful comment from the 'mainstream' of the profession. More substantial and more sophisticated sociological (and joint psychological and sociological) research should focus upon the questions of why skin disease should attract such intensely stigmatizing responses. Such enquiry is an essential prerequisite of attempts to mount 'counter-stigma' programmes (cf. Jobling, 1977). It must also probe more deeply into the illness behaviour of psoriasis sufferers, and their partners. Finally, as in this short paper, attention must be given to the ways in which the content and organization of therapy constitute social phenomena in their own right. Psoriasis as experienced in the lives of sufferers depends heavily upon its organization by professionals with given therapeutic approaches and ideologies. It almost goes without saying that patients' organizations, like the dozen or more national psoriasis associations around the world, must also be collectively self-reflective about the 'ideological' and social dimensions of the work which they do in the field.

Sociologists, too, have something to learn. There is a professional reluctance, to put it no stronger, to accept biological disease entities as diagnosed by doctors, as an acceptable basis for analysis. The sociology of a particular disease like psoriasis, or an organ-specific group of diseases like 'skin disorders', is a legitimate focus of enquiry if only because of the fact that people subjectively experience diseases as diagnosed, understood, treated, and responded to by the world. If sociologists are to speak to those they study, be understood, and have their lessons learned, this fact demands attention. The case of psoriasis illustrates the point.

Notes

1 Dennis Potter's *The Singing Detective* (1986) has been broadcast and published since the submission of this chapter. The drama has offered the public additional significant insight into the psychological and social impact of chronic severe psoriasis. Moreover, the character of the substantial press review and discussion of the television series has revealed some of the ways in which the mass media can play a major role in the attribution and amplification of stigmatizing connotations where disabilities and the disabled are concerned. For preliminary exploration of these processes in relation to *The Singing Detective* and psoriasis see Jobling (1986, 1987b). Gartner and Joe (1987) offer a more general discussion of the role of the media in the projection of images of the disabled.

References

British Medical Journal (1976), 'Washing away at acne' (editorial), 9 October.

Coles, R. B. (1965), 'The treatment of psoriasis in groups', *Medical World*, vol. 2, pp. 1–8.

Coles, R. B (1967), 'Group therapy in the skin department', *Transactions of St. John's Hospital Dermatological Society*, vol. 53, pp. 82–5.

Coles, R. B., and Jobling, Ray (1985), 'Associations for psoriatic patients', in H. H. Roenigk and H. I. Maibach (eds), *Psoriasis* (New York: Marcel Dekker), pp. 645–54.

Coles, R. B., and Ryan, T. D. (1975), 'The psoriasis sufferer in the community', *British Journal of Dermatology*, vol. 93, pp. 111.

De Korte, J., *et al.* (1977), 'Psychosocial aspects of PUVA-treated psoriasis patients', discussion paper.

Douglas, M. (1973), *Natural Symbols* (London: Penguin).

Duller, P., and M. van Veen-Vietor (1986), 'Psychosocial aspects', in P. D. Mier and P. C. M. van de Kerkhof (eds), *Textbook of Psoriasis* (Edinburgh: Churchill Livingstone), pp. 84–95.

Freidson, E. (1975), *Profession of Medicine* (New York: Dodd Mead).

Gartner, A., and Joe, T. (1987), *Images of the disabled, disabling images*, (New York: Praeger).

Goffman, E. (1963), *Stigma: Notes on the Management of Spoiled Identity* (London: Penguin).

Gussow, J., and Tracy, G. S. (1968), 'Status ideology and adaptation to stigmatized illness: a study of leprosy', *Human Organization*, vol. 27, pp. 316–25.

Hulse, E. V. (1975), 'The nature of biblical "leprosy" and the use of alternative medical terms in modern translations of the bible', *Palestine Exploration Quarterly*, vol. 107, pp. 87–105.

Jobling, R. G. (1976), 'Psoriasis – a preliminary questionnaire study of sufferers' subjective experience', *Clinical and Experimental Dermatology*, vol. 1, pp. 233–6.

Jobling, R. G. (1977), 'Learning to live with it: an account of dermatological illness and patienthood', in A. Davis and G. Horobin (eds), *Medical Encounters* (London: Croom Helm), pp. 72–86.

Jobling, R. G. (1978), 'Nursing, with and without professional nurses – the case of dermatology', in R. Dingwall and J. McIntosh (eds), *Readings in the Sociology of Nursing* (Edinburgh: Churchill Livingstone), pp. 181–95.

Jobling, R. G. (1986), 'Medicine and the media', *British Medical Journal*, vol. 293, pp. 1488–9.

Jobling, R. G. (1987a), 'How do you treat your patient? The patient's perspective', *Skin Forum*, vol. 6, pp. 1–2.

Jobling, R. G. (1987b), 'Medicine and the media', *British Medical Journal*, vol. 295, pp. 1054–5.

Jobling, R. G., and Coles, R. B. (1985), 'The skin patient – the need for information', *Dermatology in Practice*, December, 6–7.

Kahn, Jack (1975), *Job's Illness: Loss, Grief and Integration* (Oxford: Pergamon).

Potter, Dennis (1973), *Hide and Seek* (London: André Deutsch).

Potter, Dennis (1976), 'Wrestling with a vision', *Sunday Times* 18 November.

Potter, Dennis (1986), *The Singing Detective* (London: Faber & Faber). First broadcast on BBC TV November–December 1986.

Reif, Laura (1975), 'Ulcerative colitis – strategies for managing life', *American Journal of Nursing*, vol. 73, pp. 261–4.

Roth, Julius (1963), *Timetables* (Indianapolis: Bobbs-Merrill)

Shuster, Sam (1976), 'Biological purpose of acne', *Lancet*, 19 June, pp. 1325–9.

Stekel, W. (1949), *Compulsion and Doubt* (London: Heinemann).

Strauss, Anselm, Fagerhaugh, S., Suczek, B., and Wiener, C. (1982), 'The work of hospitalized patients', *Social Science and Medicine*, vol. 16, pp. 977–86.

Swanbeck, Gunnar, and Jobling, R. G. (1984), 'Organisation of psoriasis treatment and psychosocial aspects', *Acta Dermato-Venereologica*, supp. 112, pp. 61–3.

Turner, Victor (1965), 'The ritual process', in M. Gluckman (ed.), *Politics, Law and Ritual in Tribal Society* (Oxford: Oxford University Press).

Updike, John (1955), 'Personal history – at war with my skin', *New Yorker*, 2 September, pp. 39–57.

Updike, John (1963), *The Centaur* (London: André Deutsch).

Updike, John (1976), 'Journal of a leper', *New Yorker*, 19 July, pp. 28–32.

Wittkower, Eric, and Russell, Brian (1953), *Emotional Factors in Skin Disease* (London: Cassell).

Conclusion

In the opening paragraph of his review of trends in contemporary sociology, Giddens (1976) raises the question of how the discipline is regarded by the man or woman in the street. Although sociology offers a variety of 'critiques' of social institutions and other disciplines, it must, says Giddens, face up squarely to the charge of reproducing common sense and in a language remote from everyday experience or comprehension. Medical sociology, for example, may be prone to state the obvious about illness experience, or the doctor–patient relationship, in a form which irritates those concerned, when it is not ignored.

It is, therefore, with a sense of modesty that the present volume has been compiled. The editors and contributors have been aware of the limits as well as the strengths of research methods and their execution in the study of chronic illness. Indeed, much of what has been done in this field (particularly as represented in the present volume) seeks to establish the grounds for more systematic work. In developing a specifically *social* perspective on chronic illness (one that differs in important respects from both medical and psychological perspectives) it is clear that the complexities of experience are uncovered. This, however, is partly to be expected, given that such research has often stemmed from simplistic medical and psychological assumptions about the experiences of patients and their families.

Part of the task in hand is to give full recognition to these complexities without being overwhelmed by them. Though it is clear (at least on the evidence of the present volume) that severity of symptoms or formal diagnosis on the one hand, and 'coping' strategies or personality traits on the other, are inadequate by themselves for a full understanding, it is important that social research does not generate a sense of insurmountable and unsolvable problems. Such research is unlikely to be attractive to either lay or professional audiences unless a glimmer of optimism is visible.

It is intended that the present volume of essays should be read in this more positive light, in spite of the necessity of drawing attention to the real privations and difficulties faced by patients and their families. There has been a lack of published material providing a sociological perspective on specific disabling conditions, with a few notable exceptions (for example, Strauss, 1975), and it is with this in mind that the present volume has been produced.

At the same time, the methods of enquiry used here are varied, bringing together both qualitative and quantitative approaches, in an attempt to highlight the variety of responses and strategies employed by patients and their families. Although the realities of disease and disability have not been ignored (indeed, the contributors share the view that 'condition-specific' social research is important, if only because such categories are important to patients and carers) attention has been focused on the material, cognitive and emotional aspects of experience which go to make up the fabric of everyday life. The physical and functional limitations created by chronic illness will always be central to its experience, but, with the passage of time, social and emotional consequences may come to be more important, especially for the family.

The result of this approach has been to give particular emphasis to the meanings attached to chronic illness and to its consequences, as they unfold. The research reported here can thus be seen as an elaboration and extension of pioneering work of sociologists such as Strauss and Glaser (1975) in the USA and Blaxter (1976) in the UK, both of whom were concerned to develop a view of chronic illness and disability from the viewpoint of the sufferer, in contrast to official medical and administrative definitions. Their argument was that professional responses to patients' problems can only be appropriate when such meanings are *systematically* appreciated by professionals and when the latter have a more consistent approach to their role in this regard. Many of the contributors to the present volume emphasize in various ways this general point; the adequacy of health-care providers' recognition of psychosocial issues (indeed, claims to be experts in this field) can only be judged in relation to the display of worked-out approaches to them. Scambler (Chapter 7), for example, calls for an explicit 'ideology' which places everyday experience and meaning at the centre of a professional ethic (see, also, Kestenbaum, 1981).

Patients and their families need to feel confident that relevant information and support will be available from professionals when they turn to them. Of course, individual professionals do respond positively, but it is clear from the studies reported here that such support is often unsystematic, or based on inadequate understanding of the social realities of chronic conditions. Expectations do of course vary and some can be unrealistic, but at the least, those who are experts in chronic disease or disability should be able to appreciate the burdens sufferers and their carers carry. It is to a better understanding of these experiences that the present volume is directed.

Though medical and rehabilitative interventions may reduce impairments or the degree of disability, it is clear in many cases that there are real limits to such efforts. As stated at the outset, under such conditions it is the consequent disadvantage or *handicap* that really matters, and it is this which needs to be the centre of attention, both of providers and planners. It is frequently the social environment that determines the outcome of chronic illness and its impact on sufferers' and families' lives, and this approach to handicap has been a common theme running through the chapters. Having said that, let us specify a little more closely what the research and policy implications of this approach are.

Implications for Research

Contributors to the present volume have underlined the fact that many of the meanings attached to chronic illness are part of a range of strategies aimed at minimizing the deleterious effects of the *social responses* to chronic illness, as well as its ravages at the biological and psychological levels. In Pinder's and Kelleher's chapters, for example, we see patients making strenuous efforts to 'normalize' their symptoms and disabilities, though Kelleher shows the different meanings involved in normalizing. Normality may mean relegating diabetes to a minor part of life, or making it a 'normal' feature of adapted living.

Unlike professionals, patients *must* deal simultaneously with the biological and social dimensions of experience. In spite of an apparent wider acceptance and recognition of chronic illness and disability in modern society, efforts to deal with these reactions frequently produce substantial disadvantage. In a highly competitive and precarious environment this is hardly surprising; time spent on managing symptoms and treatment regimens cannot be used elsewhere. Individuals and their families do not have limitless resources, and part of the handicap produced by chronic illness is as the result of the redirection of these resources (see also Locker, 1983).

In attempting to broaden our understanding of the 'resource implications' of chronic illness, as viewed by patients and their families, therefore, it is important not to lose sight of the material issues which mean a great deal to patients, especially those concerning money and work. Chronic illness involves problems of immediate additional costs, as well as a threat to employment prospects. Several chapters in this volume, especially those by Morgan and

Robinson draw attention to such problems and this is clearly a matter of growing concern in a period of high unemployment. The impact of occupational social class and financial hardship on the 'social patterning' of chronic illness is important and received some attention in the period before the recent rise in unemployment (Conover, 1973; Townsend, 1979) but needs continual scrutiny. Substantial financial disadvantage stems from the experience of chronic illness and contributes to it, and it is important for sociological work not to lose sight of this fact (Bury, 1979; Whitehead, 1987).

It is also clear, from much of the research presented here, that gender has a considerable effect on illness experience. Robinson, Anderson and Bury, in particular, indicate the 'double disadvantage' that chronic illness may involve for women. Although changes in domestic roles are possible, and as Anderson shows, men can and do perform caring roles it is clear that women are particularly vulnerable to the effects of chronic illness; most starkly, Robinson shows that they are more likely to be abandoned following the onset of a chronic illness than men. Paradoxically, because women survive longer than men they are also more likely to be alone when chronic illness or disability occurs. In addition, women's 'survivorship' may itself create additional difficulties in that social attitudes may influence decisions about caring, and this may be reflected in the fact that the proportion of older men being cared for by their family is greater than that of women (Central Statistical Office, 1987). Though research has paid increasing attention to gender differences in welfare entitlement and caring, it has only just begun in relation to the experiences of health and illness and the use of health services.

That these experiences vary between social groups is hardly a surprising contention, though, as we have seen, systematic research is only now under way. In pursuing such tasks terminology needs to be consistent and where possible precise in its employment. The terms used to describe and delineate these experiences need to be handled with care, and where possible we have drawn on the approach adopted by the World Health Organization in 1980 (Wood, 1980). At the same time it is clear that health, chronic illness and disability are not mutually exclusive terms when seen from the patient's viewpoint. Official definitions may differ considerably from lay ones. As indicated earlier, individuals frequently 'normalize' by redefining their health status to incorporate their condition. Thus it is possible to be healthy and have a disability. The need for research on the ways in which patients and health-care providers define the problem at hand, and the outcomes of treatment under these conditions, is now being recognized and is underlined by the present volume.

In addition, the research presented here highlights the need to understand more fully the potential discrepancy between patients and their families in the way they view health and disability. Scambler and Robinson show, for example, that the reality and seriousness of a condition can be viewed quite differently by family members, and sometimes over long periods of time. Anderson and MacDonald also show that personality change or deterioration in interpersonal relationships may stem from the continuing effects of a condition or its treatment. The quality of lif' in chronic illness is contingent on a variety of social factors, aud these may change considerably over time, influencing both present circumstances, and most importantly, future outlook.

Providing, therefore, a summary of the quality of life of a patient and their family living with a chronic illness presents particular difficulties. Whereas Anderson, Badura and others have here tackled quality-of-life issues in their contributions, the present vogue amongst economists in particular for numerical summations, in order to inform decisions about 'best buys' in health care, needs to be treated with caution. It may have serious unintended consequences in the field of chronic illness and disability. The quality of life for many of those living with chronic illness is dependent on the lessening of its handicapping consequences, and this outcome is not a fixed entity.

Under such conditions, reductionist exercises in quality-of-life research may only add insult to injury. What may be a significant amount of change to someone with a chronic illness (a lessening of anxiety over money or a marital relationship, for example) may appear marginal or not measurable on a calculus constructed from the outside. This may, of course, amount to a call for better measurement and this is an issue raised by contributors here. However, the overall emphasis in this volume has been to call for a clearer recognition of the uncertainties in experience. It is this which health-care providers need to understand and tackle, if they are to improve the quality of life of patients and their carers.

The quality of life in chronic illness, then, is a product of complex interactions between subjective health, disability and the social environment in which the individual lives. It is on these interactions that the research presented here has concentrated. Several of the contributors have also emphasized one other element in the picture which often goes unrecognized, namely treatment. Living with a chronic illness involves not only changes in the body, and the responses of significant others to them, it also means, in most instances, dealing with medical treatments and their effects. As medical treatments are developed and applied more widely they become a feature of living with illness in their own right. Thus, strategic decisions about the disguising or displaying of symptoms become caught up with the handling of treatment regimens. Living with renal failure, diabetes, or psoriasis all involve important, indeed critical, day-to-day decisions concerning the biological *and* social implications of living with treatment. Frequently, families have to deal with the intrusion of treatment, as well as illness and disability, in their daily lives.

What were once life-threatening conditions have now, in many instances, been turned into chronic ones. An 'extension of morbidity' occurs (Bury, 1987) often involving the unintended consequences of treatment. MacDonald's study of rectal cancer, reported here, graphically illustrates the considerable burden that developments in surgical techniques may involve, and not only on the individual. Spouses and partners are also affected, and research on the outcome of treatments cannot stop short at discharge from hospital. We have, as yet, few accounts of what exactly is involved in coping with modern medical treatments in chronic illness. A medical model of disease is simply inadequate for this task, taking us, as it does, into complex social and emotional areas such as changes in body image, self-medication, and growing expertise amongst patients and families themselves. All of these matters pose new problems for patient–provider communication and need, therefore, systematic and careful study.

One of the major consequences of chronic illness and its treatment, which has been emphasized in the present volume, and which has long been central to a sociological perspective of chronic illness, is that of stigma. From its earliest discussion by Goffman (1963) to more recent elaborations (Gerhardt and Wadsworth, 1985) stigma has been central to an appreciation of societal reactions to chronic illness and disability. The potential spoiling of an individual's identity, by the negative reactions of others to changes in normal bodily or behavioural appearances, is at the centre of much of the misery of chronic illness and its handicapping nature.

As Scambler and MacDonald point out here, however, it is 'felt' or 'perceived' stigma which is important. Actual discrimination may be less in evidence, especially in a period marked by considerable public discussion which emphasizes treating 'normally' those affected. Yet evidence presented here shows all too clearly that many individuals living with chronic illness also live with the fear of stigma. Indeed, the emphasis on behaving towards those with disabilities as if they are normal may reflect, in part, an idealized view of disability, to which only the 'good and the great' amongst sufferers may aspire. Fear of failure against the standards of a Sir Douglas Bader, Jacqueline du Pré, or Barbara Woodhouse, appears as a real possibility in today's achievement-oriented society. What is an inspiration to one person may be an added burden to another.

It is no wonder that under these conditions many patients adopt a strategy of reducing the amount of their 'public appearance'. Social isolation amongst those with chronic illnesses reflects as much these social processes as it does the direct effects of functional disability. As Dartington *et al.* (1981) point out, the able-bodied project many fantasies on to the disabled, partly as a desire to be reassured that damaged bodies can be coped with. Such complex attitudes 'surrounding the disabled' suggest caution, therefore, in delineating 'stages in coping'. In arguing for such stages we may well be pursuing the needs of the healthy and the able-bodied, rather than the needs of people with disabilities and their families.

An emphasis on felt, or perceived, stigma suggests that sufferers fear the potentially discrediting aspects of living with a chronic illness. Contributors to this volume argue that the fear of stigma may be greater than the actual experience of stigmatizing behaviour by others, but they refrain from normative statements about how patients should, or should not, regard such discrepancies. Sensitive and careful study of the relationship between felt and enacted stigma is called for, in a spirit of empathy, both for the disabled and those with whom they live and come into daily contact. Only then can practical decisions about the management of stigma and the role of professional intervention be tackled.

Part of the need for caution in this area stems from the considerable ambiguity which exists at the heart of contemporary cultures in their views of chronic illness and disability. On the one hand contemporary culture has a strongly 'prescriptive' ingredient. Responses to social and health-related problems, in terms of entitlements to formal assistance are prescribed or codified, often in legal forms. State benefits revolve round the operation of such rules and their resource implications. Chronic illness and disability have become, in this respect, important political issues in the workings of the modern welfare state (Stone, 1984). In the UK there has been a minister for the disabled since 1974, and a panoply of regulations govern the rights and welfare of people with disabilities. Indeed, the assertion of 'rights', in the context of chronic illness and disability, itself pays testament to the prescriptive nature of modern culture, where formal procedures producing equality of opportunity can be called for and laid down in law.

On the other hand, contemporary cultures also contain a strong 'performative' ingredient. Modern societies are based on an increase in the division and specialization of labour, and this involves an increase in the level of personal skills and the display of 'cultural competence', including, most importantly, the ability to handle social interaction. Indeed the 'consumer society' involves an expansion of fashions, styles and choices all of which require an ever more active consumer (Featherstone, 1987). As Norbert Elias has described in detail (Elias, 1978) this development of modern 'civilization' can be seen in many different aspects of everyday life, where self-restraint and controlled behaviour have superseded earlier forms. The simplest of behaviours can be called on to illustrate the point, be they of table manners, the eating of food, or behaviour in the bedroom. For example, Elias documents the slow change in the way bodily functions are performed, and the rise in the 'threshold of shame' attached to such behaviours. This long and deep-seated process has involved many changes in personal conduct and a parallel rejection of 'uncivilized' behaviour.

It is clear, from this vantage point, that much of the interactional difficulty facing those with chronic illness stems from this particular cultural milieu. Formal 'rights' and a public emphasis on accepting or 'normalizing' disability exists side by side with a tacit, but by no means less substantial, emphasis on performance, consumption, self-control and the display of interpersonal skills. The display of this 'cultural competence' involves the ability to be physically co-ordinated, and psychologically 'well organized' in everyday life (Hirst and Woolley, 1982). Disability nearly always involves a potential for failing in one or other of these performance areas, and thus evoking social and emotional responses in others. Of the contributors to this volume, Jobling and MacDonald make these processes particularly clear. Living with a colostomy or severe psoriasis involves a constant burden of worry about personal hygiene and body waste. However much the individual may 'cope' with the problems this creates, the potentially 'shameful' and embarrassing aspects of the condition are ever present, even if they can be partly hidden from view.

There is a danger, from this viewpoint, of people with a chronic illness or disability being encouraged to participate more fully in public life, yet having to operate in a cultural context of considerable ambiguity. Under these circumstances it is not surprising that people with disabilities become sensitive to sources of 'invalidity' or stigma, even when, at a formal level, these are denied. Thus 'activities of daily living', such as dressing and personal cleanliness, are only in part neutral functions. They frequently touch on areas of deep symbolic significance, even though daily life would appear to be more relaxed in these respects than in immediately preceding historical periods. Discussions of policy in the field of chronic illness, therefore, need to proceed with care. A balance needs to be struck between the integration of people with disabilities into public life and the need to avoid constant exposure to the risk of breaking the rules that govern the performance of everyday life. Research on chronic illness thus takes us to the heart of contemporary society and throws into relief important dimensions of social structure and segments of the cultural order.

Policy Implications

Against this research backcloth, let us, finally, consider some of the policy implications in the field of chronic illness and disability. First and foremost is the problem of medicalization. Calls to widen the terrain on which professional care operates, to include the psychosocial aspects of experience, are made here with due care. Just as the experience of chronic illness varies, so too does the need for professional support, beyond the management of symptoms. The contributors to this volume are persuaded that such wider support should be given by health professionals, but it has also been emphasized that this should be developed on an informed basis.

All too often professionals regard themselves as experts in the field of living with chronic illness, when their professional background and training has not fully prepared them for the task. There is an urgent need for health-care providers to work out their approach to social aspects of illness and disability, in order to act as a resource to patients and their families, while minimizing the 'medicalization' of such problems. It is clear from the present findings that intuitive responses of professionals to such matters as the disclosure of diagnosis, information regarding the condition and its treatment, and the recognition of the social consequences of a chronic medical condition, suggest the need for specific education and training, if an 'enabling' role is to become firmly established in this area.

Second, there is a need for careful thought concerning policies of 'community care' in the chronic illness and disability field, in the light of evidence about the realities of life 'in the community'. The tendency for professional elites to advocate forward-looking policies in this area, without a clear assessment of the realities of the delivery of such care, is becoming marked. As several contributors here show, the vast bulk of the caring is provided by patients and families, with help from friends and perhaps neighbours on the periphery.

As Allen (1985) has recently argued, such family-based care is probably the norm, with help from the wider community being either absent or confined to limited, non-intimate, tasks such as help with shopping (though there may, of course, be exceptional neighbours or friends). As far as formal help is concerned, even in conditions such as stroke or rectal cancer, relatively few patients are actively supported at home by general practitioners, and the continuity of care between the primary and hospital sectors is frequently poor. This is not to ignore the energetic work of individual professionals, nor to belittle their activities. On the other hand the voices of many patients and families in the volume are clear; patients frequently report that they do not feel that their particular problems or views on the consequences of their condition are taken seriously, and families are left to provide what support they can. The current vogue for voluntary action and community care is all too often advocated by those wishing to reduce the role of welfare provision, and the vital role of formal services. Such a view receives no support from the research presented here. Patients and their families do need appropriate help from health and welfare services, and there is no real substitute for such help in chronic illness.

This raises a third issue which unites both research and policy, namely the issue of patient expectations. In speaking of developing more responsive professional attitudes to social aspects of chronic illness, and the need for more systematic research on them, there is a need for more direct attention to the views of patients, regarding their experience of services. Here, too, we must expect to find considerable variation. Patients and their families are bound to approach health services, however highly valued, with mixed feelings and expectations. Some will have definite expectations, with which to judge their experiences, others will not know what to expect. In addition, patients and carers may well differ in how much professional help with personal and social problems they desire. A uniformity of attitude should not be presumed, and, as has been shown here, patients and their carers may well have quite different views of the progress and future outlook of a condition, against which they will judge the relevance and effectiveness of services. Patient and family expectations need careful assessment in their own right if services are to be more responsive and 'customer'-oriented.

Fourth, and related to the last point, is the problem of 'who cares for the carer'. Much of the work on chronic illness in the past has been focused on the individual, or made only passing reference to the position and views of informal carers. The present volume, however, has given particular emphasis to the burden of care carried by families, and especially spouses. We have shown that families play a critical role in caring for chronically ill persons, but it is also clear that sufferers and their carers often differ in their perception of the illness and its effects. This warns against a further set of idealized policies being projected on to carers. Families constrain as well as support, make demands as well as succour, and are as likely to reach the 'limits of tolerance' as to provide 'a haven in a heartless world'.

Just as chronic illness disrupts the performance of the sufferer's social roles, so it threatens family life itself. Overprotection, dependency, and fears of rejection or intolerance are all reported here, as well as care and support. Health policy, first and foremost, needs to recognize the contradictory elements involved in the care of the chronically sick and disabled. A simplistic emphasis on care in the family may turn out to be a recipe for neglect. As yet, little work has been done on the experiences of family members, and other informal carers, but the present volume does indicate its importance, and the need for health services to make families and carers a legitimate focus of their activities. Only in this way will a policy of 'shared care' become a reality.

We must surely move away from the situation described by Robinson and Scambler here, where family members are taken into a professional's confidence concerning diagnosis or other critical information about a patient's condition, without regard for the consequences of so doing. Again, there is an urgent need for professionals in training, and in particular service settings, to work through such issues, so that they have at least working guidelines to inform their actions, even if these are necessarily open to revision and change.

Finally, there is the issue of communication and information. As with other research in this area, the present volume contains evidence of dissatisfaction with the information received from professionals concerning diagnosis, prognosis and treatment. In part this arises from an understandable reluctance by doctors and others to rehearse 'worst case' scenarios in front of newly diagnosed patients, especially where outcome is difficult to predict. However, this should not be used as an excuse for avoiding the need to establish a policy, and a working ethic of 'shared care'. Chronic illness often involves patients and their families becoming knowledgeable about medical information and technical detail, as the studies of psoriasis, diabetes and others testify here. Under these conditions a false attachment to 'expertise' by professionals can only hamper communication.

Patients are expected to be rational users of services, but defer to professional judgement once in the clinic (Bloor and Horobin, 1975). Of course patients and their families wish to learn and gain from professionals' expertise. But all too often this means that patients and their families are not able to communicate their own views, and their questions are treated as if 'compliance' were the only issue involved. Professionals, especially doctors, are typically unused to treating others, patients included, on an equal footing. From their earliest days in training they are led to believe that medical science is inherently superior to common sense and lay views.

Yet in facing up to chronic illness, its meaning and its consequences, the limitations of a medical model of disease are all too apparent. Disease occurs inside or on the surface of the body, but living with illness and disability involves coping with the reactions and responses of others as a central part of the experience. That experienced professionals know this only too well is not in doubt, but what is called for, and underlined again and again in this volume, is the need for a more cogent and systematic response by professionals, one that places the experience of patients and their families at the centre of the caring process. If we have been able to convey what this entails then we will have accomplished our main objective.

References

Allen, G. (1985), *Family Life* (Oxford: Basil Blackwell).

Blaxter, M. (1976), *The Meaning of Disability* (London: Heinemann).

Bloor, M. J., and Horobin, G. W. (1975), 'Conflict and conflict resolution in doctor–patient interactions', in C. Cox and A. Mead (eds), *A Sociology of Medical Practice* (London: Collier Macmillan), pp. 271–84.

Bury, M. R. (1979), 'Disablement in society: towards an integrated perspective', *International Journal of Rehabilitation Research*, vol. 2, no. 1, pp. 33–40.

Bury, M. R. (1987), 'Arguments about ageing: long life and its consequences', in N. Wells and C. Freer (eds), *The Ageing Population: Burden or Challenge* (London: Macmillan).

Central Statistical Office (1987), *Social Trends 1987* (London: HMSO).

Conover, P. (1973), 'Social class and chronic illness', *International Journal of Health Services*, vol. 3, no. 3, pp. 357–67.

Dartington, T., Miller, E., and Gwynne, G. (1981), *A Life Together: The Distribution of Attitudes Around the Disabled* (London: Tavistock).

Elias, N. (1978), *The Civilizing Process: Vol. 1, The History of Manners* (Oxford: Basil Blackwell).

Featherstone, M. (1987), 'Lifestyle and consumer culture', *Theory Culture and Society*, vol. 4, no. 1, pp. 55–70.

Gerhardt, V. E., and Wadsworth, M. E. J. (eds) (1985), *Stress and Stigma: Explanation and Evidence in the Sociology of Crime and Illness* (London: Macmillan).

Giddens, A. (1976), *New Rules of Sociological Method* (London: Hutchinson).

Goffman, E. (1963), *Stigma: Notes on the Management of Spoiled Identity* (London: Penguin).

Hirst, P., and Woolley, P. (1982), *Social Relations and Human Attributes* (London: Tavistock).

Kestenbaum, V. (ed.) (1981), *The Humanity of the Ill* (Knoxville: University of Tennessee Press).

Locker, D. (1983), *Disability and Disadvantage: The Consequences of Chronic Illness* (London: Tavistock).

Stone, D. A. (1984), *The Disabled State* (London: Macmillan).

Strauss, A., and Glaser, B. G. (eds.) (1975), *Chronic Illness and the Quality of Life* (St. Louis: Mosby).

Townsend, P. (1979), *Poverty in the United Kingdom* (London: Allen Lane).

Whitehead, M. (1987), *The Health Divide: Inequalities in Health in the Nineteen Eighties* (London: Health Education Council).

Wood, P. H. N. (1980), 'The language of disablement: a glossary relating to disease and its consequences', *International Rehabilitation Medicine*, vol. 2, pp. 86–92.

Index

For Product Safety Concerns and Information please contact our EU
representative GPSR@taylorandfrancis.com
Taylor & Francis Verlag GmbH, Kaufingerstraße 24, 80331 München, Germany

www.ingramcontent.com/pod-product-compliance
Lightning Source LLC
Chambersburg PA
CBHW071848270326
41929CB00013B/2144